FINDING
OUR WAY

FINDING OUR WAY

Jewish Texts and the Lives We Lead Today

BARRY W. HOLTZ

SCHOCKEN BOOKS · NEW YORK

Library of Congress Cataloging-in-Publication Data
Holtz, Barry W.
    Finding our way: Jewish texts and the lives we lead today/by Barry W. Holtz.
        p.   cm.
    Includes bibliographical references.
    ISBN 0-8052-4068-3
    1. Jewish way of life.   2. Judaism—20th century.   3. Tradition (Judaism)   I. Title.
BM723.H65   1990
296.7'4—dc20   90-52535

Book Design by Stephanie Bart-Horvath

Manufactured in the United States of America

First Edition

For Bethamie, with much love

CONTENTS

PREFACE AND ACKNOWLEDGMENTS   ix

NOTE TO THE READER   xiii

Introduction
FROM LIFE TO TEXT, FROM TEXT TO LIFE   3

One
TRADITION   15

Two
HOLY LIVING   39

Three
BEING SERIOUS: FIRST THOUGHTS ABOUT GOD   64

Four
GOD   83

Five
THE HEART'S WORK   110

Six
THE CIRCLE OF COMMUNITY   136

Seven
A WORLD OF JUSTICE   160

Eight
HOLY LAND   187

Nine
GROWING   211

GLOSSARY   231

NOTES   235

INDEX   247

Preface and Acknowledgments

Like most educational endeavors, this book first began to germinate with questions asked by students. The students in this case were, by and large, groups of adults at synagogues and Jewish community centers around the country whom I was teaching and meeting, particularly after the appearance in 1984 of a book that I edited, *Back to the Sources: Reading the Classic Jewish Texts*. In that book a group of scholars argued for the intellectual viability of the great Jewish texts. The book addressed the question: What are the great Jewish books and how does one read them?

These adult students (and they included as well the rabbinical students and graduate students in education whom I teach at the Jewish Theological Seminary) were interested in the enterprise of *Back to the Sources,* but they were pushing me to take the discussion one step further: If that book addressed their questions about the structure, style, and worldview of the Jewish classics, what could be said about the way those great texts might speak to our human situation now? Can these works be of more than *historical* interest? Can they, in other words, address the religious concerns of people today?

It was with those questions that this book began—with a desire not to try to represent a "mainstream," all-inclusive, or historical approach to Judaism, not, in other words, to try to assert, *"This is what Judaism says about X."* But rather to look at a set of issues that are both crucial to Judaism and of personal concern to contemporary people who wish to find ways of connection to this religious tradition.

So my first thanks goes to those questioners, with the hope that I will have made some start here in doing what they challenged me to do.

I never would have had the time to embark on this project were it not for a sabbatical leave granted to me by the Jewish Theological Seminary of America, for which I am profoundly grateful.

Much of the thinking behind this volume emanates from the educational work I have done with colleagues at the Seminary's Melton Research Center. My thanks to the Center's educational staff, especially to Gail Dorph and Miles Cohen for our work together around issues of prayer; to Vicky Kelman for the work in adult and family education; to Ruth Zielenziger for our Bible projects; and to Brenda Bacon, Elaine Cohen, Mimi Cohen, Sylvia Ettenberg, Tzipi Harte, Carol Ingall, Marcia Kaunfer, and Ruth Raphaeli for the chance to think together about the key issues of Jewish religious life during the past ten years. Thanks as well to Pauline Rotmil for holding the whole show together.

In particular, I want to thank my colleague and friend, Edy Rauch, the Melton Research Center's other codirector, for his continuing insights and wisdom and for taking on the burdens of running the Center single-handedly during the year I was away on sabbatical.

Since I see this book as an expression of my work in Jewish education, I wish to acknowledge also my great teacher in that field, Seymour Fox, whose own broad vision of the concept of "education" has expanded the way that I and so many of his students have thought about what we do.

I had the great pleasure of working on this book with Bonny Fetterman, a kind and enthusiastic editor at Schocken Books. Bonny's perceptive "dialogue" with the manuscript was enormously helpful, and her gentle prodding helped me write the book I wanted to write. Others in the Schocken/Pantheon circle were very supportive as well. Thanks in particular to André Schiffrin and David Rome.

As always, I received enormous help from Nessa Rapoport, who helped me think through the original proposal for this book, who encouraged me to think clearly and ambitiously about the project and who read and reacted to parts of the manuscript with kindness, support, and intelligence.

Having Pam Bernstein for one's literary agent is truly a privilege. Pam loved the idea for this book from the first moment and she was unflagging in her encouragement and optimism.

The major portion of this book was written during the sabbatical year I spent in Jerusalem. My enduring thanks to my friend Alan Hoffmann, academic director of the Hebrew University's Melton Centre for Jewish Education in the Diaspora, who invited me to spend a year on the "other" Melton Centre's faculty. There I had the chance to teach an interesting mix of students and to lead a seminar of the Centre's faculty, from whom I learned an enormous amount. Special thanks to Hinda Hoffman, the academic administrator of the Melton Centre, for helping to ease my transition to life at the Hebrew University in many ways, large and small.

While in Israel I had the chance to talk about this book with a number of friends and colleagues as it was in progress: In particular, ongoing discussions with Noam Zion, Mike Rosenak, and Marc Bregman were very helpful to me. In addition, others gave me help, perhaps without knowing it, when I needed advice with specific questions—in particular, Marc Saperstein, Elan Ezrachi, and Michael Fishbane. I also wish to thank Moshe Greenberg and Moshe Idel for their kind invitation to participate as a guest in the "Interpretation" seminar at the Hebrew University's Institute for Advanced Studies during 1988–89. I had an opportunity to learn a great deal from the lively discussions.

I was delighted and fortunate to find my cousin Bruce Elman on sabbatical at the Hebrew University during the same year that I was there. Although the subject areas we were working on were very different, the chance to share the ups and downs of writing lengthy works on an almost daily basis made the task considerably easier.

At the end of the project two friends, Art Green and Bob Goldenberg, took time from their busy schedules to read the draft of the manuscript and give me their reactions and suggestions. I appreciate this generosity enormously and I take the care and seriousness they gave to the assignment as a great personal gift.

As usual, my parents, sister, and assorted brothers-, sisters-, and parents-in-law encouraged this work with warmth and good cheer. Thanks to them all.

My wife, Bethamie Horowitz, to whom this volume is dedicated, lived through this project from start to finish. She never flagged in her love and support—despite her own busy work schedule and the added demands of being pregnant—even when I must have driven her batty.

Just about the time that the first complete draft of this manuscript was completed, our daughter Sophia was born, giving me the chance to understand what it really means to feel blessed.

Note to the Reader

I follow the conventional style in this book, using "R." (as in "R. Eliezer ben Hyrcanus") to mean either Rabbi or Rav. "Rabbi" was the classical term for ordination used in the Land of Israel; "Rav" was the term used in ancient Babylonia. ("Ben," or "bar," means "son of.")

Jewish sources prefer to use the terms B.C.E. (see the Glossary) or C.E. in dates (as in "the year 70 C.E."), rather than the Christian oriented terms B.C. or A.D., respectively.

In general, for biblical quotations in this book I have used the new Jewish Publication Society translation *The Tanakh* (1985). *Tanakh* is the traditional Jewish acronym standing for the three main sections of the Hebrew Bible: *Torah* (the first five books, Genesis to Deuteronomy), *Nevi'im* ("Prophets"), and *Ketuvim* ("Writings," e.g., such books as Proverbs, Psalms, Lamentations).

FINDING OUR WAY

FROM LIFE TO TEXT, FROM TEXT TO LIFE

We open a book and look at the writing. The page stands before us: black figures on white paper, squiggles and lines, lifeless, inert. But of course we know it isn't like that at all. Open a page of Japanese and for most of us that will be true. We'll look at dead letters on the page. But in a language we know, as soon as the cover is opened, we are reading. Indeed, we are reading before we are even aware we are reading. Since leaving childhood, for the majority of us reading is as natural as breathing the air.

Reading is a living process. It almost seems to happen *to* us. It's only in watching a child struggle with the alphabet or in pushing ourselves to decipher a foreign tongue that we remember a time in which reading was less a part of us than it is now. But there is a danger in this as well. Words wash over us. Thousands of words every day. When do words begin to lose their impact? In what way does reading still affect our lives? How does reading define who we are? As a Hasidic story has it, the question is not how many times one has been through the Talmud, but how much of the Talmud has been through you!

The connection between the words we might read and the lives we are living is the concern of this book. But I am talking about reading a very specific type of book here, those works which comprise the literature that the Jewish tradition calls Torah.

"Torah" is a multifaceted term in the history of Judaism, for it means not only the Bible, but also commentaries on the Bible, legal codes and compendiums, mystical and philosophical works, commentaries on commentaries, and other texts as well.

These texts are linked by webs of interpretation, by readings which expand and develop across time and space. Each generation rereads Torah in the light of its own experience and rethinks the meaning of these texts for the world in which it lives. In the same way, individuals find their own path into the sources and read the words in ways that speak most directly to their own situation. Jewish mystics expressed this idea by saying that there are thousands of aspects and meanings in the Torah and that each individual soul has its own particular way of understanding the sacred words.[1]

I take this idea to mean that the texts of the Jewish tradition have the potential to speak quite personally to anyone, and I remember quite clearly my own discovery of the way that a text of Torah might speak to the concerns in a person's life. As a teenager years ago, I was studying a midrashic work—one of the ancient rabbinic texts that interpret the Bible—with a teacher and a group of friends. We came upon a little homily based on the verse Genesis 37:1, "And Jacob dwelled. . . ." The text reads like this:

> At the time that righteous people "dwell" in tranquility and wish to dwell in tranquility, Satan comes and accuses them saying, "It's not enough that the world-to-come is appointed for them—they also wish to dwell in tranquility in this world too!" You should know that this is so—our father Jacob, because he wished to dwell in tranquility in this world was attacked by the troubles he had concerning Joseph. . . ."
>
> (Genesis Rabbah 84:3)

Jacob tried to dwell in tranquility, this interpretation claims, but he should have realized that such peace is denied to the truly righteous. All the trials he suffered with his son Joseph—the son whom he thought had died, the son sold into slavery and lost to the family for many years—all this is meant to teach us about the suffering that the righteous must endure in this world.

4

What was it about this text that spoke so powerfully to me back then? To me it had something to do with the sad realization that the righteous people in the world cannot—as Jacob tried to do—escape their tragic fate. That being righteous means being involved in the world and not hiding from it "in tranquility." That the big questions of life and death are not simple ones to answer.

There was also much in this text that didn't interest me—the issue of Satan, the question of a world-to-come—but the heart of the midrash was what mattered more; these other points seemed irrelevant. It may have been the times I was living in: The heroes of the civil rights movement and the death of John F. Kennedy surely had an influence on the way I found meaning in the texts I encountered. But what caused that powerful sense of engagement is of little consequence. For whatever reason, what that one evening taught me was the possibility of connection between text and life.

The relationship of text and life is an issue that has troubled many thinkers and none has written more eloquently about it than the great German-Jewish philosopher Franz Rosenzweig. Speaking seventy years ago, Rosenzweig addressed the question of the meaning of Jewish study in a modern world. We live in new times, Rosenzweig asserted, and "the old form of maintaining the relationship between life and the Book" will no longer work. Unlike our ancestors, we must discover a new way of Jewish learning:

> It is a learning in reverse order. A learning that no longer starts from the Torah and leads into life, but the other way round: from life, from a world that knows nothing of the Law, or pretends to know nothing, back to the Torah. That is the sign of the time.[2]

Rosenzweig saw the need for this new approach because he understood very well the fruits of modernity and both the positive and negative consequences of Jewish emancipation. Entering the mainstream of Western culture and society, the modern Jew now "finds his spiritual and intellectual home outside the Jewish world."[3] The challenge today, Rosenzweig claimed, was "finding the way back into the heart of our life"[4] through Jewish learning.

Almost three-quarters of a century later these words still strike home. The dissociation of Jews from tradition and traditional learning is no less true than it was in Rosenzweig's time; possibly the alienation today is even more profound. And this despite a recent revitalization of Orthodoxy in America. But what does it really mean to move in Rosenzweig's "reverse order"? What does it mean to go from life to text?

But then perhaps he had it wrong. Or at any rate, not quite right. Perhaps the process is more complicated than the phrase "from life to text" makes it sound. For just as surely as "life" determines the concerns that call out for "text," the "Book," as Rosenzweig put it, establishes the language in which those concerns are voiced and the categories by which they are understood. In other words, we may start with our lives in order to help us understand our books, but what we read and study will in turn redefine the ways we see our lives. Text and life, in that case, are intertwined in a complex dance: we hold up the mirror of words and find it reflecting the story of our lives; we understand each—the books we read and the lives we lead—in the light of the other. Thus, after reading that midrash about Jacob, I could never again think that a righteous person could escape from engagement in the concerns of the world. And understandings deepen with time and reflection.

Like Rosenzweig we are talking here about Torah, works which in addition to their inherent personal interest are the sacred books of a people. This is a library, in other words, rooted in a context, and if that fact is ignored, one misses an essential point. For throughout most of Jewish history the texts Jews called Torah defined a world of real lives and national hopes. This was a community whose existence was defined by sacred language, a community that was required by Scripture to see itself as a "holy people." Of course, like all human beings they had their failings along with their dreams. The gap between reality and aspiration, between what they wanted to be and the inarguable facts of the human condition, is spanned by the bridge of meanings found in these books. These books were meant to help them make sense of their lives, both as individual Jews and as a nation.

What Rosenzweig was trying to address was the world of modernity and its effect on our relationship to Torah, a question that will reappear in many chapters of this book. Once upon a time, he says, in the intact world of medieval Jewry the connection between text and life was clear and the *authority* of the classic sources to influence, indeed to determine, the destiny of one's life was beyond question. But here we now stand, no longer part of that reality, confronted by a now unfamiliar literature once as close to us as our skins. To be sure, Rosenzweig's view may romanticize the past. We cannot go back in time; we cannot really know what it meant to see the world as our ancestors did. But his point about the present is clear: What previously defined us as a people now both literally and figuratively reads like a foreign language. So what are we to do about the library?

For many Jews that decision was made long ago, perhaps by their parents, even by their grandparents. The library is closed; the books gather dust; eventually, the key gets discarded along with other mementos of the past.

But there are other possibilities as well. Perhaps—despite the difference between our world and the world of the past—these texts can speak to us too. The question is how to find a way into reading them?

One option is obvious: We can look at these works in the way that we look at any literature of the past. Like any great literature, Jewish sources are intellectually challenging, and the excitement of reading is its own pleasure. Thus, Israel Scheffler, a leading philosopher of education, rightly points out a fact that we have all experienced: Intellectual enterprise has its own powerful *emotional* content that cannot be underestimated.[5] Some contemporary educational thinkers have argued that there is a dichotomy between two approaches to learning—"cognitive" experiences versus "affective" experiences. The former are seen to be matters of the intellect; the latter occupy the realm of the emotions. But, as Scheffler shows, such a polarity is misleading; it overly simplifies a complex matter.

7

When Scheffler speaks about emotions that can occur during a scientific inquiry—such as "the joy of verification" and "the feeling of surprise"—we can appreciate the "affective" dimension of such "cognitive" experiences. Indeed, psychological research about infant development suggests that the connection between learning and emotion is with us from the earliest days of our lives.[6] The demanding work of Jewish study clearly offers these powerful emotional rewards too. Like the disciple learning the art of Zen archery or the musician struggling with a Bach fugue, we are involved in the pleasure of learning a difficult thing.

When we read and study Jewish texts, we are involved in another task as well: an attempt to understand those who came before us. What did the rabbis of the past believe and care about? What did the Jews of the Middle Ages feel as they wrote their poetry and philosophy? Why did the Hasidim of the eighteenth century need to create their own religious path? We can study the Jewish classics in the manner that we read the Greeks, the Romans, the ancient Chinese, and that would be fine. Except for us there is something different here too, something beyond an inquiry into history. These, after all, are *our* predecessors. We trace these works the way we follow the lines on a family tree. It is where we come from. And like a relative one may not know very well, may be meeting for the first time in fact, we feel a kind of obligation to pause a moment to see who this member of the family really is. In that sense to study these texts is a debt we feel we owe to our ancesters and our collective past.

But that too is not enough. I believe that anyone who studies the works of the Jewish past must begin with a kind of faith assumption. It may differ from that of our ancestors, but it is serious nonetheless. Simply put, it is this: We believe that there is, to use an old-fashioned word, *wisdom* to be found in this library. The texts of the past can teach us something, can speak to our lives. This book is an attempt to see the way that these sources might do just that.

It seems to me that this "teaching" can occur in two different ways. First, there are times when we will read a text and discover within it an idea or insight which we had simply never thought about before. Perhaps it's a matter of finding a personal connection to a text that is well known to us. Or perhaps it is a new discovery altogether. But even when that does not happen, there is a second way that a text can give us understanding—it is a reminder of that which we knew but had forgotten or put aside. And it brings with it the authority and weight of an ancient tradition as well, a fact we will explore in more detail in the first chapter of this book. That one's own thoughts are confirmed or supported by an older wisdom can be a powerful anchorage in an individual's life.

So we begin with a commitment to give the texts their due. And that means wading through some difficult waters—some strange vocabulary and different assumptions, for example. Most of all, it will mean patience. In recent years we have heard a good deal about the *baalei teshuvah,* those people who have "returned" to Judaism.[7] But these seekers are to be found not only in yeshivot for Americans located in Jerusalem. Among uncommitted Jews, among synagogue members, among those whose affiliation is not with synagogues, but in community centers and Jewish Y's, as well as among deeply committed and ritually observant Jews, there is also this kind of seeking.

What I wish to do in this book is to show how the great texts of the Jewish tradition can speak to the concerns of contemporary life. This book addresses the situation of people who live in a secular world, but who want to explore the ways that Judaism might relate to central issues in their lives, to dilemmas that religion has always tried to confront. It uses the resources of the Jewish tradition to help people grapple with questions of meaning, faith, and religion and it does that through an exploration of some of the essential issues discussed by the classic Jewish sources.

In each chapter I have tried to discuss a small set of relevant texts from traditional literature, reading them and organizing them in an order that reflects a certain approach to the issue at hand. In addition, I have attempted to point out something about the *way* one goes about reading such works, what characterizes the literature that we are looking at, and how the reader might examine other sources of a similar sort. Although I offer a "reading" of each particular text, I try to distinguish, as best as I am able, between what the text may have meant in its historical context and the way I am looking at it now.

Of course, the texts chosen reflect, not surprisingly, my own personal interests and concerns. The traditional literature I turn to is that which I know the best and which speaks to me the most. In particular, the book is weighted toward writings from the formative period of classical Judaism, the rabbinic age, and especially toward texts of the type called midrash.[8]

Rabbinic Judaism began in the early years of the Common Era and produced a literature which continues to influence Judaism up to our own age. Originally, this was an oral tradition—the teachings and sermons of the rabbis were passed on from generation to generation, and the status of these rabbinic teachings was important indeed. Thus, one rabbinic tradition claimed that the "oral Torah" (as this tradition was called) had been given by God to Moses on Mount Sinai along with the "written Torah." This is a perplexing idea but, as one contemporary scholar has put it, "From the standpoint of modern literary studies, this is actually a rather sophisticated insight: a way of saying that a text contains its own potential interpretations from the start."[9] We shall have more to say about this concept in the next chapter.

Eventually, these teachings were edited, organized, and written down. Therefore, what we today call rabbinic literature represents a long oral tradition preceding the written document. Thus, to know that a certain statement appears in a sixth-century work actually tells us less than we might think about the historical facts surrounding any given statement. Did the rabbi to whom a text is attributed in fact speak those words? Even that is difficult to determine. But issues of historicity have not been of great moment in the life of Judaism. What matters more is the teaching itself.

Rabbinic literature is made up of a number of different kinds of genres. One finds sermons and prayers, stories and parables, laws briefly stated and lengthy legal debates. One important form of this vast body of work is midrash. Midrash is the classic Jewish literature that seeks to interpret Scripture. Midrash takes many different forms and interpretation may serve a number of purposes. It may, for one, wish to elucidate law and behavior. Thus, when the rabbis wished to know what the Bible meant by its statement to "remember the Sabbath day and keep it holy" (Exodus 20:8), they interpreted various verses in the Bible to understand the commandment. The relationship between law and midrash is made additionally complex, however, by the fact that we do not know if the interpretation preceded the practice or if a practice already in place, say about the Sabbath, eventually demanded a midrashic "justification" based in Torah.

This type of midrash—known in Hebrew as *midrash halakhah (halakhah,* literally the "way," being the traditional word for Jewish law)—is only one variety of text that we encounter. The other major type of midrash is that which seeks to examine the narratives of the Bible, filling in details, teaching theology, spirituality, and religious principles. That type of midrash—*midrash aggadah* in Hebrew *(aggadah,* literally "telling," is the general term used for Jewish literature that is *not* expounding law)—also responds to the biblical text. And both types of midrash look at the Bible with enormous care, trying to find significance in every word, in every slight oddity of language. Biblical phrases are weighed and considered for meaning; words that we might easily skip over as a matter of biblical "style" are mined for secret significance.[10] To the rabbis, therefore, the Bible appears as a monumental code waiting to be unlocked. The rabbis were able to see the Torah in this fashion because of their conception of its authorship. For them this document was a matter of God's revelation. And every word of the Perfect Author required scrutiny.

There is no single work called "The Midrash"; instead midrashim (plural) were collected in various works, most of which were arranged according to the order of biblical verses. A midrash about Abraham, for example, will appear in the midrashic work Genesis Rabbah, which arranges its interpretation by following the book of Genesis in almost a verse-by-verse fashion. But midrashic texts appear in other places as well, most significantly in the Talmud.

There are two talmuds, the smaller Jerusalem, or Palestinian,

Talmud and the far more significant Babylonian Talmud, a work edited in the sixth century of the Common Era, the product of the great Jewish community of Babylonia. The Talmud is a massive and wide-ranging work. Ostensibly organized into six large thematic "orders" within which are various "tractates," the Talmud will often juxtapose various topics and materials in surprising fashion. Midrashic texts on various biblical verses can seem to appear out of nowhere: a story about Jacob's wives Rachel and Leah in the middle of a discussion about prayer; a midrash about Abraham in the midst of legal debate. Nonetheless, the typical features of midrashic literature will also obtain—careful discussion of words, puns, allusions to other verses as "proof texts," and all the other characteristics of midrashic exploration.

As I have said, most of the texts used in the following chapters come from rabbinic literature, many from the Babylonian Talmud, others from midrashic collections. And the texts chosen here lean toward the side of aggadah rather than halakhah. Another writer with different interests and abilities could base a book like this one on texts or literary genres that I do not address. There is an enormous richness in the tradition and I do not mean to imply that the sources I have used are the only ones relevant, even to the topics that I explore.

My point is that the vast tradition called Torah can be read by the contemporary reader in meaningful ways. Therefore, I have given myself the liberty of looking at other traditional sources too, if they seem particularly relevant to the issue at hand. The great law code of Maimonides, the Mishneh Torah, will have a role here, and in the chapter on prayer, I turn toward eighteenth-century Hasidic texts, partially because of the great importance that prayer held for Hasidism.

Finally, I must admit to one final prejudice: Not every text in the traditional literature will speak to a contemporary ear. There are rabbinic texts that seem obscure or dated—texts, for example, espousing values about the status of women or non-Jews, that represent another historical or sociological reality. And there are texts that are simply dull or pedantic. Because my goal here is not to construct an inclusive historical survey of traditional literature,

I have, by and large, avoided choosing texts like these. Certainly, there are others who can find contemporary significance in these writings, but I have stuck with the sources that seem to me most meaningful, even when they are provocative. The texts here are not unproblematic, but the problems they raise are fruitful ones and to my mind there is nothing less interesting than dealing with a text from the past simply so we can point out its supposed inadequacies.

Martin Buber, writing about the mission of education, argued that through a nation's education "the generations which are growing up are made conscious of the great spiritual values whose source is the origin of their people. . . ." That much may be obvious, but Buber makes another point as well. Education necessitates that "these values are deliberately woven into the design of their lives."[11] Learning and reflection, in other words, must point in two directions—toward the past, toward the values at the source of what one is as part of a people, but also toward the here and now, toward the "design" of our lives today.

How can tradition be understood, Buber asks? He sees three different possibilities. One approach is what he calls "negative." The impact of the tradition is "warded off as neither credible, nor usable, nor timely."[12] But those who reject the tradition are only part of the story. Perhaps even more debilitating is the approach Buber terms "fictitious." In this case

> those who follow it exalt the works and values of national tradition, regard them as the subject of pride and piety, and point to them with the mien of collectors and owners, as though they were the coronation robes in a museum, not, of course, suitable apparel for a living sovereign. While they boast of their tradition, they do not believe in it. They teach it in school but not with the purpose of seriously integrating it into actual life. All that seems necessary to them is to "have" it.[13]

It seems to me that a good deal of talk about Judaism today seems to be taken up with this kind of attitude. We take "pride" in being Jewish, in "having" a tradition, even in teaching it to our

13

children, but not because we believe in it or really hope to see it have a role in our lives.

But there is another possibility. It is the situation in which, as Buber says, "the adherents of the movement open their heart to the tide of the elements, absorb and transform what they have absorbed in response to the demands of the hour."[14] That is the task before us: to see in what ways those words on the page can come alive, listening to the voice behind the text as it speaks to us, indeed, as it aims to move us toward change.

TRADITION

When I think about religion, I often imagine a kind of intersection where two roads converge. One road represents the world of powerful personal experience, the moments in which I have felt some profound connection to meanings beyond my self. These experiences may be of joy or of pain; they may occur in conventional "religious" settings like in a synagogue or at a holiday celebration, or more mundanely when I'm staring out the window or dusting the furniture. In fact the element of *surprise* seems to typify these breakthrough moments. One can sit many hours in a synagogue and nothing like it might happen. And then all of a sudden, you are *there*. To use the conventional language of religion, it is the world of the sacred, a moment of holiness.

And these times do tend to be *moments*. As much as surprise is part of them, so too the fleeting quality of these experiences is typical. We want to hold on to them, but in essence they are the present moment come suddenly alive. And then the present passes. Of course, even after the moment itself is gone, we retain it in our memories. It becomes part of us. For a while we can conjure up a strong echo of the experience itself, but slowly and inexorably it becomes memory or, as people say, "only a memory."

Some years ago toward the end of my grandmother's life, my

15

father and I went to visit her in the hospital. It was a beautiful day, a sudden thaw in the late winter, and the three of us took a walk around the grounds. My father talked with his mother and I walked in silence with nothing much going on in my mind but thoughts of the pleasantness of the day. Then all of a sudden and quite by accident, it seemed, I looked up and found myself staring directly into my grandmother's eyes. She was not a sentimental person and though I had always been quite close to her, she was not the kind of grandmother who pinches you on the cheek and gives you a hug. Nor did she do that on this day. But she gave me a small, remarkable smile and appeared to step right outside the pain of her illness. Without words she seemed to say to me, "We do know each other, don't we?" And I had a sense of connection to her unlike anything I had ever experienced. All the while my father continued his conversation with her, but to my grandmother and me it seemed irrelevant, and my father was completely unaware that this something else was happening between my grandmother and me.

For many years I thought about this occurrence and tried to figure out what actually had happened. I never talked to her about it. It didn't seem necessary. In fact, after she died I was glad I had never mentioned it to her, perhaps because I was afraid she might not have remembered it at all. Yes, of course it is possible that "I made it all up," whatever that means. But that doesn't really matter—the historical accuracy of the event has little significance. What matters is what I felt happening then and the way that that perception lives for me over the years. Of course, now, after all this time, it has become memory. I cannot really reexperience the moment; I know that it happened, but it has faded into personal legend. It has become the past.

It is the past that forms the other metaphorical street of that intersection called religion with which I began this chapter. If one aspect of religion is the immediate "now" of my experience, like that moment of communication with my grandmother, the other is the "then" of the past. We all have the memories of our own past experiences, but for a religion like Judaism, there is also a larger picture: the echoing tales of our people's ancient ways. To

16

be sure, we like to believe that this vast repository of the past emanated from actual experiences. Indeed, the sacred books of Judaism recount those very moments: the stories of Abraham, the revelation at Mount Sinai, the wanderings in the wilderness, and many others. But for us these records of experience have become the past and even their factuality remains a mystery. They have become memory, or to put it another way, they are tradition.

Tradition. It's hard to imagine talking about Judaism without using the term. But what do we mean when we say it? Tradition, from the Latin *traditio,* "that which is handed down"; in Hebrew *masorah* from the root *masor,* also meaning "to hand down or hand over." The classic statement in Judaism is the beginning of the Mishnah's tractate *Avot:* "Moses received Torah at Sinai and passed it on *(m'sarah)* to Joshua, Joshua to the elders, the elders to the prophets, and the prophets handed it over to the Men of the Great Assembly."[1] Thus, tradition moves through the generations.

But what is that "Torah," that "it," which is being handed down? Literally, "Torah" means teaching or instruction, but is that teaching something fixed and tangible? Is Torah like the old family heirloom, that ceramic vase or gold watch, which one generation gives to the next? The object never changes; the vase is beautiful and fragile and pristine. We guard it and protect it, and from one generation to the next it remains the same. Indeed, that is the nature of its beauty and value—its stability over time. Is that what we mean by tradition, the careful preservation of the past?

For the classic Jewish writings, as we shall see, this is a complex and central problem. It is at the very heart of what our ancestors were about—trying to figure out what is being "handed down," what is the nature of tradition?

The question of tradition goes beyond the issue of permanence and change. Tradition also carries with it authority and demand, a point which we today are likely to overlook. For us tradition has become synonymous with "custom." True, it is custom with the weight of precedent—we might say, for example, "In our family the tradition is to serve hot dogs or (as is the custom in

New England) salmon and peas on the Fourth of July." Or "In our college we walk around the Quad three times on Homecoming Weekend." But what if one year we serve chicken instead or skip the walk because of the weather? In other words, tradition, at least as most of us use it, is a combination of custom, sentiment, and stability. It is not authority beyond the individual. You don't "have to" do it; it is your own choice.

But for Judaism, at least classically, "tradition," as we use the term, is not even a category in the vocabulary. What matters is *mitzvah,* not in our watered-down sense of "a good deed," but in its essential linguistic meaning, "that which is *commanded.*" Thus, for us today tradition raises two crucial questions: what is the content of that which is handed down, and what demand does that content make? Or, to put it another way, how does one determine what the tradition is, and once we know what it is, is there anything that it can make us *do*?

I think it is fair to say that most of us today are ambivalent about the whole notion of tradition. On the one hand, we *want* tradition—we live in an uncertain world with few easy answers, and the apparent certainty of tradition is terribly attractive. And yet we are moderns: We believe in personal autonomy; we want the power to control our own lives; we feel that we should participate in the decisions that affect us. Rules make us nervous; indeed, answers make us nervous. Any authority over us is subject to question. We don't want anyone to tell us what to do or how to think or what to believe. For us, thinking about religious questions raises the issue: Can anyone or anything, including a tradition, speak to us with authority, and how is that kind of authority going to be established?

As a religion of tradition, Judaism presents us with this dilemma. And as we look at it further, things become even more complicated. To begin with, above I have lumped together both how we act and what we think, but within the Jewish tradition there is a long-standing distinction between matters of behavior and issues of belief. Thus, as one writer has put it, "Classical Judaism, drawing directly on its biblical antecedents, tends to emphasize act over intention, behavior over thought. Righteousness is chiefly a matter of proper behavior, not correct belief or appropriate intention."[2]

But even separating belief from action does not really help solve our original problem about the nature of authority. Of course, if I were a Hasidic Jew living in Borough Park or Jerusalem there would be no question. My religious master, my *rebbe,* would direct the spiritual concerns of my life, and even some aspects of my "nonreligious" life, such as whom I would marry or what career I would enter, might be determined by my *rebbe*'s advice. (For after all, it would be argued, is there anything *outside* the realm of religious concern?) As we well know, there are gurus in other traditions with similar authority. But for most of us, such a route is not going to work.

Even outside the world of Hasidism, throughout much of Jewish history, the rabbi served in an authoritative, though perhaps more limited, role. He acted as the arbiter of Jewish law—halakhah as it is known in the language of tradition—and he served as a kind of interpretive teacher of Torah. But even here modernity has changed the nature of things. Many Jews are not interested in the fine points of halakhic argument; indeed, even to care about "what is the law" is to have already accepted a major form of authority. By doing so, one is stating: I will do what the tradition wants me to do and therefore I will find a rabbi who will tell me with accuracy (or compassion or sensitivity—traditional Jews choose their rabbis not just because the rabbi will "get it right!") what that traditional demand is.

But once again, for most Jews today halakhah is not the prime focus of their lives. It is not accidental, in that sense, that in modern times the role of rabbi has undergone a significant change. With the waning of that sense of tradition and halakhah (and, I think, with the rise of psychology as a kind of surrogate religious path), rather than a source of traditional learning, more and more the rabbi is seen as a kind of counselor in times of need as well as a "priest" in the ceremonial pageant of the large "cathedral" synagogues that blossomed in the post–World War II era.

And so once again we are back to where we started. Where neither gurus nor conventional halakhic categories are acceptable for most Jews as sources of authority, is there any way that Judaism can speak with authority in a time when we wish to find a connection to the stability of tradition? Nor is this only a question for the so-called liberal denominations of contemporary Judaism. Even Jews who accept the authority of traditional Jewish law cannot ignore the conflict of tradition and the world of modernity. This is certainly true of the world of "modern Orthodoxy," that is, among Jews who wish to remain faithful to tradition while enjoying the accoutrements of contemporary life—television, fashion, university education, and the like.[3] To live in the modern world means to face questions about the nature of tradition.

Interestingly enough, these very questions are raised with considerable passion and insight within the classic Jewish sources themselves. By looking at some of those texts, reading and interpreting them, a kind of response for our times may also begin to emerge.

I want to begin by turning to a famous story from the Talmud that speaks to at least one dimension of our concern. The context of the tale is this: During a dispute among the rabbis over the ritual purity of a certain oven (the specific details are not relevant for our discussion here), Rabbi Eliezer ben Hyrcanus, a distinguished sage of the first century, has taken the position that use of the oven is permissible; the other rabbis disagree. But the story rapidly goes far beyond the technical matters of ritual purity. It becomes an examination of the very nature of the issue of human versus divine interpretation of the text of tradition:

> . . . On that day Rabbi Eliezer brought all the proofs in the world, but the other masters would not accept them.
>
> He said to them: If the law is according to me, let this carob tree prove it. And the carob tree moved a hundred cubits. Some say four hundred cubits!
>
> They said to him: We don't learn proofs from a carob tree.
>
> Then he said to them: If the law is according to me, let this stream of water prove it. And the stream of water turned and flowed backwards.
>
> They said to him: We don't learn proofs from a stream of water.

> Then he said to them: If the law is according to me, let the walls of the House of Study prove it. And the walls of the House of Study began to topple. . . .
>
> Then he said to them: If the law is according to me, let the heavens prove it.
>
> A voice came forth from heaven and said: Why do you dispute with Rabbi Eliezer? The law is according to him in every case.
>
> Rabbi Joshua rose to his feet and said: "It is not in heaven" (Deut. 30:12).
>
> What is the meaning of: "It is not in heaven"?
>
> Rabbi Jeremiah said: The Torah has already been given once and for all from Mount Sinai; we do not listen to voices from heaven. For You have already written in the Torah at Mount Sinai: "After the majority must one incline" (Exod. 23:2).
>
> Some time later Rabbi Nathan came upon Elijah. He said to him: What did the Holy One, blessed be He, do at that moment?
>
> Elijah said to him: He was smiling and saying: "My children have defeated me, my children have defeated me."
>
> (Talmud, *Bava Metzia* 59b)

In this tale Rabbi Eliezer appears to have heaven itself on his side. Although the other sages disagree with him in the matter at hand, Eliezer seems to win the case handily by bringing a series of miraculous occurrences—the carob tree that flies, the stream that flows backward, the leaning walls of the House of Study—to support his position. Finally, a voice from heaven tells the sages, "Eliezer is correct!" But Rabbi Joshua will not be moved—even if heaven tells us differently, the human process of interpretation is what matters. The Torah is not in heaven, he quotes, and we can't be expected to rely on miracles for the system to work. Human agency, *even at the expense of "truth,"* is what really matters.

Interestingly enough, Rabbi Joshua wins his case by quoting Torah itself. This is the meaning of the lovely coda to the story in which Elijah the Prophet tells the reader what God really thought about this whole business. "My children have defeated me," God says. How? By using the Torah against me! And of course, like the parent who must accept the child's own autonomy, God is delighted. (Indeed, it seems that this tale, like others in the Jewish tradition, also recounts a learning experience for God.) This epilogue assures the reader that divine blessing rests upon the victorious rabbis. They have gained their maturity, no longer dependent on miracles or even on divine prophecy.

Clearly, as in other talmudic stories, one thing this tale expresses is the rabbinic antipathy toward miracles and the rabbis' belief that relying on the supernatural threatens the continuity of the Jewish tradition. Since no one can count on miracles or prophecies, a religion cannot *depend* on the supernatural for its future. To be sure, the rabbis believed that such events can and do occur in the world, but far more important for the perpetuation of Judaism is the rational argumentation of human deliberation and the majority rule that determines the final law. For the rabbis, despite their belief in the divine nature of revelation, authority rests with the human court.[4]

For us, of course, the rabbinic polemic against the authority of miracle is not much of a concern. We do not worry about the perpetuation of a tradition by prophecies and divine revelations. We do, however, know of such traditions alive in the world today. Indeed, examples of prophetic fanaticism today, whether they be in Iran or among Christian fundamentalists, may indicate something of what the rabbis were concerned about.

But the story of Rabbi Eliezer and the other sages is not only of historical interest. Beyond learning something about the concerns and circumstances of the rabbinic world, I think we can begin to see an approach to matters that are of more immediate concern to us as well: What is tradition, and where does its authority lie? This tale, to begin with, suggests that the issues are human ones. We are not trying to discern voices in the heavens, but rather tradition is in the hands of human beings. But who those human beings are and how they may be invested with authority requires further examination.

Another talmudic text begins to deal with those issues:

> R. Eleazar ben Azariah opened his discourse:
> "The words of the wise are as goads and as nails well planted are the words of the masters of assemblies, which are given from one shepherd" (Eccles. 12:11).

Why are the words of Torah compared to a goad? To teach you that just as the goad directs the heifer along its furrow to bring forth life to the world, so the words of the Torah direct those who study them from the paths of death to the paths of life. But you might think that just as the goad is movable so the words of the Torah are movable; therefore the text says "nails."

But you might think that just as the nail neither diminishes nor increases, so too the words of the Torah do neither diminish nor increase; therefore the text says "well planted"—just as a plant grows and increases, so the words of the Torah grow and increase.

"The masters of assemblies": These are the sages [*talmidei hakhamim*: literally, "students of the wise"] who sit in assemblies and study the Torah, some pronouncing unclean and others pronouncing clean, some prohibiting and others permitting, some declaring unfit and others declaring fit.

But a person might say: How, then, shall I learn Torah? Therefore the text says—all of them "are given from one shepherd." One God gave them, one leader proclaimed them from the mouth of the Lord of all creation, Blessed be He; for it is written: "And God spoke all these words" (Exod. 20:1).

(Talmud, *Hagigah* 3a–b)

This text is a midrash, a rabbinic commentary that attempts to expand and illuminate a passage from the Bible. This particular midrash, in fact, is of a particular sort—a proem or introductory commentary that scholars believe represents in some edited form a version of an actual sermon from ancient times. In fact, the text above has been discussed in a famous and masterful scholarly essay by Joseph Heinemann, one of the great experts on midrash in this century.[5] Heinemann demonstrated the "oral" nature of this type of text, seeing it as a kind of public performance in which the preacher (*darshan* in Hebrew) tried both to instruct and to entertain through his skill in public performance.

This midrash is a commentary on the biblical passage "And God spoke all these words" (Exod. 20:1), a passage immediately preceding the giving of the Ten Commandments at Sinai and therefore one of great significance and interest in rabbinic literature. But, Heinemann points out, this text, like most sermons of the proem form, does not begin by quoting the passage from the Torah reading; rather it quotes "a verse from afar" (here Eccles.

12:11) which appears to have nothing at all to do with the business at hand—revelation at Sinai. The skill of the preacher, as Heinemann describes it, is in building the links between "the verse from afar" and the opening verse of that day's Torah reading (here the beginning of Exod. 20) with which the sermon must conclude.

Heinemann paints the picture of the *darshan*'s oral presentation before the appreciative crowd. The speaker must create a structured presentation in which the two unrelated verses are imaginatively connected:

> As the preacher approaches his aim, step by step, the sense of anticipation on the part of the audience—who know towards which passage he is striving, but do not know how he is going to forge the required link—mounts up; but while building up the tension, the homilist also evolves a set of ideas which reaches its summit at the very end. . . .[6]

In our consideration of this text we are less concerned with its formal structure, interesting as that may be, than with the ideas that the *darshan* is presenting as he moves from the verse in Ecclesiastes toward the Torah reading in Exodus.

Of course, the Ecclesiastes verse is a puzzling one, a fact that no doubt accounts for the interest it generates throughout rabbinic literature. Its cryptic style calls out for interpretation. Here Rabbi Eleazar ben Azariah begins by breaking the verse down into three parts: Torah, he says, should be connected to three words— "goads," "nails," "well-planted."

We note right away that Rabbi Eleazar has made an important homiletic point at the very beginning of his sermon. Our text is talking about "the words of the wise," but without a moment's hesitation Rabbi Eleazar is speaking of "the words of Torah." "Words of the wise" and "words of Torah" are immediately and almost casually identified in his presentation.

How can we define the nature of Torah, asks Rabbi Eleazar. His answer is to see each of the three terms in Ecclesiastes as a metaphor that gives us another dimension. Torah, he begins, is a "goad." Its strictures, its clear teachings, push us like a goad along the path toward life and away from death. But, Rabbi Eleazar continues, a goad is something "movable" and lest you think that that is true of Torah, we learn from our verse that Torah is fixed like "nails." And yet that too might be misleading: A person might then think that Torah never changes and develops. Therefore, the text tells us that Torah is like a plant—the words of Torah "grow and increase."

Now, of course, we might ask: Aren't these three ideas contradictory? How can something be at the same time movable, fixed, and growing? For Rabbi Eleazar this does not seem to be a problem. Perhaps it is merely a matter of the sermon's "performance" aspect; perhaps Rabbi Eleazar doesn't really worry about the inherent contradictions as he builds the links leading up to the Exodus verse, but I don't think so. To my mind the multifaceted, seemingly contradictory aspect of Torah is at the heart of Torah's mystery and fascination for people like our preacher. Torah is all these things. And that, in fact, is the direction toward which the sermon itself is headed.

Rabbi Eleazar paints a portrait of the great teachers of Torah, the "masters of assemblies," all engaged in the act of interpretation—some saying one thing, some saying the opposite! In this din of interpretation, Rabbi Eleazar realizes, "a person might say: How, then, shall I learn Torah?" In other words, *amid all of this conflicting interpretation, who is the authority that I should listen to?*

To that crucial question Rabbi Eleazar has a simple answer, almost shocking in its implications:

> . . . all of them "are given from one shepherd." One God gave them, one leader proclaimed them from the mouth of the Lord of all creation, Blessed by He. . . .

In other words, don't worry—even though the interpretations may differ, may even contradict one another, all of them are Torah nonetheless. When Rabbi Eleazar quotes the verse from Exodus "God spoke all these words," he means to supply the emphasis—*all* these words: The Torah at Sinai and the Torah of human interpretation, even in the cacophony of readings that cannot be harmonized, all emanate from God.

But what are we to make of this? Rabbi Eleazar has moved us

beyond the story of Rabbi Eliezer ben Hyrcanus and the problematic oven, but he still has left us with the issue of authority. In the previous story we saw that authority is a human matter; we cannot expect miracles nor turn to a divine presence to help us interpret the nature of tradition. In the sermon we've just looked at we see that many interpretations, many authorities, may speak "the truth." In fact, there is no one single reading, no one single authority. But does that mean there is no authority? That in having many teachers we no longer have *a* tradition? Where does that leave us?

One possibility is that we should find security in the "true" teachers of the past. By turning toward the old ways we can cut through the confusions of our times. One talmudic text tries to deal with this issue: If Torah is increased through the interpretations of its teachers, what then is the relationship between the weight of the past and the demands of the present?

> Rav Judah taught in the name of Rav: When Moses ascended the mountain, he found the Holy One, blessed be He, occupied in attaching little crowns to the letters of the Torah. [In a Torah scroll, unlike printed Hebrew script, seven of the letters have the ornamentations or "crowns" referred to in our text.]
>
> Moses asked Him: "Master of the Universe, why are You attaching those crowns?"
>
> God replied: "Someday in the future, a man will appear named Akiva ben Joseph and he will be able to make heaps of interpretations just based on these little crowns."
>
> Moses said: "Let me see him."
>
> "Turn around," God said.
>
> Moses found himself in Akiva's academy and sat in the back to listen to the class. But he was unable to understand what was going on and he was distressed.
>
> Finally a certain subject came up and the students asked Akiva, "How do you know this?" and Akiva replied "This is a teaching from Moses on Sinai." And Moses was pleased. . . .
>
> (Talmud, *Menahot* 29b)

Tradition tends to put us under the shadow of the past. We think about those who came before us and believe ourselves to be inadequate to the vision and authority that they possessed. The rabbis lived under a similar burden. They deferred to their own predecessors and believed that the further back in time one could trace an argument, the more authority that argument would have. Thus, in a talmudic argument a quotation from a first-century C.E. source generally has more weight than one from a fifth-century authority. In that sense they did not seem to see *progress* in history, but rather a decline, as if the message of Sinai, like a recording heard in the distance, fades from hearing and becomes less reliable the further we move from the source.

But history moves forward as well, as the text above testifies. In this remarkable story, Moses "our teacher," as the tradition speaks of him, cannot even understand Akiva's words. He is like a simpleton sitting in the back of the class. And God assures Moses that the crowns on the letters, mere irrelevant decoration to Moses' eyes, will become the source of numerous interpretations in Akiva's hands.

Of course, this tale, like many others in the rabbinic sources, raises as many questions as it answers. One of the pleasures of this literature is precisely that the enigmatic nature of the utterances and the richness of the tale leads to many different readings. In this story, for example, we wonder about the resolution of the difficulty. Moses is assuaged by hearing "this is a teaching from Moses on Sinai." But why should he be pleased? And is it really a teaching of Moses after all? It seems quite obviously *not* to be: Since Moses himself cannot understand the discussion at hand, how could it be "from Moses on Sinai"? What seems to perk up Moses is the mention of his own name. So is it only ego? Is that why Moses is happy, because he hears his own name quoted after so many generations?

In a certain sense that does seem to be it: Moses is pleased because he knows that he will be remembered. Or, to put it more generously, he knows that there will be a continuity in tradition —Moses' words and teachings will form the basis of that which will come after him. But—and this is a big but—the text also suggests that tradition will evolve so much that even Moses himself will not be able to understand what the later interpreters have to say.

Perhaps we could say this means that the later thinkers will somehow capture the spirit of Moses' meaning, that they will interpret as Moses would have if Moses had lived in their times. But this is a tricky point. How exactly are we to know that one interpretation is attached to the line of Moses from Sinai? Indeed, in our text, how does Moses know that Akiva is in that line? After all, Moses doesn't even know what Akiva is saying! So in what sense is it "Torah from Moses on Sinai"? Surely the answer cannot simply be that by stating you are part of it (as Akiva does), you *are* part of it. So what then?

Perhaps we should consider the story from Akiva's point of view. Let us assume, since the text doesn't really tell us, that Akiva does *not* know that Moses is sitting in the back of the room. (Of course, looking at it the other way adds a whole new and tantalizing wrinkle to the story: If Akiva recognizes Moses sitting there, his attribution of the tradition to Moses is only a response to the distinguished guest in the classroom!) No, let us assume that Moses is sitting there invisibly, or at least incognito. So the following question is raised: What does Akiva mean when he says "from Moses on Sinai"? Is he aware that Moses would not have understood anything he had been saying? Or maybe the nature of the present is such that we don't ever think about the way we unknowingly transform the past?

But we'll take Akiva at his word: He indeed believes that his teaching is from Moses on Sinai. Perhaps he means that he received this very teaching from his own teacher and he assumes that that teacher received it from another, and so forth. Therefore, he believes that these interpretations do go back a very long time. "From Moses on Sinai" becomes, in that case, a metaphor for "a long-standing interpretation." Now, of course the beginning of the story actually argues against that reading. At the beginning of the tale Moses is told exactly the opposite: Someday, God tells him, a great innovator will come along who will be able to find numerous meanings in each of those little crowns. Not someone who will pass on the old traditions very well, but rather someone who will find new meanings.

And perhaps that is what it is about. To be in the line of Moses on Sinai means to go beyond Moses. It means to be able to interpret with depth and insight and innovation. Is that, perhaps, why Moses is pleased at the end—he is reconciled to the passage of time, to the ongoing evolution of tradition? Looking at it this way, Moses is pleased because he recognizes his own fundamental role in the design of tradition and he accepts the brilliance of Akiva as innovator.

But like a hall of mirrors the story has one more turn to make. The text with which we began above concludes with a whole new twist:

> . . . Moses returned to the Holy One, blessed be He, and said to Him: "Master of the Universe, You have such a person and yet You are giving the Torah through me!"
>
> "Be still!" God replied. "This is My decree."
>
> Then Moses said, "Master of the Universe, You have shown me his teaching, now show me his reward."
>
> "Turn around," God said.
>
> Moses turned around and saw how [after Akiva died a martyr's death] Akiva's flesh was being weighed out in the marketplace.
>
> "Master of the Universe," Moses cried, "this is his teaching and this is his reward!"
>
> "Be still!" God replied. "This is My decree."
>
> (Talmud, *Menahot* 29b)

After seeing Akiva's genius, Moses—known even in the Bible as an exceedingly humble man—wonders why he should be chosen to receive the Torah and not Akiva. God curtly tells him to be still: This is a matter of divine fiat that cannot be questioned or understood. This first part of the ending is, I think, quite intelligible in the light of what has gone on before. We have just learned that the relationship between the past, even with the founders of tradition like Moses, and the present interpreters must inevitably be one of distance, even of incomprehension. To say that Akiva should have been the one who received the Torah misses the point implied in the earlier section of the tale: Others will come after Akiva whom even *that* great sage, if he were granted Moses' experience of looking into the future, would not be able to understand. According to the thinking of this talmudic passage, would Akiva, if placed in the classroom of a later interpreter like Maimonides, be able to understand him? Absolutely not. This is the way of history; in fact, one could just as clearly argue that the present cannot comprehend the consciousness of the past. Akiva understands Moses as little as Moses understands Akiva! God tells Moses to be still because Moses has misunderstood the essential nature of interpretive "evolution."

But of course it is the last few lines of the story that we are most concerned about. It is hard to read the tale and not feel uneasy. A talmudic story about the nature of tradition and interpretation suddenly has become a discussion of the problem of evil. Why should Akiva, the greatest of rabbinic interpreters, be the object of torture. This is his teaching and that is his reward! Moses is incredulous. But the tale, almost in a kind of restating of the conclusion of the Book of Job, allows Moses no answer. The relationship between human accomplishment and human suffering is not to be spelled out.

Note here that the rabbis do not give us an easy answer to the question. The Talmud doesn't have God tell Moses that Akiva will be rewarded in heaven or that a martyr's death is a noble death or that God sees the big picture while we are stuck in our merely human consciousness. Their answer is stark and bold: Such things human beings—even Moses himself!—cannot fathom; answers, if there are answers, remain in the mind of God.

So the text seems to move into reflecting about the issue of evil and divine decree, and we are told that even "our teacher" Moses did not understand such matters. What we do on earth—even interpreting Torah—cannot be judged by standards of reward and punishment. We do not study in order to receive the good life, the life of ease. After all, Akiva is murdered *because* he violated the Romans' law and did teach Torah.

Nonetheless, I am left with an uneasy feeling. And a different, almost heretical interpretation comes to mind: Is it possible that Akiva is being *punished* for his innovative interpretations of Torah? Perhaps the whole slant is exactly the reverse of what we have been suggesting up to now: The rabbis, through means of this parable of Moses on Sinai, are suggesting that Akiva went too far. In interpreting Torah so that even Moses could not understand it, Akiva went beyond the range of interpretation "permitted" by tradition and for that he is punished—hence, "Be still! This is My decree." Or perhaps we are being taught that the big questions of life and death are so unfathomable that even the great Akiva can come to such an unhappy end.

Rabbinic tales, like this one, often reverberate with ambiguity. Is this tale, we might ask, meant to praise Akiva or to bury him? I think the latter reading can be argued, perhaps can even be supported, but the weight of evidence in the tale pushes the interpretation in the other direction, toward Akiva as martyred hero. Why otherwise would the legend begin with God Himself crowning the letters of Torah and proclaiming to Moses that a great scholar would arise someday to interpret this divine handiwork? Indeed, one clear theme in the tale is that God *intends* Torah to be interpreted throughout the generations. God even supplies levels of meaning (here symbolized by the crowns on the letters) to give human beings the opportunity to interpret. Akiva's terrible death, according to this view, is a separate matter from his accomplishments as an interpreter of Torah.

Reading this story, we ourselves become part of the same complicated saga. Almost unwittingly—through our own reflections and hesitations, questions and resolutions—we have become participants in the drama of interpretation. And the very ambiguity of our tale, the possibility that a completely different interpretation may be lurking before our eyes, is what keeps that process alive.

But this very fact, so well exemplified in our wrestling with the tale of Moses and Akiva, raises an even deeper question that lies at the heart of what we've been looking at throughout this chapter: Once again, what is the source of authority? That is, when I read any text—this tale, for example—and try to figure out what it means, who is to say if I "got it right"? Is my reading as good as anyone else's? Is there no "authority"?

To me the three texts that we've looked at in this chapter suggest an *approach* to this problem, though they do not supply a crystal-clear answer. To begin with, tradition lives through the human power of interpretation. The story of Rabbi Eliezer and the sages points toward the idea that authority can only make sense in the human realm. We do not seek authority from "the heavens" but we rely on the skill and intellect of human beings. Indeed, the very process of reading that we have been doing here is a kind of message in its own right: The seeds of a contemporary understanding of Judaism can be found in the heart of the tradition itself—its texts and tales.

Is there one answer, one correct way? Our second text, Rabbi Eleazar ben Azariah's sermon about the "words of the wise," suggests that there is not, that there are many readings, many interpretations, "all of them given from one Teacher." Indeed, in our own lives as we grow and change over time, these readings and understandings, like anything else, will—must!—give way to other understandings. The din of Rabbi Eleazar's study hall thus resembles the panorama of understandings that live in my own mind—from my youth, from yesterday, from teachers whom I accept and others I reject.

Innovation and the insights of today, as we learn from the last story of Moses and Rabbi Akiva, do not necessarily indicate inferior understanding. This legend implies that the interpretations of our own time may actually outstrip those which came before. But the story has another meaning as well: The interpretations of one generation have a limited relevance to the world of another age. Perhaps Moses did not understand Akiva because Akiva's views simply did not speak to Moses and his vision of reality. In that sense, as we have suggested above, Akiva would have had as much trouble understanding Moses as Moses did Akiva. Which is to say, the tradition we create for our own time is that which the time and the individuals who live in it demand. We could have no other.

Tradition is, in other words, what we ourselves make of it. And, as I've suggested earlier, even those who define themselves as "Orthodox" recast Judaism in the light of who they are and the milieu in which they live, although they may not always recognize or be aware of the reshaping as it occurs. In each generation certain aspects of the past—whether it be rules of sexual behavior or stringency in observing the dietary laws or commentaries that are valued or devotional practices that are emphasized—receive emphasis while others recede in significance. We ourselves are the source of tradition.[7]

But it's fair to ask in that case: Is there any limit? Is tradition so flexible, so much within ourselves, that *anything* we call Judaism is Judaism? Or, to put it another way, are there limits to interpretation, to midrash?

We live in a world very different from that of our rabbinic forebears. For them the hierarchy of authority was very clear. In Rabbi Eleazar's sermon the creators of tradition are not the nation as a whole, but the *talmidei hakhamim,* the rabbis themselves. True, they may contradict one another, but the tradition is secure because at least you know that the opinion you are listening to is from a person *qualified* to give it. A trained interpreter. A rabbi.

I am reminded of a wonderful scene in a story by the great Hebrew writer S. Y. Agnon, "Two Sages [*Talmidei Hakhamim*] Who Lived in Our Town."[8] Agnon paints a vivid picture of the two rival sages battling over Torah in front of the congregation, one trying to give a sermon as the other keeps interrupting. The battle is conducted with words, with verses, but it is a battle nonetheless and at the end one has emerged the clear victor. The townspeople, in this tale set in Eastern Europe before the war, do not *themselves* try to "create the tradition." They are observers of the struggle between their qualified leaders. True, the congregation will judge who wins and who loses, but as audience, not as actors in the contest.

We today do not live in Agnon's traditional world. We are not prepared to be spectators on the sidelines. Obviously, the populist traditions of the West have had a tremendous impact on almost all of us. Hierarchical worlds are not very comfortable for us. But at the same time I wonder if we really are ready to take the opposite position—*everyone* is a rabbi. Everyone interprets.

One possible compromise would be to say that we ourselves want the right to create and be our own authority, but we will use the *methods* of interpretation used in the past to create that tradition. This is an attractive idea, but it has its own inherent difficulties. We must remember that the midrashic methods used by our ancestors in interpreting biblical texts were founded upon a view of the Torah that most of us simply do not share. For them the Torah was a kind of monumental code. As we saw in the legend about Moses on Sinai, God is understood to be the source of this code: It was God, after all, who added those crowns on the letters. The human interpreter seeks to unlock that code, and of course it's a code that has more than one solution, for many solutions come to light over the course of generations.

Now we too seek meaning in the sources. We too wish to read Torah for its significance. But we do not use the methods of "decoding" used by our ancestors—the wordplays, the proof texts, the rules of interpretation.[9] We can appreciate their artistry and their inventiveness the way we might admire Aristotle's physics or Shakespeare's use of the cultural assumptions of his time—but the premises under which they worked cannot be ours. Thus, to say that we will invest authority today in those who use the same *methods* that were used in the past is not going to solve our difficulty.

The problem with "tradition," of course, is the problem of *power*. What tradition seems to be saying is, "I have the truth; I have the final word and your role is to accept what I am giving to you." But I suspect that very few of us today are going to accept unreservedly such a position.

It seems to me that we must aim toward something like the following: First, we must recognize that there will be no *one* right answer (and no one "rabbi") for all of us. Second, if we are going to be our own interpreters, we better do it with a very healthy dose of self-criticism and modesty. It may be that the interpretations of the past cannot be our own, but we have got to recognize both our own personal limitations on the one hand and the contributions of the past on the other.

Is there a source of truth? Can we get the "right" answers? As long as we remain committed to our own populist or democratic ideals, we are not going to find any easy answers. But perhaps the idea of tradition itself can offer a kind of midway solution if we think about it in a different way. I am drawn to a definition of tradition that resembles the way in which the psychologist Jerome Bruner speaks about "culture." Bruner talks about culture as "transactional," something that is "constantly in process of being recreated as it is interpreted and renegotiated by its members." As he puts it:

> In this view, a culture is as much a *forum* for negotiating and renegotiating meaning and for explicating action as it is a set of rules or specifications for action. . . . It is the forum aspect of a culture that gives its participants a role in constantly making and remaking the culture—an active role as participants rather than as performing spectators. . . . [10]

If for culture here we read "tradition," we come up with something different from seeing it as a fixed source of unchanging authority. Rather, viewing the Jewish tradition in this light, we can see our task as conducting an ongoing *conversation* between ourselves and that tradition. At times we will bend our wills to the demands of the tradition; at other times, like Akiva teaching in front of Moses, we will reconceptualize what the tradition itself is. Judaism becomes the grounds for a living debate and deliberation in which we share power with tradition rather than live under its unbending authority.

Certainly, in such a system those individuals who have knowledge about that tradition must be valued. Such people are our "rabbis"—using the old term in a more inclusive way, to mean "those who are learned about the tradition." We cannot base such explorations on a foundation of our own ignorance. And even more than that, if we value a democratic vision, we are going to have to take that task of learning upon ourselves and not leave it to a body of "experts." In a certain sense, therefore, the traditional Jewish commitment to study and learning becomes even *greater* in a time when reliance upon expert authority becomes less desired.

Moreover, although we recognize that in the past, in that which is handed down, there is a source of wisdom, we also understand that, in the transactions between tradition and ourselves, that wisdom is not always going to be relevant to us. There are times— *after* we give it its due, *after* we take it as seriously as it deserves— that we will have to say that particular aspects of tradition are not going to work for us today and no elaborate fiddling is going to make them work. Our relationship to tradition is going to have to be an activist one—if tradition is going to live, we are going to have to make it live. We may need the assistance of wiser minds than our own, but in the long run we're going to have to do it for ourselves.

One can find occasional support for such a view, surprisingly enough, within the classical sources as well. The midrashic text below, in fact, takes the same line from Ecclesiastes which we have seen before to make a completely different point—wisdom need not come only from a rabbi, but it can come from an ordinary person as well:

> "My commandments which I command you this day."
> (Deuteronomy 11:13)

> Where do you learn that even if one learns an interpretation from the least learned of the Israelites, he should consider it as if he had learned it from a sage? From the verse "which I command you" (Deut. 11:13). And, more than that, it is not as if he had learned it from only one sage, but as if he had learned it from many sages, as it is said, "the words of the sages are as goads" (Eccles. 12:11): just as a goad guides a cow along its furrows, thus producing livelihood for its owners, so do the words of Torah guide a person's thoughts toward knowledge of God.

> And more than that, it is as if he had learned it not from many sages, but from the Sanhedrin itself [the rabbinic court of the most learned of the sages], as it is said, "masters of assemblies" (Eccles. 12:11), "assemblies" meaning the Sanhedrin. . . . And more than that, it is as if he had learned it not from the Sanhedrin, but from Moses, as it is said, "they are given from one shepherd" (Eccles.

12:11). . . . And even more than that it is as if he had learned it not from Moses but from the Almighty One, as it is said, "they are given from one shepherd" and "Give ear, O Shepherd of Israel, You lead Joseph like a flock" (Ps. 80:2) and "Hear O Israel, the Lord our God, the Lord is one" (Deut. 6:4).

(Sifre Deuteronomy 41)

The text begins with a simple assertion: Learning Torah from a simple Israelite is equal to learning it from a sage. Of course, it is possible that the use of the word "Israelite" here is meant to imply that we are referring to the ancient Israelites—those who crossed the sea with Moses and experienced revelation at Sinai—and there is a rabbinic tradition that those people had been given a special level of wisdom and connection to the divine. But, given the standard usage of rabbinic Hebrew, it is far more likely that the midrash simply means an ordinary Jew. Indeed, the term used in the original, *katan,* means literally "small," a "small person," either in learning or in social status. The text takes the verse from Deuteronomy, as is typical of midrash, in an almost overly literal way. "The commandments which I command *you*" comes to mean "you" in the sense of any "you" within Israel. Everyone is commanded directly by God and therefore anyone can offer insight into Torah.

The text proceeds to develop its assertion using, for the most part, the lines from Ecclesiastes that have been seen earlier in this chapter. Here the midrash lays out a series of building blocks, starting with the idea that the ordinary Israelite's wisdom is as important as that of a sage, moving to assert that it is as if the words of the ordinary Jew had the weight of words spoken by a member of the elite body of sages, the Sanhedrin, continuing by stating not just that but that these words are as if Moses himself (the shepherd) had spoken them, and concluding in startling fashion by equating the words of that simple Jew with those of the ultimate Shepherd, the Almighty One!

Each of us may feel *katan,* "small" in learning, but this text seems to demand something else of us: that we take our own insights seriously, that we not let the weight of tradition feel too much like a burden. Between humility on the one hand—our sense that indeed there is much to be learned from the past, that we today do not hold the copyright on the wisdom of the ages— and the assertion of the validity of our own insight on the other, we today look to find our own way of connection to tradition, both respecting it for what it is and reshaping it as well.

TWO

HOLY LIVING

I have spoken about one way of looking at our relationship to the Jewish tradition: as a kind of "conversation" between the tradition and ourselves. But I suspect that there are probably no times in which that discussion is more heated and more strained than when we consider the way the tradition makes demands upon our behavior. Being an adult, we like to feel, means having nobody tell us what to do, and yet here is the Jewish tradition with its almost overwhelming lists of prescribed and proscribed actions trying to direct our lives.

Consider the classic model of a traditional life as exemplified by the Talmud's description of Rabban Yohanan ben Zakkai:

> He never engaged in ordinary conversation, nor did he ever go four cubits without studying Torah, nor four cubits without wearing his Tefillin, nor did anyone ever get to the Study Hall before he did, nor did he ever sleep or nap in the Study Hall, nor did he think about Torah while in alleys where there was any filth. . . .
>
> (Talmud, *Sukkah* 28a)

Here we have Judaism's highest ideal, the portrait of a man whose entire life is devoted to holiness. But is it, we might ask, a life one would want to live?

I was brought up with the idea that one of the characteristic features of Judaism was that it made no distinction between sacred and secular moments—everything could and should be infused with holiness: how we pray, of course, but also how we eat, how we deal with matters of property and business, how we celebrate a wedding or conduct a divorce. Everything, in other words, is "religious."

Things would be a lot simpler, of course, if we always lived in that sacred dimension of time, that world of the present moment, which I tried to describe at the beginning of the last chapter. If every instant of my life were as powerful, as meaningful and alive as that five minutes of interchange that I remember from my visit to my grandmother at the hospital, I suppose I would have very little problem in living a "holy" life. By "holy" here I don't mean simply an ethical or ritual life, although those dimensions are certainly part of it, but rather living with a sense of meaning and significance informing everything that I do.

In the history of Judaism there is probably no stronger statement of this view of life than that which was presented in the early writings of Hasidism toward the end of the eighteenth century. This revivalist movement urged people to conduct even their most ordinary daily affairs with the same intentionality and intensity usually reserved for "religious" activities such as prayer. *Avodah begashmiut*, serving God in the midst of the events of ordinary life, is what they strived for, as we can see in the following text:

> Through everything you see,
>   become aware of the divine.
> If you encounter love, remember the love of God.
> If you experience fear, think of the fear of God.
> And even in the bathroom, you should think—
>   "here I am separating bad from good,
>   and the good will remain for His service."
>   (*Tzava'at Rivash* 3b)[1]

It is a remarkable statement, a daring statement, in fact. In the same text the writer expresses not only lofty sentiments about the love of God, but he brings matters down to the most mundane of human activities with a startling directness.

And note how much further such a text goes than the classic Jewish prayer from the morning liturgy that praises God for fashioning within the human body "numerous openings and passageways . . . so that if but one of these were impaired, we could not long continue to exist." The prayer, like the Hasidic text above, also deals with matters of the body, but it does not connect bodily functions to acts of spirituality. In the Hasidic statement even the bathroom can become a place of meditation on the divine.

What a vision of living this text suggests! It's almost as if the Hasidic master is trying to shock his disciples: "Every moment should be infused with holiness," he teaches. "Are you listening?" he shouts out. "Do you understand me? I mean *every* moment!"

It is a stunning demand, powerful and uncompromising, but I wonder about the poor disciple at the other end of the text. What does *he* say? Obviously the popularity of Hasidism in its early years, its success in recruiting followers as it swept across the Jewish communities of Eastern Europe, is a testament to the compelling power of the message, although to be sure the teachings of Hasidism contained more than this one direction. But there must have been some listeners who shared my own reaction two hundred years later: at once admiration for the seriousness of what the master taught and at the same time a strong dose of skepticism about my own ability to live according to those prescriptions.

And though the Hasidic rendition of this idea is unusual, the point of view behind the text does not come out of thin air. It is a kind of spiritual descendant—and more radical version—of older tales from the Talmud in which disciples try to learn the ways of holy living from the example of their teachers. Thus, we have incidents reported in which Rabbi Akiva followed his teacher Rabbi Joshua into the bathroom and Rabbi Kahana hid under his teacher's bed—in both cases to learn rather personal things from their masters. When they were questioned about such extraordinary behavior, they each replied, "This too is Torah and I need to learn it!" (Talmud, *Berakhot* 62a). And in a famous utterance many years later the Hasidic Rabbi Leib the son of Sarah put the same idea this way: "I did not come to the Maggid of Mezeritch to learn interpretations of Torah from him, but to watch how he tied his shoelaces."

In a certain way such behavior is not difficult to understand. There are people whom I admire and whose opinions and behavior I count on as a kind of guide to my own—personal "opinion-makers" we might call them. And most of us rely on certain public thinkers as well: if an event happens in the political arena, we value the reactions of those particular columnists or philosophers whom we always find interesting or challenging. That's how people like George Will and Flora Lewis earn their daily bread.

And of course we remember those people who profoundly affected our lives when we were young. But in adulthood it's rare for anyone to have a personal role model who can so influence one's behavior in all aspects of life. We are simply too aware of the feet of clay hiding beneath the robes. A friend of mine says that he never wants to meet the writers that he admires—he'd prefer not to have to deal with the character flaws that he's sure he would see. The books themselves should be sufficient.

But the declarations by Rabbi Akiva and Rabbi Kahana that "this too is *Torah*" and the comments of Leib, son of Sarah, are more than reflections about the importance of having a religious role model. They represent a position which asserts that we should *always* be engaged in Torah—in a "religious" life. And it is a similar principle that drives the classic Jewish conception of the *mitzvot*, the commandments. According to the classical view, God has given us a set of acts that we are expected to perform, or in the case of the negative commandments, to avoid. These commandments include areas of ritual life, certainly, but also matters of property, criminal behavior, and domestic life as well. Fulfilling the requirements of the mitzvot is a Jew's primary obligation.

But why, following this view, were the commandments given? This is a matter of considerable debate in the traditional literature. In one famous midrashic explication we read:

> Rav said: the mitzvot were given only in order that human beings might be purified by them. For what does the Holy One, blessed be He, care whether a person kills an animal by the throat or by the nape of the neck? Hence their purpose is to refine human beings.
> (Genesis Rabbah 44:1)

The allusion in the passage is to the method of killing an animal in the fashion appropriate to the requirements for kosher meat. But Rav's main point seems to be that the mitzvot are not so much significant in their particularities, but become significant in the *process* of fulfilling them. When the commandments are performed, something else happens—human beings are "purified."

But of course we are still left somewhat puzzled. What does "purify" mean? And equally important, what is Rav's view about the very nature of the mitzvot? Is there no specific meaning in the actions we are required to perform? Are they mere divine whim? Or to put it another way, were the mitzvot given simply to teach us how to obey God's will? That is, since human beings need to be taught the discipline of divine service, God gave them the mitzvot. The specific content of the mitzvot is irrelevant—our job is to learn to obey.

This is a view that certainly has had its advocates throughout Jewish history, but it is balanced by the opposite pole—the mitzvot *are* rational, the specific actions that are required *do* have a meaning. God would not give human beings a set of meaningless commandments.

But another problem can be raised nonetheless. Let us say that the mitzvot do have meaning. Isn't it possible that despite their rationality, the meaning may be unintelligible to the human mind? That is to say, perhaps God has given commandments that are important at *His* plane of reality but to us they remain incomprehensible. This too could be argued based on Rav's statement in the midrash above: We are being "purified," but because of our limited capacities, we don't know in what way that purification is taking place.

This idea—that the mitzvot are rational but we are inadequate—seems almost cruel. And it was rejected by a number of thinkers, most importantly by Moses Maimonides in the Middle Ages.

Maimonides made the distinction between the mitzvot in general and the specific details of their actualization. These details, he said, may be without specific meaning, but the mitzvot as a whole are certainly available to the powers of human reason:

> The generalities of the commandments necessarily have a cause and have been given because of a certain utility; their details . . . were given merely for the sake of commanding something. For instance the killing of animals because of the necessity of having food is manifestly useful. . . . But the prescription that they should be killed through having the upper and not the lower part of their throat cut . . . is like other prescriptions of the same kind, imposed with a view to purifying the people. . . . In my opinion all those who occupy themselves with finding causes for something of these particulars are stricken with a prolonged madness in the course of which they do not put an end to an incongruity, but rather increase the number of incongruities. Those who imagine that a cause may be found for suchlike things are as far from truth as those who imagine that the generalities of a commandment are not designed with a view to some real utility.
>
> (*Guide of the Perplexed* III, 26)[2]

Maimonides is taking a double-edged approach to the problem of the mitzvot: On the one side, the commandments as a whole are seen as meaningful and intelligible; on the other side, the little details of their performance serve to train human beings to submit to God's will. And it is through that submission that people become "purified." "Purification," then, occurs through a life of obedience to divine will.

Others in the tradition took a different tack. Even the little details were meaningful, according to this view. And what is interesting is that the more mystically oriented thinkers within Judaism did not reject the commandments, as we might have predicted (since why would those at the lofty heights of mysticism care about the petty details of the mitzvot?), but rather they emphasized, in contrast to Maimonides, that even the smallest details of the mitzvot had significance—holiness could be found in *everything,* they argued.[3]

But where does that leave us? Today we seem to be in exactly the opposite situation from the one addressed by Maimonides. For us the problem is not in the small, seemingly irrational details of the mitzvot, but in the whole general structure. That is, if I felt confident about the mitzvot as a whole, I would probably have a good deal less difficulty with the specific details of observance.

Our problems begin with the whole question of the holy life that I raised earlier: I am not sure that I would *want* to live in a world so infused with holiness, even if I could do it. We live in secularity and as part of modernity. For most Jews today the world of the nonholy is attractive and compelling, and there is no denying that. Of course, this may be our own weakness, and I'm sure there are those who would see such a position as just that. Certainly, there is much that is wrong with Western secular modernity. But we are part of it and that is not going to change. What we want to do is find those places where modernity simply doesn't seem to work, where modernity fails to address our hunger for a sense of deeper meaning in our lives. But drawing that line is not always easy to do.

I remember walking to the movies in New York one Saturday night some years back and bumping into a group of *hasidim* hurrying off in the opposite direction. "Where are they going?" I thought, and then I realized they were on their way to a *melave malke,* a Saturday night celebration that tries to extend the spirit of Shabbat into the week. I too had had Shabbat, but now I was on my way to the movies. And my first reaction was: Haven't they had enough holiness for today? Don't they want a little time off? I certainly did. For me it was the perfect image of the world of tradition versus the world of modernity. I live a Jewish life; I feel connected to the mitzvot. But on Saturday night I'm more likely to go to the movies than to a *melave malke.* Yet once again I am not sure which of us is mistaken. Perhaps my desire for secularity is not a quality to be admired, but one which shows my own inadequacies as a religious soul.

Still, in recognizing the pull of secular life on me, I am not denying at the same time my desire to live part of my life in that world of holiness. That is, there is something in the midrash quoted before that seems right on the mark when it says that the purpose of the mitzvot is to purify human beings. The mitzvot can do something for us: they give us a chance to move away from the claims of secularity and toward a sense of the holy in our lives, and in that way they become a kind of "purification" from both the positive and negative aspects of contemporary life.

Thus, one midrashic text talks about the reasons behind the mitzvah of lulav and etrog, the palm branch and citron waved by Jews during particular moments in the prayers of the holiday of Sukkot: "The Holy One, blessed be He, has said 'I have given you many commandments—because I needed them? . . . It is not for My sake that I have given you these commandments, but rather to benefit you' " (Midrash Tanhuma, *Parshat Emor* 24).

To my mind the crucial idea about the commandments is their power to give one's life a sense of wholeness. The mitzvot are about the integration of human experience. And more than that, they are about an apprehension of meaning that is beyond the self, something, I would argue, that even the most secular person needs. When I look at the varied activities of my life, I try to find some sense of meaning, some thread of connection among all the things that I do. There is within the system of the mitzvot the power to accomplish just that. The "benefit" is precisely that sense of connection, that feeling that there is both integration and a greater significance in my harried and disconnected life.

Part of that sense of integration comes out of the fact that the mitzvot carry with them the weight and power of tradition. Like other aspects of tradition that I explored in the last chapter, the mitzvot have the advantage of antiquity; when I perform these deeds, I have not invented them out of the air, but I have put myself into a larger sense of wholeness, not only tying together my own life, but joining me to those very things that my great grandparents and theirs before them had done in their lives. And these actions are the same deeds that have engendered pages of explication and years of pondering throughout Jewish history.

But it is not just the significance of the past that matters. Even more significant, it seems to me, is the inherent power of *deeds,* of action. This connection strikes me as a very deep one. For it is not merely what flashes through my mind, my thinking, that the mitzvot are about, but activities in the world of materiality, the world of my body. It is what my ancestors *did,* not what my ancestors *believed,* that matters here. In all likelihood I am very far away from the intellectual world of those who came before me. As I tried to show in the last chapter, over time tradition evolves and deepens through interpretation, through acts of mind. Akiva lives in a world very far from the world of Moses. And his Judaism is different as well.

And so I do not believe that my great grandfather and I would really have much to talk about if we could meet: I would seem bizarre to him and he would seem antique to me. Our beliefs and our attitudes would be very different, shaped by the age in which each of us lived. The historian Robert Darnton in writing about his approach to eighteenth-century French history brings home the same point as he comments on the gulf that separates us from the past:

> Nothing is easier than to slip into the comfortable assumption that Europeans thought and felt two centuries ago just as we do today— allowing for the wigs and wooden shoes. We constantly need to be shaken out of a false sense of familiarity with the past, to be administered doses of culture shock.[4]

But one of the powerful dimensions of Judaism is the sense that despite the passing of time, of generations in fact, I am tied to those who have gone before me not by "thoughts and feelings" as Darnton puts it, but by the physical deeds that I do. If I wave the lulav and etrog at Sukkot, I know that my great-grandfather —no matter what his beliefs and worldview—would have done that very act as well.

I have said that part of the sense of integration comes from connection to the past, but, for me at least, that level of meaning only tells part of the story. To say "I do these deeds because they were done before me" ultimately seems to me like an insufficient, perhaps even circular argument. The actions in and of themselves have to resonate with a level of meaning.

In a way, some of that meaning does come out of their antiquity. That is, doing the mitzvot is not just a matter of doing things that my ancestors did—it's doing things that my ancestors felt to be meaningful as they did them. And I'm sure that part of the weight of meaning my great-grandfather felt in, let's say once again, waving the lulav and etrog came because he knew that it was meaningful for *his* great-grandfather.

But beyond the chain of the generations, we want there to be something else for it to work. For Jews throughout history, and for some today as well, that something may have been the clear sense of obeying God's will and command. But although there are times in which I do feel that too, my own connection to the mitzvot comes mostly out of another sensibility.

In fact, classical Jewish literature abounds with interpretive explication of why we do these deeds. Rarely are we left with no explanation, and the phrase "this is what God wants of you" tends to be the *beginning* of inquiry, rather than its conclusion. For an example we shall look at a set of rabbinic interpretations about the lulav and etrog. I have mentioned lulav and etrog in this chapter a number of times precisely because unlike, say, giving *tzedakah* (charity), it is a mitzvah that is hard to justify on the grounds of rationality or societal needs. *Tzedakah* in that sense is an easy case (though not always very easy in the doing!) because it is obvious that any community needs to find a way to take care of its poor. Now, of course, we know that societies—America today, for example—are not always committed to this task. But the case for *tzedakah* is not a difficult one to make.

In lulav and etrog, however, we have an example of a mitzvah that appears to be without an easy explanation. Obviously, as we can see in the midrashim below, the rabbis felt a similar need to understand this commandment. From the rabbinic period onward a considerable literature evolved concerning this particular practice. In one place in the Talmud, for example, waving the lulav and etrog was compared to the biblical[5] waving of the sacrificial loaves:

In the Land of Israel they taught the following: Rav Hama b. Ukva stated in the name of Rav Yose the son of Rav Hanina—the priest

> waves them [the loaves] to and fro in order to restrain harmful winds;
> up and down, in order to restrain harmful dews. . . . In connection
> with this Rava stated—And thus with the lulav.
>
> (Talmud, *Sukkah* 37b–38a)

The comparison to the sacrificial "wave offering" is of less interest to us here than the underlying reason stated by these rabbis—the waving of the lulav has an almost magical significance. It affects the fall of rain and dew.

What is interesting about this reading is how close it seems to the most elemental dimension of the ritual and probably to its origins in prehistory. Even today when we watch or participate in the ceremony of lulav and etrog, there is that sense of the "primitive" that cannot be ignored. Shaking the palm and the citron in the classic four directions of the compass, as well as upward and downward, and chanting "Please, O Lord, deliver us" puts the worshiper in touch with an ancient human ritual.

And yet, of course, at the same time that elemental quality can easily make us uncomfortable too. The thought intrudes: What am I doing, a sophisticated modern man, shaking these plants and asking for salvation? After all, I don't really believe that I am going to effect the rain and dew by performing this ritual.

That that same self-consciousness was shared by our rabbinic forebears seems to be indicated by the enormous number of classical interpretations that are precisely *not* like the text quoted above. The rabbis developed a vast symbolic literature on lulav and etrog that undermined the more "primitive" dimension and emphasized instead the almost allegorical nature of the ritual. Since by biblical injunction the lulav and etrog are bound together with two other native plants of the Land of Israel—the willow and the myrtle—these four "kinds" or "species" form the basis of a vast array of symbolizing midrash. (During the ritual of "waving" itself the citron is held in one hand while the palm, to which willow and myrtle branches are attached, is held in the other. The four species are held right next to one another during the ritual.) For example:

> Of the four plants two bear fruit and two do not. The ones that bear fruit must be bound closely to the ones that do not. The former represent disciples of the wise whose prayers . . . are meant to bear fruits of mercy for ordinary householders, delivering them from all degrees of poverty and kinds of affliction. . . . On the other hand, the plants that do not bear fruit must be bound close to those that bear fruit since the former represent those persons who are meant to provide a shelter of physical comfort for the Sages and their disciples.
>
> (Pesikta Rabbati 51:2)[6]

This tendency to compare the four species to different kinds of Jews is typical of the symbolizing efforts of the rabbis, as we see in one of the most well known of such readings:

> "On the first day you shall take the product of goodly trees, branches of lulav, boughs of leafy trees and willows of the brook, and you shall rejoice before the Lord your God for seven days."
>
> (Leviticus 23:40)

> Just as the etrog [understood by the phrase "fruit of goodly trees"] has taste as well as fragrance, so Israel has among them those who possess both learning and good deeds. As the lulav has taste but not fragrance, so Israel has among them those who possess learning but no good deeds. Just as the myrtle [understood by the phrase "leafy trees"] has fragrance but no taste, so Israel has among them those who possess good deeds, but not learning. And just as the willow has no taste and no fragrance, so Israel has among them those who possess neither learning nor good deeds.
>
> What then does the Holy One, blessed be He, do to them? To destroy them is impossible. But, He says, let them all be tied together in one band and they will atone for one another.
>
> (Leviticus Rabbah 30:12)

But this is not the only interpretive tradition. In other rabbinic texts the four species are compared to God or to the great biblical heroes and heroines or to the limbs and organs of a human being or to the scholars and judges of Israel. And there are more. In fact, it seems that the example of lulav and etrog is an almost unparalleled opportunity for symbolic explication in Jewish religious literature. Perhaps this results from the rabbis' discomfort with these "primitive" ritual devices, or perhaps the very physicality and richness of the objects inspired them to new heights of interpretation. But for whatever reason, we have an enormous body of material that deals with the reasons behind the ritual. And these texts about lulav and etrog provide only one example of a whole bookcase, as it were, within the classic Jewish library, the literature of *taamei hamitzvot*—"reasons for the commandments."

The *taamei hamitzvot* literature clearly shows that the rabbis believed there was a legitimacy in pursuing the reasons behind the commandments. It may be that absolute obedience to God was the most fundamental "reason" of them all, but the rabbinic interpretive imagination—as evidenced by the example of lulav and etrog—was not inhibited by that fact.

And yet I wonder about *taamei hamitzvot*. In the long run, what is the relationship in real life between the *taam,* the reason, and the mitzvah? What, if anything, does the reason do for the person actually performing the prescribed act?

While I am waving the lulav and etrog, am I really thinking about the four kinds of Jews or the four limbs of the body or anything else? The connection between the experiential dimension of performing a mitzvah and *taamei hamitzvot*—the intellectual reasons behind the mitzvah—is what I am trying to get at here, and I suspect in real life the link is not very strong.

In fact, I suspect that *taamei hamitzvot* are effective really not *during,* but *before* the actual mitzvah: the "reason" may be what gets me to do the mitzvah in the first place. Thus, waving a palm branch and citron may seem rather silly at first blush, but once I am convinced that there is indeed a symbolic dimension to what I am about to do, I can then go ahead in good conscience and perform the deed. It is a kind of antidote to my own self-consciousness if I can see that, yes, very rational people can perform ritual acts such as these.

Taamei hamitzvot work in the realm of rationality, but mitzvot themselves, I think, tend to affect us in some other aspect of our nature. When I myself am actually waving the lulav and etrog, do I really think much about that whole library of explanation? To be fair—only sometimes. On occasion, it does slip into my head: "Ah yes, the four types of Jews. As I am doing this, I am symbolizing my aspirations for a Jewish community bound together in common purpose." But mostly I am not experiencing the "waving" as allegorical. Now of course if you stop me in the street and ask, why do you Jews wave those silly plants on Sukkot, I would have a ready answer: "Silly? They certainly are not silly. Let me tell you about some of the symbolic reasons. . . . " And off I'd go with my *taamei hamitzvot*.

But that is more for public, or at any rate rational, consumption. The *experience* of the ritual is something very different. The deed as it is performed is far more than the explanatory reasons, whether they be the classic allegories or the ones that I have invented this morning. The deed includes my rationality, of course. I certainly have not expunged those *taamim* from at least the level of my subconscious. And a new "reason" that I might create or hear will have the power to engage me. Living interpretation is always fascinating. But as I perform the actual ritual, the reasons may only float occasionally into mind, if at all.

Along with rationality, waving the lulav also carries with it a sense of the ancient and the nonrational that is missing from most of my modern existence. It also gives me the simple and incommunicable pleasure of the ritual and its physicality. I am taken back to some ancient form, but I differ from those ancestors (I suppose, although who can tell?) because often I am both performing the ritual and watching myself perform it at the same time. The thought intrudes: "Hm. Here I am waving the lulav and etrog. Strange ritual, isn't it." Such it is with modernity: Ritual is not an easy thing for any of us.

But what's interesting is that *despite* this self-consciousness, I continue to wave the lulav. Of course, there are times in which the ritual does not seem strange at all. I am on occasion struck by how interesting this ritual is, how the symbolism seems so right. And there are other times still: times when I am not *thinking* about the ritual at all. I am just doing it. And I experience a kind of consonance between the interpretative reasons that I carry with me and the actual performance of the ritual act.

I suspect, however, that despite the nonrational heart of ritual that I have been trying to describe, the rational *taamei hamitzvot* still may play a crucial role in all of this. Because of my modernity not only do I need that rational substructure, that introductory push that allows me to throw off my rational inhibitions, but I also need to be *educated into ritual*. I need to learn to enjoy the ritual, to love the ritual, we could even say. And that affection comes first through the route of reason, bolstered over time by habit. It may be that Jewish rituals, like any difficult discipline, only make sense and come alive after years of concentrated practice. In its own way waving the lulav and etrog is like being the Zen archer or the practitioner of other arcane and demanding arts: At first it just doesn't make too much sense, but over the years one finally comes to see the depth of the experience.[7]

For some, of course, the path takes a different route. For those raised with the early habit of the mitzvot, the role of the "reasons" may be different. In that case *taamei hamitzvot* may become the intellectual bulwark to bolster those habits of childhood acquired long ago. Of course, a person raised with the mitzvot has the advantage of long practice and practical knowledge. Knowing the rudiments of Jewish practice is in itself an accomplishment; after all, even waving the lulav and etrog is a complex and minutely regulated ritual. In addition, such a person has the psychological connection to ritual that goes back into the world of the prerational. If you cannot even remember a time in which you didn't experience lulav and etrog on Sukkot or see the candles being lit before the Sabbath, the mitzvot are in some sense part of your deepest self, an inner world older than memories.

But there are prices to be paid even there. For some the connection to childhood means never coming to see the adult dimension of ritual. For those people the meaning of ritual is always stuck in the past. They may never outgrow the understanding of their youth, and as time passes that fact may inhibit the ritual from growing with them as they get older. And for others the associations with childhood are too tied up with the other things of youth that we all throw off as we get older. Ritual in that case is tied to the psychological constraints of the past—to parents and home and family. To be free of ritual becomes symbolic of being free in general. (In my mind this resembles the story of the second-generation Jews in America who in throwing off their parents' East European ways for the attractions of the Golden Land saw Jewish ritual practice as intricately tied to that "Old World." They felt that in throwing out the past, they had to throw out *all* of the past—the accents, the ways of dress, *and* the Jewish ritual life as well.) Yet despite these impediments, the person raised in Jewish ritual practice enters adulthood with great advantages of knowledge and familiarity.

This is assuming, of course, that one wants to enter into any of this at all. I have said above that the literature of *taamei hamitzvot* can provide a way into ritual practice or a rational substructure upon which to base such practice, but what gets a person to want to open up those books of interpretation to begin with? Most people living in secular modernity live very far away from the world of ritual and religion, and, unlike the situation of our great-grandparents, we can easily choose to opt out of ritual life. Indeed, most people have. It is this reality that is captured by the sociologist Peter Berger in his book *The Heretical Imperative*. Here is how Berger describes the change from the world of the past to the religious situation of today:

> Sociologically speaking, premodern societies are marked by the fact that their institutions have a very high degree of taken-for-granted certainty. This is not to say that this certainty is total; if it were, there would never have been any social change. But the degree of certainty, when compared to that of modern society, is very high indeed. . . .
>
> The modern individual . . . lives in a world of choice, in sharp contrast with the world of fate inhabited by traditional man. He must choose in innumerable situations of everyday life, but this necessity of choosing reaches into the areas of beliefs, values, and world views.[8]

I have said before that I believe that the mitzvot offer an opportunity to give one's life a sense of wholeness and meaning. Such rituals can give one a sense of personal integration within the context of a larger history of one's people and one's past. They offer the power of tradition. I am not saying that this is guaranteed; I am not saying that this works all the time or that it's easy to do. Nor have I yet tried to spell out in detail how this sense of the mitzvot may relate both to the classic demands of the tradition and to our desire to remain part of the modern world. But I do believe that the many achievements of modernity—most of which we would find very difficult to give up—may not offer the final answer to the deepest desires of human beings for meaning, continuity, and wholeness. And I believe that some of that meaning can be found within Judaism's own approach to living in the world. Or at least to the way we can interpret that approach for a contemporary consciousness.

But I think it's clear that despite my own assumptions about the mitzvot and their contemporary power, not everyone will agree. Not everyone will want to begin to explore those rituals or will find them to be meaningful even if they do give them a try. To use an image that I've suggested elsewhere,[9] sometimes I think about the Jewish world today as one traversed by a kind of imaginary line. I picture a large group of people assembled around a swimming pool. On one side of the line are those—by far the larger majority—for whom Jewish symbols, rituals, and literary sources mean very little. Perhaps out of a kind of nostalgia they may attend a Seder or even light candles for Shabbat, but aside from that Judaism does not speak to them in a meaningful way. They are standing around the swimming pool fully dressed; they never really take the plunge.

The other group, considerably smaller, is already in the pool. Sometimes as they splash around in the ambience of Jewish content that is their world, they are aware of that larger group, sitting by the sidelines occasionally peeking in but by and large taking little notice of the swimmers.

For a long time as I thought about the people standing around that pool, I think I operated under a particular delusion—something that could be called perhaps "educator's optimism." I believed that all one had to do was teach people the extraordinary symbolic significance of the mitzvot—*taamei hamitzvot*, the reasons behind practice—and with little hesitation they would leap to embrace them. Of course, in retrospect this seems very naive.

It underestimates exactly what Berger has pointed to—the very nature of modernity makes such a possibility difficult indeed.

But more than naive, I think I was missing something very crucial about the nature of the mitzvot themselves—how deeply they are tied to the nonrational side of reality. It is not simply giving some interesting "reasons" for the mitzvot that will lead people to observe the commandments; because that behavior, as I tried to show earlier, is something much larger than the work of rationality. Studying the symbolism of ritual can help people appreciate why others might want to perform these rituals, but it may have very little influence on their own actions. Or at least that is true for most people. For it's clear that since the mitzvot live in some realm beyond or behind reason (and therefore beyond or behind "reasons" for doing them), in some way the decision to explore the mitzvot and to consider actually practicing them in one's own life is going to have to be in large part a matter of individual temperament. That is, there are people who, because of who they are, will just not want to enter the pool.

And I would not even want to begin to define what the "mitzvot-oriented" temperament would be. The many aspects of the mitzvot themselves would preclude that. I have known people who performed mitzvot out of sentimentality, or mysticism, or obedience, just to name a few motivations. But what is clear is that some people will never find a way in or want to.

The question of temperament was probably always with us. But until the ancient structures of Jewish communal and religious life began to break down, it was irrelevant. People observed the commandments because it was part of the rich fabric of the community's life. For some the commandments were no doubt very meaningful; for others the mitzvot were merely a regular part of ordinary life. Some may have wondered in passing about the whole enterprise of the commandments, but for the most part they were simply what one did.

Nor, despite our idealization of the past, was the observance of mitzvot at the same level of intensity for every Jewish community and in every age before modernity. These matters surely differed among localities and across time. But for the most part, the mitzvot were part of the central structure of the community. We can probably think in our own lives of similar communal structures that we sometimes care deeply about, but which we seldom question even if they don't seem terribly meaningful to us. In our society, for example, just about every child goes to school. We never think much about that fact, even though throughout human history (and in some places even today), most children *didn't* go to school. For us it's simply a fact of life. For some people it is very important and compelling—they love school or they passionately argue about it; for others it is a necessary burden.

Going to school is the expectation of our society as Jewish ritual practice was once the expectation of the community of the past. But with modernity the attitude toward ritual practice changed. When the practice became a matter of choice, temperament and inclination began to become significant factors. (Of course, we should not forget that there are many communities of Jews today in which the communal expectation of ritual practice still obtains. But—excepting the world of the ultra-Orthodox—interactions between the Jewish and non-Jewish culture are so plentiful that Berger's point about choice is very much a reality.) [10]

Thus, there are many who will always stay on the sidelines. But what about those who are open to the exploration? In this case too the "reasons" for the mitzvot are only a partial solution. The fact is, finding *taamei hamitzvot* is not the crucial problem people have in performing the commandments. As I have said before, since the "reason" is only one part of the experience of the ritual itself, having a quiver full of *taamim* may still not lead you to load up the bow. There are many rituals for which I could enumerate lovely explications; but I still might not perform the mitzvah.

Of course, this may itself be one of the dangers of the whole enterprise of *taamei hamitzvot*. The rabbis worried about rationalizing the commandments because they feared that knowing the *reason* might lead someone to say, "Well, in that case I don't have to perform the act. Isn't knowing the reason enough?" [11] Focusing on the reasons, the rabbis argued, no matter what one's motivation, can lead you away from actually performing the commandments.

And for us the difficulty is even greater because the view of the commandments that I suggested before is not based on a sense of the will of God behind the deeds we do. That is, if I live with a consciousness of God's stringent demands upon me, I may perform the mitzvot, as the rabbis had hoped, out of obedience if for no other reason. But without that, performance of the commandments can easily lapse.

We live in a time and culture which does not easily embrace external authority. But we should be cautious about too lightly dismissing the power of "being commanded" as motivation for religious action. The sense of discipline and order that such a sensibility brings, and even the exhilaration of feeling oneself to be serving God's will was a profound force in the lives of Jews for generations, and for many today as well. Those who can hear the clear voice of God's command and who can focus their lives upon it are blessed with a kind of religious confidence that brings rich rewards.

But what about those who do not hear that voice, who do not accept the authority of a greater external will? One can only be honest: You cannot make yourself believe in divine command and practice obedience if you do not feel yourself to be commanded. And although there may be moments when one might very well believe "this is what God wants me to do," most of the time such a belief may simply not be there. Instead, it is the personal significance of the mitzvot that motivates one to perform them. In that case you *choose* to follow that path, rather than feel you are *commanded* to do so.

One possible solution to the dilemma is to take an "as if" approach to the situation. That is, to act "as if" I really did believe that God wanted my steadfast obedience to the divine will, even if I don't feel that all the time. And there are times that such an attitude may allow me a way into observance. I do not expect to perform each mitzvah with perfect concentration; as I said earlier in this chapter, it is precisely that kind of demand within Hasidism that I find daunting. I am perfectly willing to accept the fact that many times I will perform mitzvot without such concentration and intentionality, the quality the rabbis called *kavvanah* (to be "directed"). No, the structure and regularity of the mitzvot is one of its appealing qualities; *kavvanah* in performing the mitzvot is what we can hope for, though not what we need expect.

But despite all that, a consistency in performing the mitzvot is not easy to attain and "as if" is not going to work all the time. Nor am I talking about the more difficult, demanding, or ideologically remote commandments. For example, simply saying the blessing before eating—only one sentence, and an idea that I find completely reasonable and unproblematic—is something I cannot easily find the motivation to do at every meal.

Why should that be so? I have come to see in my own life that there are times that some kind of natural laziness or secular stubbornness is just going to fight against performing the mitzvot. In a way—to take a secular analogy—I sometimes think of the mitzvot as being like exercise or avoiding foods that are bad for you —you know what you should be doing, you know that it's good for you, but it's still hard to do what's right.

Most of us, if we do wish to find a way into the commandments, are going to have to deal with the fact that we have been shaped by modernity. I am reminded of an oft-quoted talmudic dictum of Rabbi Hanina which states, "Greater is he who is commanded and fulfills the commandment than one who is not commanded and fulfills the commandment" (Talmud, *Bava Kamma* 87a). In other words, what really matters is your relationship of service to the divine, not your own human inclinations, even if they are positive ones. This expression of the classic underpinning for the mitzvot, it seems to me, is one that seems very far away from the central values of modernity and one that most of us will have difficulty embracing. For us personal autonomy and decision-making, even in our religious lives, are going to have to be at the heart of who we are.

In that regard we should not forget that our ancestors also understood the difficulty of fulfilling the commandments. After all, the classic literature often refers to the mitzvot as a "yoke" that human beings must bear. Indeed, there is a dangerous side to Torah as well:

> "This is the Torah which Moses placed [Hebrew: *sam*] before Israel. . . . "
>
> (Deuteronomy 4:44)

> If he is worthy, it becomes for him a drug [Hebrew: *sam*] of life, if not it is a drug of death. That is what Rava meant when he said: If he uses it the right way, it is a drug of life to him; if he does not it is a drug of death.
>
> (Talmud, *Yoma* 72b)

Like many midrashic texts, this one bases itself on a wordplay. In this case the Talmud associates the Hebrew verb meaning "to place" (*sam*) with a different word pronounced the same way, "medicine" (also *sam*). Because of the word order of the original, the Talmud is able to read the biblical text as "This is the Torah which is a drug . . . ," an effect that can't quite be captured in translation. And since in classical Hebrew, as in contemporary English, the word "drug" has both positive and negative connotations, an additional dimension is added to the interpretation.

Torah is not a simple thing—it has a two-sided nature. For those who are "worthy" it brings life; for those not worthy, death. (Of course, paradoxically, one of the reasons classically given for the commandments in general is *l'zakot etkhem,* to *make* you worthy.) And what might Rava mean when he says "using it the right way" will make it a drug of life to you? How could one use Torah in the "wrong" way?

One could simply say that the rabbis believed that violating the mitzvot of the Torah would bring a person death, either in the literal sense or in terms of the future punishments that such a person would receive. Thus, if you are unworthy—a sinner—you will eventually find Torah to be "poisonous." But I suspect that the text is somewhat more complex than that. It seems to me that in some way the rabbis here recognize the difficulties of the yoke of Torah and in this utterance, at least, we have an opaque, almost allegorical representation of the darker side of the mitzvot.

But such warnings aside, it is clear that the mitzvot generally were seen as opportunities for joy. *Simha shel mitzvah,* the joy of performing a commandment, was a key element in the traditional understanding of the mitzvot, as was the notion that the highest ideal was to perform mitzvot for "their own sake." Performing a mitzvah for its own sake is a difficult concept, far more so, I think, than the more familiar idea of *Torah lishmah,* study for its own sake, another common rabbinic aspiration. The latter case resonates with all that we know about experiences of learning for the simple joy of learning, both in secular and religious contexts. But what does it mean to perform a mitzvah for its own sake?

Of course, it obviously means not to think about the reward that such a deed may bring. The rabbis wanted to discourage too much focus on the divine ledger of reward and punishment. Indeed, they tell us that the reward of a mitzvah is the chance to do another mitzvah (Mishnah, *Avot* 4:2)! But more than that, the concept of mitzvot for their own sake seems to speak of that inner dimension of connection and integration that I tried to explore earlier in this chapter. At that point I was speaking about a ritual mitzvah, lulav and etrog, but I think that the joy of mitzvah for its own sake can come out of other practices as well. I have noticed in myself over the years that kind of reaction personally whenever I give *tzedakah.* Why this should be I don't know. But I find that after writing out a set of donation checks, there is something that just simply makes me feel good. And I think that it is more than the sense of helping people in need (though that too is powerful), but it also comes out of the feeling that I have just performed a mitzvah!

Now, I am perfectly willing to admit that not everyone is going to feel this. Obviously, one has to care about mitzvot before this can work. Nor, I think, did I myself always have this same kind of reaction. But I've noticed in recent years something that I can only call the joy of mitzvah for its own sake. And I think that comes out of a feeling of relationship to something larger than my own personal whim: my people's history, a sense of my place in the universe.

The growth of this attitude toward mitzvot happened for me

over the course of time, and there is something to be said for the incremental, organic sense of doing mitzvot that the tradition was well aware of. There is no way around the fact that to find "deeds" meaningful one has to do them. As the rabbinic sage Rav said: "From doing mitzvot from ulterior motives you will eventually come to do them for their own sake" (Talmud, *Pesahim* 50b).

Of course, mitzvot were never seen as a field you could wander around in based on your own fancy. Mitzvot were intricately bound, one to the next, in a much larger system or fabric. Yet while it is clear from rabbinic declarations and warnings that every age had its own set of "difficult" or lapsed commandments, what distinguishes our age, and indeed Jewish history since the Emancipation, is the breakdown of the whole acceptability of that larger fabric. In the past there were some Jews who observed the commandments with rigor and others who were less punctilious, but only society's true "outsiders" denied the centrality of the mitzvot themselves. But today, in a world of many options, the norms have changed and the outsiders and insiders have switched positions.

In this kind of world it is probably necessary to rethink the role that mitzvot can play in the lives of most Jews. For some people any commitment to the commandments is going to be gradual and ultimately only partial, if at all. For some a beginning exploration of the mitzvot will lead to other mitzvot. This is the way that the ancient rabbis envisioned it—"a mitzvah will inspire another mitzvah." For reasons I have explored earlier in this chapter, it seems unlikely that everyone will come to find a connection to the whole system of commandments outlined by Jewish tradition.

But more significant, I believe, is the possibility that there are many people who might want to find their way into those commandments, to try them on, so to speak, and perhaps to grow into them. Here I think there are possibilities. To begin with there is one dimension of the commandments that I have touched upon only slightly in my discussion here, but it is not to be underestimated. I have focused mainly on the element of personal significance found in the mitzvot, but we should not forget that many of the commandments are performed within a social context, a community of like-minded people. If the personal-significance side of the mitzvot might be seen as the vertical dimension of the commandments (at least in the traditional imagery—one's connection to God, let us say), this other side of the commandments is its horizontal dimension. Performing the mitzvot—waving the lulav and etrog for example—with others around you doing the same deed gives the individual a sense of belonging, a feeling that one is part of something larger than oneself.

I think in that sense of the feeling I have had attending an early morning weekday service. Not all the people that show up are great spiritual masters, seeking communion with the holy. Very few are, I suppose. But starting the day in communal prayer, seeing friends and neighbors in the first hours of the day, gives everyone—even the least devout—a sense of being bound up in the framework of community and a sense of shared purpose in an enterprise sanctioned by history and tradition. In a time such as ours, characterized by loneliness and displacement, the attraction of a welcoming community needs no explanation.

In addition to that horizontal domain, of course, I do believe that there is an openness in people today toward finding ways of enriching and deepening the experience of their lives in the "vertical" plane. And for that the mitzvot, to be sure, are only one part of a larger picture. But what I have tried to argue in this chapter is that one can find in their symbolic weight and in their very physicality a sense of integration and of joy that is both meaningful and compelling. That, as I have said, does not ease the difficulty of living the life that they demand, particularly given who we are today, but there is a sense around us that secularity, attractive though it is, may not hold every answer. And Judaism, it seems to me, with its complement of ritual and deed, represents a challenge to that secularity, a different kind of echo that we hear behind us.

THREE

BEING SERIOUS: FIRST THOUGHTS ABOUT GOD

In an early work of midrash called Sifre, we find the following remarkable statement:

> ... If you wish to come to know Him who by His word created the world, study *aggadah* for by doing this you will come to know Him ... and will cling to His ways.
>
> (Sifre Deuteronomy, *Ekev* 49)

What does it mean to come to "know" God through the study of aggadah, the imaginative literature of rabbinic interpretation? Examined from one point of view, one might argue that this text provides a kind of easy way out of a difficult problem. Instead of thinking about the question of God, it seems to say, one might be better off simply studying aggadah. For most of us, confronting what we really believe about God is a good deal more difficult than studying texts. In fact, for a religion as intellectually oriented as Judaism, the allure of study can come dangerously close to replacing the hard, personally challenging work of thinking about the big questions of meaning implied by the word "God."

In a similar vein a colleague once pointed out that people find it a good deal easier to talk *about* prayer than actually to pray. "Studying aggadah" broadly defined (that is, to include the study of Jewish texts of all sorts) is an opportunity to talk and argue and

64

debate—all very good things, all meaningful and stimulating. But it is also a chance to *avoid* thinking about bigger matters, words we may feel uncomfortable about—belief, faith, God.

Of course, to be fair, I must quickly point out that in locating these comments in the midrash from Sifre quoted above, I have been unfairly taking shots at an inappropriate straw man. I have used the text as a way to introduce the question of our reluctance to think about God, but in fact the point of the midrash is actually something else. If we look at the section immediately preceding our opening quotation, we see that the text is asking how it is possible for any mere person to come close to God, to understand God:

> "And cleave to Him."
>
> (Deuteronomy 11:22)

> How is it possible for man to ascend to heaven and cleave to fire seeing that it has been said that "the Lord your God is a consuming fire" (Deut. 4:24) and "His Throne was fiery flames" (Daniel 7:9)? Rather, cling to the Sages and to their disciples and I will evaluate it as if you had ascended to heaven and had received the Torah there.
> . . . If you wish to come to know Him who by His word created the world, study *aggadah* for by doing this you will come to know Him . . . and will cling to His ways.
>
> (Sifre Deuteronomy, *Ekev* 49)

God, according to this text, is like fire, something no human being can touch without harm. In the next chapter we will look more carefully at this metaphor for God, but it is clear at this point that the midrashist is suggesting how impossible it is for human beings to know God. It is a profoundly difficult task open only to the most religiously gifted, if even to them. What we can do, says this midrash, is to watch the behavior of the Sages, those spiritually advanced individuals from whom there is much to learn.

It is at this point that our previously quoted section appears, offering an alternative approach. Aside from looking at the exemplary lives of the Sages and their disciples, in trying to understand God we can also turn to the resource of aggadah. The study of Torah, in other words, can be a way into religious insight.

But our midrash seems to imply something even more specific about the nature of Torah study. Religious texts may be sophisticated or simple, abstruse, speculative, philosophical, or argumentative. But behind them all, we are being told, we should not forget that these texts are human attempts to express something about the real experience of what we call religion, namely, the sense of what it means to live one's life in relationship to the holy. By "the holy" I mean, at the most basic level, the sense that there exists a realm of meaning greater than oneself. That reality may or may not bear the name "God," but a sense of the holy is at the heart of all religious expression. Religious texts of many varieties are all in some way trying to capture something of that experience.

Some of these works, such as mystical texts, emanate from a direct encounter with the holy experienced by the writer. These experiences are often seen as being something "beyond words," and yet at the same time, their elusive quality pushes people to try to understand them through the only means we have, that of language. Thus, the literature occasioned by such experiences tries to interpret and explain them, attempting to show others the meaning of such events and, just as importantly, in doing so helping the writers clarify for themselves what they had experienced.

Mystical works, of which there are vast numbers within the Jewish tradition,[1] present an obvious example, but nonmystical writings also emanate from an encounter with the holy. The complicated pages of a talmudic argument represent something more than mere mental gymnastics. In these debates the rabbis of the talmudic age were trying to answer questions they felt to be of monumental significance: What, they wanted to know, does God expect of me? What does it mean to live a holy life?

Classic religious philosophy is another example of the same inclination. Behind the ordered arguments is an urgency as well. We are not reading idle speculations when we pick up Maimonides' writings, for example; we are looking at that thinker's attempt to understand something that was very real and very pressing for him: What is the nature of God and God's relationship to human beings? I say quite carefully here "for him," because this was the way that Maimonides might have framed the question. But it's important to ask also: What about us? How do we think about the question of God?

And here we face a different problem. For the religious writers of the premodern age, the existence and reality of God was a given fact. They knew it through two paths, which we shall look at below—*tradition* and *experience*. But for us each of these paths that once led to faith has become problematic. Before we look at the issue of God specifically, I would like to consider the situation in which we find ourselves today.

Our ancestors believed that tradition—as preserved in both written and oral form, in holy books and in interpretations passed on by word of mouth—represented evidence able to support their faith. These traditions—in particular the Bible itself, since it was seen as the word of God—reported as accurately as any modern news broadcast the deeds God performed and the words God uttered. To paraphrase the medieval philosopher Judah Halevi's view of the reliability of tradition: Six hundred thousand people standing at the foot of Mount Sinai could hardly have been mistaken![2]

By and large, it did not trouble these tradition-oriented people, as it would others hundreds of years later, that they were working out of a self-enclosed system, that the argument for the validity of tradition was in essence a circular one. That is, how do we know the Bible is true? Because the Bible tells us so. But during the Middle Ages questions about the authorship of the Bible began to be raised, and later thinkers such as Spinoza pressed the case further. Eventually, by the mid nineteenth century, a view of the Bible that stressed its *human* origins began to undercut its authority as a source for faith.[3] If the Bible is the work of human beings, this argument proposed, how can we base our beliefs about God on the accuracy of its reports? How do we know that it is telling us what God actually did or said?

Of course, one could still fall back on the second path, the argument of experience. Looking at history, one could say that the Bible and other holy books may be of human authorship, but nonetheless they accurately represent how human beings actually experienced God's presence in the world. These human beings, the biblical authors, have done us the favor of passing on in reliable fashion what really happened. Thus, the Bible gives us the words and deeds of God as reported by the Israelites in ancient times in the same way and with the same reliability that Walter Cronkite reported the landing of the first man on the surface of the moon.

But unfortunately for us today this analogy is not terribly convincing because our difficulties with the entire position are at a deeper level: Almost all of us today are suspicious of the very existence of anything called "the experience of God." We know about technology; we have seen rockets with our own eyes, and when CBS News tells us that a rocket has landed on the moon—with videotape to boot!—we are prepared to "believe" it. But do we "believe in" the experience of God?

When we talk about what is "real," we like to think that we are examining objective facts. But in fact all of us experience the world through the filter of expectations and preconceived categories of understanding. Whenever something happens to us, the categories of understanding that we all walk around with help us to make sense out of that experience. Most of the time we are not even aware that such interpreting is going on. But particularly when we come upon something new or unexpected, we can see it operating. We try to make sense of what happens in the light of what has happened to us before and what we understand to be possible.

The categories of interpretation with which we operate come first of all from our biology, the physical limitations and advantages we possess as human beings: We cannot fly; we cannot see in the dark or breathe under water; but we can process information, use and make tools, and think abstractly. Our biology as humans means that we will see and understand reality differently from the way other living creatures experience it.

And beyond the effects of biology we see the world through

the eyes and expectations of a culture that we were born into and a history that we learn about as we grow up. In other words, the experience of what is "real" is not something neutral, something that just happens *to* people, but rather, expectations—formed by our biology and our culture and our past—*shape* what we take to be real. Thus, for people today it may be that our biology (that is, the brain cells we were born with) and our past (the record of our ancestors) could lead us to accept experiences of God, but— and this is a very big "but" indeed—the culture that most of us were born into strongly pushes us in the other direction, toward doubt or denial.

We can imagine, by analogy, a tribesman arriving from Africa on the day of the American moon launch. This representative of a so-called primitive culture has never seen a television screen, but if we put him in front of the tube and explain to him what is happening before his very eyes, how might he react? Quite possibly he would tell us that of course no man can land on the moon, that only gods live on the moon, that Walter Cronkite is a sorcerer and the little bright box we call a television is really a magician's trick. Some years ago there was a science-fiction film whose plot involved a phony space launch perpetrated as a giant ruse by the government for some nefarious purpose. Everything had been staged for the unwitting TV cameras and the entire world had been fooled. In its own paranoid way that movie confirms the tribesman's perception—after all, how do we know that it "really" happened?

Now what if we visited the tribesman's world? What if we were presented with a people who saw living spirits in the fire of the stove or demons in the trees around the huts? To our eyes, that understanding of the world is as absurdly inaccurate as ours was to the tribesman.[4]

Of course, for the most part, none of this is a matter of choice. We do not choose the culture that we are born into. It is true that the tribesman could decide to emigrate to America and we might find him years later wearing a three-piece suit and working on Wall Street. And certainly, to look at the flip side, there are tales of anthropologists "going native." But by and large we tend to stay part of at least the larger culture that we were born into. And that culture, that world we call modernity, is one that has conditioned us to view with suspicion, even ridicule, any experience called God.

Modernity, of course, encompasses a complex set of beliefs and influences. These include our faith in science and technology as well as our respect for the thinkers who created that worldview. We are the heirs of the European Enlightenment, which placed its emphasis on human rationality. The experience of God, though it may have its rational side, is much more closely allied to the nonrational side of human consciousness. Thus, through the influence of rationalism, those experiences not subject to the rule of reason became suspect. One important thinker, the early-nineteenth-century philosopher Ludwig Feuerbach, helped shape modernity's conception of religion by seeing religious ideas as mere "projections" of the world of humanity onto the plane of divinity. Later Marx saw humanity as driven by the economic realities of class structure, while Freud suggested that human experience emanates from darker forces of aggression and will and sexuality. For Freud and for Marx—in different ways—religion was a mask for the world of the merely human.

For our times Freud in particular has been a strong factor in the way we tend to see the world. Let's say, for example, one morning you were to wake up and have a vision in which an angelic being dictated wisdom to you. How would you react? For Joseph Karo, the great sixteenth-century Jewish legalist of Safed, there was no question: He had been visited by a heavenly messenger, a *maggid,* who could reveal secrets of the upper worlds.[5] Nor did Karo see any conflict between his role as legal authority and his visions of a messenger from heaven. But in the world after Freud, for most of us such a vision would be more likely to occasion a visit to one's psychotherapist than an affirmation of religious faith.

And what would it take to make us see things differently? Could anything? If I prayed in the evening to win the state lottery and the phone rang the next morning with the news that I had won a fortune, would *that* make me change my mind? Or would I say, as I suspect I would, "What a strange coincidence that was!"

Now of course there is another way we could look at it. We could argue that in ancient times people did indeed have experiences of God, but that for whatever reason—perhaps our unworthiness—people today are not granted that privilege. Thus, even in the Talmud (*Berakhot* 20a) we find Rav Papa asking Abaye why miracles happened to their ancestors but none happen in their time. (Because, Abaye answers, in the past they were willing to martyr themselves and we are not. And in a symbolic sense perhaps Abaye is correct!) But the reasonable explanation is not that things happened in the past that don't happen today, but rather that our sense of the absence of God is a matter of perception and interpretation in the way I have been suggesting above. That is, human beings' understanding of their experience is generally based on the expectations and categories of explanation found in their culture. And in our culture no such expectations and categories about experiencing God exist, while in the past they did.

Thus, if I am visiting our African tribesman and a tree falls on his neighbor's head, my explanation would probably be "bad luck," while the tribesman might say "the gods have punished him." And of course—as we rationalists often forget—*either* explanation is plausible. Despite the accomplishments of Western science, I cannot prove to the tribesman that there are no gods who were out to punish the neighbor. In fact, from a certain point of view, his explanation is a good deal more *rational* than mine! His, after all, is of a world ruled by cosmic order, a world in which events have clear meanings. What kind of "rationality," he well might say, is found in "bad luck"?

Our situation, then, is to find a way to think about God in a world in which neither tradition nor experience has the force it once had. Of course, we could take another route—we could decide *not* to deal with the issue of God at all. One of the interesting dimensions of Judaism as a religion is that it actually can offer this kind of possibility. Judaism, as has often been pointed out, places its emphasis on deed rather than on belief. And although rabbinic sources strongly condemn the nonbeliever—called *kofer ba-ikkar,* "one who denies the key principle"—it is clear that the crucial aspect of being a Jew was always seen as adherence to the mitzvot, to religious practice. The rabbis, of course, found it hard to imagine that a person could perform the commandments *without* a belief in God. For the rabbis, as we have seen in chapter 2, the underlying motivation behind human compliance with the commandments was the divine authority at their source. In the words of one rabbinic source, "A person does not go to commit a transgression until he first denies Him who commanded him not to do it" (Tosefta, *Shevuot* III, 7).

Aside from its theological implications, the focus on deed in Judaism served an important social function as well. For example, it meant that ten Jews, each with a different conception of God and each with a different understanding of the traditional liturgy, could all pray together in the same room without ever having to examine one another about aspects of their faith. In that way Judaism for the most part was able to avoid the kinds of schisms over belief that wracked the history of Christianity.[6] (This is not to say that in the past there were not significant differences of *practice* among Jews and Jewish communities. We can still see that today when very observant Jews from Oriental communities will eat rice and beans on Passover, while Jews from European backgrounds consider those foods forbidden on that holiday.)

I have raised this matter of the Jewish emphasis on actions over belief not for its historical interest but because one could, perhaps, use it as a convenient way out of the entire "God problem." The question of God, we might say, the issue of belief, is not a Jewish question! What matters is the system of mitzvot. That's what it means to be a Jew.

One could take, in that case, the perspective about the mitzvot that I suggested in chapter 2 and put all the theological dimensions of the mitzvot on the proverbial back burner. In that chapter I spoke of the mitzvot as the actions I use to make my life meaningful and whole, that in a world of moral fogginess and infinite choice, I have within my own power the ability to make some sense out of my life through the "old ways" of my people. Such a conception of the commandments does not depend on the traditional notion of One who Commands, and like that group of varied Jews praying together in the same room, I too can keep my private thoughts—perhaps my questions and doubts—about God and belief to myself and just get on with the business of leading a meaningful Jewish life through the practice of the commandments.

I would be less than honest if I didn't say that such an option is appealing. I cannot speak about the Jews of the past, but I think for many Jews today the focus on deed and the avoidance of questions of belief is an effective solution to the dilemma of trying to be a religious person in an age of doubt.

But as much as this is an age of secular skepticism, perhaps for that very reason, it also seems to be a time of religious search. We see that fact manifested in phenomena such as those who "return" to religion (called in Jewish circles the *baalei teshuvah*) and in the rise of Christian fundamentalism. Indeed, a visitor from Mars to the United States, placed in front of a television or radio tuned to certain stations on the airwaves might never realize he was visiting a supposedly "secular" nation!

But even those who have not "returned" are seeking ways of going beyond the secularity of contemporary life, looking for the transcendent, the meaningful, in ways that may or may not be conventionally "religious" but which nonetheless flow out of those same personal needs. Theodore Roszak has called this phenomenon the "contemporary hunger for wonders" often found in

> a vast popular culture that is still deeply entangled with piety, mystery, miracle, the search for personal salvation. . . . Charismatic faith, mystical religion, oriental meditation, humanistic and transpersonal psychotherapy, altered states of consciousness . . . there are obviously many differences between these varied routes. Yet, I would argue that they point in a common direction.

73

This, he claims, is the desire to find some "personal knowledge of the extraordinary."[7] And Roszak is not alone in pointing out other elements of that same religious "hunger" around us.[8]

All of which convinces me that there is no way we can avoid exploring the issue of God, even if Judaism *might* possibly allow us a way out. But when we try to think about God, I believe we must do so in the light of one crucial ground rule, an idea expressed for me in the following talmudic text:

> Ezra prayed "Our God, great, mighty and awesome God."
>
> (Nehemiah 9:32)

> R. Joshua ben Levi said: Why were one group of sages known as "the Men of the Great Assembly?" Because they restored the crown of the divine attributes to the way it had once been.
>
> Moses had come and said: "The great, mighty and awesome God" (Deut. 10:17). Then came Jeremiah and said: "Strangers are destroying His Temple. Where then are His awesome deeds?" Thus Jeremiah prayed "O great and mighty God whose name is the Lord of Hosts" (Jer. 32:18), omitting the attribute "awesome."
>
> Then Daniel came and said: "Strangers are enslaving His children. Where then are His mighty deeds?" Thus Daniel prayed "O great and awesome God . . . (Dan. 9:4), omitting the attribute "mighty". . . .
>
> (Talmud, *Yoma* 69b)

The text begins in typical midrashic fashion by posing a question about the language of the Bible. We find in the prayer of Ezra a formula that mimics that of Moses' prayer in the book of Deuteronomy in which God is described by His "attributes": great, mighty, and awesome. And yet if we look at prayers uttered by two other prophets, Jeremiah and Daniel, we find that in each case one of those three divine attributes had been omitted. Why did this happen, ask the rabbis, and how did it happen that Ezra, a later prophet, once again used the formula of Moses?

It is clear to the rabbis that what we have in the prayer of Ezra is a *restoration* of the original prayer formula, an accomplishment which the rabbis ascribe to the "Men of the Great Assembly," a legendary group of sages associated in rabbinic lore with the time of Ezra. Indeed, it appears that what made Men of the Great Assembly "great," at least according to our text here, was the fact that they were able to restore that proper ancient formula.

The core of the explication is in the way the rabbis deal with the quotations from Jeremiah and Daniel. By carefully looking at these prayers, the rabbis noticed the "omission" of certain words from the prayer of Moses. Now of course this whole discussion is based on an assumption we may not accept. Namely, we have no evidence that in biblical times Moses' prayer was seen as some kind of known liturgical formula and therefore was something *consciously* varied by the two later prophets. But in our text the rabbis seem to work on this assumption, and in fact the historical truth of their view makes very little difference in considering the key point they are trying to make. As we have seen, the factual accuracy or structural concern upon which a given midrash is based is often irrelevant to the underlying religious statement that the rabbis propose.

Here, the rabbis argue, we see that Jeremiah and Daniel leave out certain attributes about God because the prophets' historical circumstances—the events they saw happening around them—prevented them from speaking those words: How can we call God "awesome" when the Temple is being destroyed? How can we call God "mighty" when His people are being enslaved? (Of course the words "mighty" and "awesome" themselves seem almost interchangeable here, but once again we have to overlook the minor inconsistencies that are simply part and parcel of rabbinic interpretation.)

The text then continues, in a section we have not quoted here, with a complex description of the interpretive turns that allowed the Men of the Great Assembly to restore the ancient prayer, after which it concludes with the following discussion:

> . . . But how could Jeremiah and Daniel omit something established by Moses? R. Eleazar said: "Since they knew that the Holy One, blessed be He, insists on truth, they were unable to say any false things about Him."
>
> (Talmud, *Yoma* 69b)

To me this is an important piece of wisdom that should inform our own speculation about the question of God. The Men of the Great Assembly found methods of interpretation to justify the restoration of the full prayer,[9] but Jeremiah and Daniel took a different path. Faced with a discrepancy between their own perception of truth and their own understanding of the world around them, these prophets did not take the route of the Men of the Great Assembly, who solved the issue by complex interpretive twists. Jeremiah and Daniel simply stated, "We cannot say those words *because they are not true.*" Note that the text here takes a radical stand: It does not say that Jeremiah and Daniel *believed* the words to be untrue, but rather that the words *were* untrue. Of course, the Men of the Great Assembly are lauded for their restoration of the original prayer, but Jeremiah and Daniel are also praised for their espousal of truth.

To my mind there is guidance in this text about the way we should think about God. The ground rule I want to propose is that when we speak about God, we say the things we really think and not the things we *think* we should think. A good deal of discussion about God is undermined, I believe, by a kind of dishonesty of good intentions. People either feel embarrassed about their doubts or unclear about their beliefs, and instead of spelling out the "truth," they speak about God with a kind of diffidence —or confidence—that may cause more problems than it solves. Here, at any rate, I think we do better to avoid the interpretive cleverness of the Men of the Great Assembly and stick with the hard truth of Jeremiah and Daniel.

Our task then is to be honest with ourselves and at the same time to address those difficult questions that all people have, as we try to find our own relationship to the *ikkar,* that first principle of religious life.

The religious literature of Judaism is, of course, filled with statements about the nature of God. But how are we to understand those writings when their language and assumptions seem so very different from our own?

Our earlier discussion of the African tribesman may give us a place to start. The tribesman, we recall, when told about the tree falling on his neighbor's head, ascribed the event to the work of the gods, while our inclination was to view it as bad luck. On the one hand, the two explanations of the falling tree—bad luck versus the gods' will—may merely serve, as it was intended earlier, to show the power of cultural premises in predetermining our perception of "reality." Like those old visual-perception games in which black and white drawings appear to represent different figures depending on how you look at them (is it a girl with long hair or an old man with a beard?), what we *expect* to see leads us to see what we see.

But looking at it from another angle, this is not merely an exercise in exploring cultural relativism. Knowing the cultural premises behind any given idea does not necessarily undermine the power of the idea itself. Thus, we can say that just because we may know why Freud wrote what he wrote—what *his* cultural and psychological world was, in other words—doesn't mean that he didn't at least to some extent speak "truth."

In the same way, we may be able to look back at the world of religious tradition and think once again about the "truth" of what our ancestors were saying about God. In other words, even though I may know something from the psychological and cultural point of view about why Joseph Karo saw a heavenly *maggid* —he was a man of a certain background and temperament and he lived in a world in which angels were believed to be real—nonetheless, he still may have seen an angel! Or to state it more precisely: I myself do not "believe in" angels; I don't believe that they exist as a factual reality; I have never seen one and doubt that I ever will; but I am willing to believe that Joseph Karo had an insight into what I would call "the realm of the holy" which he experienced and expressed as "seeing or hearing a *maggid*."

That doesn't mean that Karo consciously decided to "choose" that metaphor to express his vision—indeed, for him an angel really was there. Karo and all the others in our tradition who had experiences of God, expressed in many different ways, may in their own way be offering us today what was seen in the past as the testimony of tradition, if we were to take them seriously enough. Simply put, what these writers are telling us is that the realm of the holy exists, is "true." The literal content of what they saw—a Karo or a Rabbi Akiva or an Isaiah—the terms they used and the specific reality that they perceived is very different from our own. But isn't it possible that, despite that, they still spoke truth?

To put it another way: If I go to watch a cricket game—something I know absolutely nothing about—I may come back and speak about it in terms completely bound by my own psychology and culture. So I may talk about the whole game in the language of baseball and I may project my own personal biases as I describe it. Other people may say "he really doesn't know anything at all about cricket. Everything he says is influenced by the one thing he does know—baseball." But that doesn't mean that a game was not played that day. Isn't there, in other words, some aspect of reality behind the story; or, as Peter Berger has put it:

> Modern philosophy and science . . . are quite correct in seeing religion as a symbolization of the human world. The gods are indeed symbols of human realities. This insight, important as it is, does not necessarily imply that the gods are *nothing but* that.[10]

The view of the last century of cultural and religious scholarship has often implied (or stated outright!) that in a way the testimony of tradition represents only the "errors" of our ignorant ancestors. I am not saying that we should give up our own rationality; we certainly should respect the insights of modern scholarship and see the historical and cultural factors behind religious thought and expression. But I think that we can use the anthropological perspective mentioned before to teach us something else as well: When we look at the life of other cultures, we find a reality and truth there no less real and no less true than our own. And that approach can be applied as well to the texts from the past that we study. The ancient texts may speak in a foreign or exotic tongue, so to speak, but that is not to say that these texts do not speak the truth.

Perhaps the old term "belief" may be relevant here. I have

always found the formulation "Do you believe in God?" a difficult and not particularly helpful question. What does it mean to "believe in" God? That there *is* a God? That God does certain things? And what did that God do? Is that God we "believe in" the God of the book of Exodus? Or Jeremiah's God? Or Maimonides'?

Instead, I would argue that the real matter of belief is connected to the way we look at the insights of tradition, preserved for us in the texts of the past. We can choose to look at those texts with the analytic eye of science; we can see them as matters of historical circumstance, of cultural values, of psychological expression; and of course all of that is legitimate. But I think belief enters when we choose to see the religious writings of the past as matters of truth as well. There is nothing that I can say to verify those writings, but that moment of belief, that place which is beyond rationality, lies in the statement that these texts, speaking in their own language nonetheless tell us something that is *real.*

To be sure, this belief is subject to doubt and questioning, but, despite that, I have glimmerings of insight from my own individual experience that occasionally help confirm it. As I've said before, if I lived in a world of continuous holy experience, I would have many fewer religious questions. Of that there is no doubt. But my own statement of faith is that my ancestors have something to teach me about God and religious experience that I should not be quick to dismiss.

When we think about belief and about the day-to-day reality we see about us, an even bigger question, it seems to me, is what we "believe" about the meaning of our own lives. How do we look at our experiences over time? Do we see our lives as random events, unconnected happenings? In that regard a powerful question about belief is raised by the following enigmatic text:

> Rava taught:
> When, after his death, a person is taken to be judged, he will be asked the following questions:
> Did you conduct your business affairs with integrity?
> Did you set aside fixed times for the study of the Torah?
> Did you fulfill the commandment of procreation?

> Did you hope for salvation?
> Did you engage in the careful study of wisdom?
> Did you learn to understand how one thing follows from another?
>
> (Talmud, *Shabbat* 31a)

This talmudic text tries to consider those things about which tradition says human beings will be judged in the last reckoning. All the questions are clear, indeed almost predictable, until we reach the last line. And there we wonder: what does it mean to "understand how one thing follows from another"? To me this text seems to be suggesting that one of the tasks we ought to do in our lifetime, is to find a sense of continuity and meaning in the story of our lives, to take the events of our own experience with a deeper level of seriousness than we might normally do.

Essentially, the question of meaning is a religious question: Are the things that happen to us a random set of disconnected events or do we find a sense of cohesion in our own life histories? In the language of the Jewish tradition this problem has been discussed as the nature of the divine hand that guides human destiny. Rabbi Akiva's famous aphorism—"Everything is seen and freedom of choice is given" (*Avot* 3:15) sets the tone for that complicated, often almost contradictory debate. For Akiva's paradoxical statement includes at once both the fact of divine foreknowledge ("everything is seen") and the opportunity for human beings to control their own actions ("freedom of choice is given"). And how could both be true at once?

But to review the long philosophical debate over human free will and divine determinism is not my concern here. Instead, what I wish to consider is the whole question of whether we see a sense of meaning in the ordinary events of our lives. It seems to me that we are greatly aided here by a central insight of psychotherapy that suggests that in some sense our lives can be seen as intelligible *stories*. That is, when we look back on events, there is a kind of wholeness that seems to emerge.

In the Talmud we find Rabbi Yohanan's statement: "A man's feet are responsible for him; they lead him to the place where he is wanted" (*Sukkah* 53a). That is, we often feel a kind of inner destiny that drives our lives, both for good and ill. Perhaps that "place where he is wanted" is the culmination of all those events of character and genetic influence and cultural milieu and parental care—most of which none of us have any control over. In that sense our lives *are* predetermined. We are the products of our own past and yet, as Akiva cautions, no one wants to live without the sense that "freedom of choice is given." Most of us, unless mental illness incapacitates us, do not feel that we are prisoners of our past. We feel we can change. Indeed, change is the very symbol of our freedom.

And we also can feel the events of our lives as a kind of story. The psychologist Erik Erikson tells of following up many years later a group of children he had once worked with. In their youth these children had been studied as they used blocks during play. What, the psychologists wanted to know, was the symbolic meaning of these play constructions? One boy, a black child from a poor family, used to imagine himself to be the Lone Ranger. At the same time, the boy, during his playtime, had built block figures representing caged wild animals that needed to be guarded. When Erikson saw him years later, he discovered that the boy had grown up to become an inspirational leader for groups of black teenagers. Erikson describes his conversation with the man:

> But when I now inquired what he thought had given him the strength to guide youngsters in a riotous mood, he said something like this: "These boys can see that I am strong and they feel that I have it in me to be violent myself. But they also know that I have my anger well in hand and they could never provoke me to act against my values. So they listen to me." This is as good a statement on nonviolence as I have heard; but it also seemed quite consonant with the repetitive theme of the play constructions that he had done when he was in his early teens, the theme of wildness contained and yet also transcended by discipline and self-expression. . . . He had become aware of his anger and yet also learned to employ it in social action. As so often, his life, when compared with early observations, was an instance of a promise kept beyond prediction, and his play constructions had a recognizable place in that life history.[11]

Here we have the story of a life whose themes have been consistent throughout. A tale, a narrative, emerges that leads from childhood play to mature adulthood. If we were to look at our experiences with the same care, a similar sense of "story" would likely emerge.

Of course, the great difference between our perception of meaning and the language of the traditional sources is that we view our lives "backward," after the fact, and the traditional texts speak about the "seeing eye" of the God who knows all in advance. And yet if freedom is indeed given, if, in other words, we are products—even as Rabbi Akiva would put it—of our own will, then the difference is not all that great. Our ancestors were able to say something we perhaps cannot—"What has happened to me is all God's plan"—but seeing our lives as meaningful involves being able to say something not so very different after all: "Yes, it does all come together. My life does make sense." It means, in other words, that we are always forced, in my phrase from before, to "be serious"; we, as the Talmud points out, are always challenged to answer that very big question from the *human* perspective: Did you learn to understand how one thing follows from another?

This way of thinking about our own stories may give us insight into the issue of belief and intimations of the power of meaning as understood by traditional religion. In this way we can, in fact, see that our "belief" about the wholeness, the structure of meaning, in our own lives is analogous to the power of belief that religion has asserted; we too believe that our destiny is shaped by forces that we recognize but only vaguely understand. But of course such a perspective still does not directly deal with the question of God. In that regard I have suggested in this chapter that the testimony of tradition, as seen in classical texts that speak about the divine, may offer us a way into thinking about God. It is to that larger matter that we turn in the next chapter.

GOD

In the last chapter I spoke about tradition and experience as two great foundations of religious faith in the past and why today each of them presents us with certain difficulties. But there is a third traditional pathway to belief that we should also put on the agenda: finding God through the path of *reason*. Isn't it possible, this position argues, that there is something about the very nature of the world that leads us, through the rational powers of our own minds, to accept the reality of God? To explore this idea more deeply we can turn to a midrash on the first great religious "call" in the Bible:

> "The Lord said to Abram: Go forth from your native land and from your father's house to the land that I will show you."
>
> (Genesis 12:1)

> R. Isaac said: This may be compared to a man who was traveling from place to place when he saw a castle in flames. Is it possible that the castle lacks a person to look after it, he wondered? The master of the castle looked out and said, "I am the master of the castle." Similarly, because Abraham our father said, "Is it conceivable that there is none to look after the world?" The Holy One, blessed be He, looked out and said to him, "I am the Master, the Sovereign of the Universe."
>
> (Genesis Rabbah 39:1)

The midrash above, like many rabbinic interpretive texts, begins with an implicit question about the biblical text: Why at the beginning of chapter 12 in Genesis does God choose Abraham as the father of what will later become the Jewish people? Why was that particular person appropriate to become "Abraham our father"? This kind of investigation is one we often find in the rabbinic literature about biblical characters. Indeed, one of the intriguing questions that any reader feels about those figures in the Bible chosen by God is, does the prophet appear to get chosen because he is worthy or is he worthy because he was chosen? In other words, does God seek out people who are already appropriate and make them into prophets, or does the very choice by God take ordinary people and make them extraordinary? Were Moses or David or Deborah or Samson—all very different characters— unusual people before the divine mission, or did the mission (and the relationship to God because of the mission) change them into something greater?

In general, when faced with this question, the rabbis argued for the first point of view and tried to find those special elements already present in the individuals that made them worthy of divine choice. Thus, midrashim about the origins of various biblical figures try to show how reasonable it was that they later became the messengers of God.[1]

The case of Abraham is particularly striking since he, after all, becomes the starting point of the entire history of Judaism. Yet before the divine command to "go forth from your native land," the Bible tells us virtually nothing about him, aside from the genealogical account at the end of Genesis, chapter 11. There his origins are traced back to Shem, one of the three sons of Noah. Why, the rabbis want to know, was this man in particular chosen by God? What had made him worthy? The legends about Abraham are a striking example of the way the so-called "laconic style" of the Bible—the way the Bible tells its tales with very few details —leads to the evolution of midrashic interpretation.[2]

The midrashim about Abraham therefore tend to stress his personal discovery of faith, his understanding that there was a God that ruled the universe. Thus, we have, among others, the midrashic story of Abraham breaking the idols in his father's home.[3] The midrashic text quoted above is also part of that interpretive tradition.

In our text Abraham recognizes the need for the castle to have a caretaker, that is, for the world to have a Master. This idea too is part of a larger midrashic family of sources. There are many texts that present the image of God as creator of a well-ordered universe: God is an architect who designed a palace or a builder who constructed a ship. In fact the Torah itself is seen as the blueprint that God consulted in creating the ordered universe.

Interestingly enough, in recent years the idea of the well-ordered universe has been getting some unexpected support from the world of science, particularly from the writing of physicists such as Robert Jastrow and others.[4] Since contemporary physics sees the universe as having a moment of origin—"the big bang theory"—it is only a short step from there to the notion of some kind of Mind behind that instant of creation.

There is a piece of common wisdom which holds that the job of science is to give the "what" and the job of religion is to give the "why." Of course, no one knows why the universe came into being, but contemporary science seems to suggest that at one specific point in time an event we might call creation did occur. Clearly, the fact that the universe had a moment of origin does not *necessarily* mean that the universe was intentionally created, but the realm of physics may move us in that direction, particularly because of the sense of rationality and order that seems to underlie the fundamental laws of physical matter. Surely, this argument goes, such rationality must emanate from some monumental Intelligence. The most famous example in modern physics of a scientist who focused on the ordering forces of the universe is of course Einstein, who saw himself uncovering the Mind of God in the deepest structures of the universe. According to Einstein, these laws of physics were not, as others have suggested, merely human fantasies about "order" projected upon a world of actual disharmony, the way that a person might think he *sees* a pattern in the picture of an inkblot where instead he is *creating* that pattern by the ordering tendency within his own mind. On the contrary, as Einstein said in a letter to a colleague:

> You find it strange that I regard the comprehensibility of the world . . . as a miracle or as an eternal secret. Now, a priori, one ought to expect the world to be chaotic, in no way comprehensible through thinking. One could (even *should*) expect the world to be governed by law only to the extent that we intervene by introducing some order. This would be a kind of order similar to the alphabetical order of the words in a language. The kind of order created, for example, by Newton's theory of gravitation, is of an entirely different character. Even though the axioms of the theory are posited by man, yet the success of such an undertaking presupposes a high degree of orderliness of the objective world, which was not to be expected a priori. Herein lies the "miracle" which is becoming increasingly deep with the development of our knowledge.[5]

The very existence of the universe is one piece of "evidence" in this position, but following along the same line, Jewish traditional texts emphasize something else as well. The *variety* we see in the natural world is another indication of a divinely planned creation:

> See how many animals there are in the world and how many beasts there are in the world and how many fish there are in the sea. Is the voice of any one of them like the voice of any other? Or the appearance of any one of them like the appearance of any other? . . . Hence it is said, "How great are your works, O Lord" (Ps. 92:6).
>
> (Seder Eliahu Rabbah, 2)

Human beings, these sources state, can scarcely understand the underlying significance of what we today would call the ecological system:

> Even creatures that seem to you completely superfluous to creation like fleas, gnats and flies are all an integral part of the creation of the world, and they all fulfill the mission of the Holy One, blessed be He.
>
> (Genesis Rabbah 10:7)

The variety of nature and the complex, subtle relationships among these creatures and between living beings and their environment is an argument, it seems, for the existence of a deeper order to the world than might be readily apparent. In fact, in our own time, as issues about the destruction of the natural world are more and more on our minds, we have witnessed a whole generation of contemporary writers such as Barry Lopez, Robert Finch, and Annie Dillard (along with the rediscovery and reprinting of earlier nature writers like John Muir and Henry Beston) whose loving description of the world of nature has expressed a deeply felt religious message about the inner life of creation.[6]

But despite the appeal of authors like Jastrow and the nature writers, I feel that ultimately there is something missing in the "theology of the physicist"—namely, what is the relationship between that Creator and that universe which was created?

If we look once again at our midrash above, we notice that the insight that Abraham gains is not that there is a *builder* (although of course there are numerous Jewish texts that do assert such a view)—for him that was an obvious point. Rather, Abraham's question was "Is it conceivable that there is none to look after the world?" In other words, is there an ongoing role for God in history?

After the act of creation ("the first three minutes," as we might say) does God, in Abraham's view, remain involved in the life of the world? Especially, if we follow the metaphor of the midrash, when we look out on a world that often appears to be "in flames." Indeed, if we press the parable of that midrash a little bit further, we can ask if there might not be a deeper set of questions underneath it: If the universe is in flames, why doesn't the Master do something about it? How does the fire "prove" that there is a Master? It might in fact prove the opposite—that the world has no one to put out the flames!

And more than that, the physicist's God presents another problem as well. It seems to me that a position about the nature of God has to make some sense in the light of people's day-to-day lives. It has to speak to the concerns of normal existence and not only to our occasional speculations about the origins of the universe. Thus, does the existence of the physicists' God help us in any way to understand the experience of the holy in our own personal lives? The God of the first three minutes seems very far away from my own existence, and though I may find some comfort in believing that the cosmos is a well-ordered creation, it does not seem to answer "the hunger for wonders" that I spoke about in the last chapter, the inner needs in a person's own life that religion has always been able to address.

In that regard the naturalists' God, the God of the many and varied species, seems to work somewhat better. I myself remember visiting the aquarium in Eilat at the southern tip of Israel and seeing the astonishing variety of tropical fish swimming in those tanks—fish in the shape of boxes, fish that looked like lions, fish that appeared to have been painted by Picasso—and without consciously planning it, the words of Psalm 92, "How great are your works, O Lord," came out of my mouth. I suspect that if we lived less of our lives in urban settings, this religious perspective might speak to us with even greater power. Indeed, it's likely that some of the fervor behind contemporary ecological concerns, as well as the interest people find in exploring the natural world through camping and hiking and wilderness programs like Outward Bound, may emanate from a secularized version of these deeper religious impulses.

What I do find compelling in the views of the physicists and the naturalists is that they both begin with a sense of mystery, and it is there that my earlier question about the importance of the *personal* dimension of religious experience begins to crystallize. For mystery is not only a matter of rational speculation about the origins of the universe or the variety of natural life; it is also a perception that is able to touch any of us at any moment. It is the sense that behind the normal world we deal with every day is a realm of the unknown, the unexplainable, that every once in a while will startle us into awareness, if even for an instant.

Thus, Akiva interpreted the verse in Exodus (33:20) "A person cannot see Me and live":

> This verse means that even the Beings who hold up the heavenly throne [described in Ezekiel, chapter 1] do not see the Glory. Shimon ben Azzai said: I do not dispute the words of my rabbi, but only add to them: "A person cannot see Me and live" means that even the angels, who live forever, do not see the Glory.
>
> (Sifra *Dibura Dinedava* 2:13) [7]

Shimon ben Azzai's midrashic point takes Akiva's comment one step further. Since we know by tradition that the angels live forever, Shimon states, that obviously "proves" that they cannot see God; for no being—even an angel—can see God and live!

But behind the explication is a deeper point: both Akiva and Shimon ben Azzai assert that there is a level of reality that even the angels cannot penetrate. In other words, behind all speculations and behind all knowledge that we might have is the realm of the impenetrable, called felicitously by later Jewish mystics the *Ein Sof,* the "without end"—the deepest mystery of the universe. It is out of the same impulse that Einstein writes:

> The most beautiful and deepest experience a man can have is the sense of the mysterious. It is the underlying principle of religion as well as of all serious endeavor in art and science. . . . He who never had this experience seems to me, if not dead, then at least blind. The sense that behind anything that can be experienced there is a something that our mind cannot grasp and whose beauty and sublimity reaches us only indirectly and as feeble reflexion, *this is religiousness.* . . . To me it suffices to wonder at these secrets and to attempt humbly to grasp with my mind a mere image of the lofty structure of all that there is. [8]

Thinking about God, then, begins less in the "three minutes of creation" than in the perception that there are things "that our mind cannot grasp." I may find those things in observing nature or in thinking about my own life. But what characterizes my experience at those times is the sense of mystery.

It seems to me also that thinking about the notion of mystery once again pushes us to confront the idea of faith. For clearly I could choose to take a very different view of this whole matter. I could say, as modern secularism often has, that essentially we see around us an intelligible reality or, at any rate, a set of questions waiting to be answered. These questions may be complex, but ultimately they can be dealt with. There is no heart of mystery at the center of this reality, only the world of fact and plausibility. Such a view surely can be held and defended, but the main point, it seems to me, is that no matter what alternative one takes it means *choosing* to do so. Or it means choosing to reject any "evidence" that may push one in another direction.

One can, in other words, choose to see one's experience in the light of mystery and religious significance or one can look at the same phenomena as "just the way things are." I can take, for example, the fact that human beings possess the capacity for memory as something that is "simply" the result of a set of electrical impulses within certain cells in the brain. I can choose to see "being alive" as another set of complex physiological phenomena. But I can also say that such explanations do not in any satisfying way explain for me "memory" or "living" or very much of anything else. For that other level of significance I may choose to say such realities are part of a deeper mystery that I cannot explain or even understand but which enriches my sense of being part of an essentially meaningful existence. Of course, scientists should strive for scientific explanation, but there is a moment—if we are not, as Einstein said, "dead or at least blind"—in which explanation will fall short and the sense of mystery will strike us as powerful and real.

I have had this feeling myself in looking at the natural world or in thinking about the very complexity of human beings themselves. It also comes, particularly as one gets older, with the sense of human finitude:

> R. Levi said in the name of R. Hama: A sculptor makes a statue; the sculptor dies, but his sculpture endures. But with the Holy One, blessed be He, that is not so. Rather the Holy One, blessed be He, made man and man dies, but the Holy One, blessed be He, lives and endures. This neither the sculptor nor the silversmith may do. The silversmith casts an image: the silversmith dies; the casting endures.

But the Holy One, blessed be He, made man and it is man who dies; it is the Holy One, blessed be He, who lives and endures for ever and ever.

(Midrash Psalms 103:2)

There is in this text a kind of rhetorical power whose repetitions hammer home its central theme with force. Even those who have the skill to do beautiful and enduring work, creations that will live after them—these people too will die.

But there is something ironic here as well. Human beings are God's "work of art," yet unlike the creations that we might make, the human being does not live on. God is God because divinity is eternal. Thus, tragically, God must watch His own "artistic" work die.

And of course behind the text lurks a deeper question: We know that flesh-and-blood artists try to ensure immortality through creations that will live on after them; but if God is to be compared to the artist, why does God choose as His creation mortal human beings? In other words, why do we exist at all? It is as central a question as one can imagine and yet no answer is attempted here. Perhaps Rabbi Levi sees this as beyond human comprehension. He focuses on what we *can* know: the simplest fact of life is that we are alive. And also that we will die. To be a human being means that one must accept the end of one's existence. God, according to this text, is that mysterious reality that exists beyond all human limitation.

But then the question arises, we say "human limitation," but how limited, in fact? Is it possible to go beyond ourselves, to know that ultimate reality, that mystery which is God?

"There is none like God, riding upon the heavens to help you, through the skies in His majesty."

(Deuteronomy 33:26)

All the people gathered around Moses and said to him, "Our master Moses, tell us what is the nature of the Glory on high?" Moses said to them, "From the lower heavens you can know the Glory." This is like one who wanted to see the glory of the king. They said to him, "Go to the capital city and you will see him." He came to the city and saw a veil spread over the gate and precious stones and pearls were attached to it. He could not look at the sight and he fell to the ground in a faint. They said to him, "If you could not look at the curtain and you fell in a faint, how much more would you have been unable to enter the city and see the Glory!"

(Sifre Deuteronomy, *Parshat Zot Haberakhah* 355)

All human beings have limitations, a fact symbolized here by the parable of the man who wished to see the king's face. But even seeing the curtain over the gate was too much for him to bear. Certainly, this midrash argues, to come face to face with God would be beyond human capacity, although our understanding of the "lower heavens"—that which we can know as mortals—gives us an inkling of what the upper heavens might be like.

It is hard for us as moderns to accept the possibility that there are things we will never know, that we have limitations. The rabbis of ancient times saw themselves as part of a kind of cosmic continuum in which their place in relationship to God and the rest of the world was quite clear. Of course, there were always people who wished to go beyond, who wished to penetrate the mysteries of the heavens. But in the ancient view this was a dangerous undertaking.[9]

Taking this midrash seriously, it seems to me, means to understand that any reckoning of our place in the universe and any thinking about the big questions of our existence must begin with the realization that there are places we cannot go. There are understandings we will never have, and like it or not, that fact, coupled with the reality of our own mortality, makes us quite small in the overall scheme of things. In other words, to think about God means to begin with an attitude uncharacteristic of contemporary life—a sense of humility.

Of course, to say that there is mystery is not the same thing as saying that there is God. In a way, we are stuck in a paradox: How is it possible to think about God if God is that mystery which is beyond understanding? I have suggested earlier that one way we can begin to explore the "otherness" implied by the word God is to turn to something we know very well, the nature of human beings themselves. Thus, we read in Leviticus Rabbah:

> **What reason did David see for praising the Holy One, blessed be He, with his soul? David said: The soul fills the body and the Holy One, blessed be He, fills His universe, as it is said, "For I fill both heaven and earth, declares the Lord" (Jer. 23:24). Let the soul which fills the body come and praise the Holy One, blessed be He, who fills all the universe.**
>
> (Leviticus Rabbah, *Parshat Vayikra* 4:8)

The text goes on to set up a whole set of convergences between the nature of the soul and the nature of God: Both the soul is everlasting and the Holy One, blessed be He, is everlasting; the soul is unique and the Holy One, blessed be He, is unique; the soul is pure and the Holy One, blessed by He, is pure, and so forth. A biblical quotation, as is typical, supports each assertion.

Though I have known this particular text for a long time, it was only in recent years that I felt it begin to speak to me. Indeed, one of the curious truths about reading Jewish texts is that at times a text that has always been familiar will suddenly take on a new life or meaning because, for whatever reason, at that moment in your own experience you are ready or able to see that meaning there. Thus, the idea of a soul separate from the body—an idea, by the way, not really found in the Bible, but one of those many accretions to Judaism in the Hellenistic environment of a later period—was one that I did not find particularly meaningful, and for a long time this midrash made little sense to me.

But lately I have begun to look at the rabbinic concept of the soul in a different way, thinking of it as something akin to what we today might call mind or consciousness, that sense of "I" which every person possesses. It is the person I know myself as, the voice inside my own head that thinks and experiences and simply is.

I have learned a good deal about that sense of self from reading about those whose souls differ from my own, "travellers to unimaginable lands," as the neurologist Oliver Sacks has called them.

I am referring in particular to Sacks' marvelous *The Man Who Mistook His Wife for a Hat* and other books, and two books by his predecessor A. R. Luria, *The Mind of a Mnemonist* and *The Man with a Shattered World*.[10] In these works we get a glimpse into the minds of people whose concepts of time and space are far from our own. And yet these are human worlds nonetheless. Sacks is interested in the convergence of brain and mind, that intersection where the physical instrument resting in our skulls becomes something more than a set of interconnected cells and electrical impulses, that place where flesh and spirit meet. We may see tragedy in the cases Sacks describes, but there is mystery and exhilaration as well. Sacks describes people who through accident or illness find themselves, sometimes unknowingly, in other worlds of reality, as palpable to them as the chair I sit on is to me.

Why, according to this midrash, did David praise God with his soul? (The allusion is to Ps. 103:1—"Bless the Lord, O my soul.") The rabbis answer that David is teaching us something here about the identification between the two elements, God and soul. The self, the "I," is something that none of us completely understands. We walk around with it (or it with us!), yet when this text says, "Let the soul which fills the body come and praise the Holy One, blessed be He," it suggests there is a connection and likeness between soul and God. The self, the inner life, may be the best device we have to help us understand the divine.

Our own experiencing of life is the most real thing any of us can know and yet it is completely mysterious. Oliver Sacks looks at one of his patients and wonders:

> Stimulate a point in the cortex of such a patient, and there convulsively unrolls a Proustian evocation or reminiscence. What mediates this, we wonder? What sort of cerebral organization could allow this to happen? Our current concepts of cerebral processing and representation are all essentially computational. . . . And, as such, they are couched in terms of "schemata," "programmes," "algorithms," etc.
>
> But could schemata, programmes, algorithms alone provide for us the richly visionary, dramatic, and musical quality of experience —that vivid personal quality that *makes* it experience?
>
> The answer is clearly, even passionately, "No!"[11]

Isn't it possible that the very nature of the mind, of consciousness, is a signpost into a more profound set of questions and speculations? Indeed, as the midrash states, the soul seems to be one of our best ways into the nature of God because it teaches us that for something to be real it does not have to be physically seen or even understood. After all, every day I can say "I" and it's quite clear to me what I mean. Sacks has shown in his work with people whose inner world has been damaged that there is nothing more real to a person than that inner life of the mind. It is more real than the body or the physical universe. It can turn a woman into a hat or left into right. It can rewrite the map of the spatial world. Isn't it possible that God—something equally unseen and ununderstood—can be real as well?

Thus, the aspect of reality that is closest to me and most with me—which *is* me, in fact—invisible, mysterious, and unique, leads me to the greatest of mysteries. What this text suggests is that the simplest thing in the world—that I wake up in the morning and there is an "I" there (indeed an "I" there in my dreams as well)—might well take me to the most complex.

It is consciousness itself, then, which can suggest that there is God. *For it is the hint that there can exist something very real that is more than the merely physical.* But ironically consciousness is so natural, so much with us, that most of the time we never think that the "vivid personal quality of experience," as Sacks puts it, that is, being alive, is something to be surprised about at all! It is one reading, perhaps, of an enigmatic midrashic text:

> "And you are My witnesses, says the Lord, and I am God."
>
> (Isaiah 43:12)

> Rabbi Shimon ben Yohai taught: "If you are my witnesses," I am the Lord. And if you are not my witnesses, I am not, as it were, the Lord.
>
> (Pesikta de Rav Kahana 12:6)

It is hard to know what to make of such a text. Often, pithy and perplexing midrashim like this one (usually the favorites of anthologizers) when put back into their context will seem a good deal less dramatic than the lone sentence plucked out of its setting. But in this case, looking at the midrashic setting in Pesikta de Rav Kahana does not give us very much guidance. There the remark is made in the context of a number of comments about Exodus 19:1 through Exodus 20:26, the story of the revelation at Sinai. And nothing in what comes before prepares us for Rabbi Shimon's teaching.

The text is attributed to Rabbi Shimon ben Yohai, known in later Jewish lore as the putative author of the Zohar, the great work of medieval Jewish mysticism. Shimon ben Yohai has a powerful mystique surrounding him in rabbinic literature. He is associated with the Bar Kokhba revolt and hence with a kind of messianic passion and personal fervor. Probably the best-known story about Shimon bar Yohai (as he is usually called, using the Aramaic "bar" instead of the Hebrew "ben"; both mean "son" or "son of") is the legend told in the Talmud (*Shabbat* 33b) that he and his son fled from the Romans and hid in a cave for twelve years. When told by Elijah that the emperor had died, they emerged out of the cave, saw a man ploughing his field, and cried out, "They forsake eternal life for temporal life!" And everything they looked at was immediately consumed in fire. God, worried that this dangerous intensity would destroy the world, has them return to the cave for another twelve months so they can accustom themselves to the realities of normal life.

Of course, it is hard to know if the general picture we get about a sage from his teachings or from stories like this one will in fact help us understand much about any particular utterance attributed to him. But there *is* something about this midrash—its short uncompromising manner, perhaps—that has the feel of an utterance from the Shimon bar Yohai of legend.[12] The text puts a midrashic spin on the verse from Isaiah, proposing a causative relationship between the first section of the verse and the second: God becomes God *because* Israel is God's witness. Certainly, this is not an idea to be found in the *peshat,* the plain contextual meaning, of the biblical quotation. And it is an idea that Rabbi Shimon also is careful to qualify: "I am not, *as it were,* the Lord." That "as it were" is a phrase one sees at times in rabbinic texts and it almost always raises a kind of flag for an interesting, often theologically "dangerous," statement about to follow. Even without witnesses, God must be God, no? But our midrash wants to make another point: Without the witness of human beings, there might as well be no God. God requires a community of belief and attestation.

To see the world through the perspective of the holy, in other words, means to be God's "witnesses." And to see the world from a completely secular or materialist point of view (that is, to say the world is only "matter"; there is nothing beyond the physical) means "as it were" there is no God. Like the old conundrum that asks if a tree that falls in the woods makes a sound if no one is there to hear it, this midrash seems to suggest that without witnesses, without people who see life through the lens of the holy, there is no God. Or to be more precise, there might as well be no God. Thus, to return to an earlier point, we may choose to take the issue of human consciousness as simply a given, a fact of life that requires little notice. It has nothing to do with holiness, nothing in common with God. Or we can *choose* to be witnesses to a sense of the divine in the world, something toward which we are led by reflection upon our own experience of mind, of being alive.[13]

This act of choosing that I have been talking about may move one toward a sense of the holy, but it does not end our difficulties with the question of God. In fact, in a way it is only now that we are ready to begin! I have spoken about the sense of mystery, the feeling that there are dimensions of reality that I simply cannot fathom. I see this mystery as an intimation of divinity. But I am still left with a basic and pressing problem: I have been thinking about God, but I am left to ask what is the nature of God? And how is God to be perceived, experienced, or understood?

For me, that inquiry begins with the following midrash:

R. Levi said: The Holy One appeared to them as though He were a statue with faces on every side. A thousand people might be looking at the statue, but it would appear to be looking at each one of them.

So, too, when the Holy One spoke, each and every person in Israel could say, "The Divine Word is addressing *me*." Note that Scripture does not say, "I am the Lord *your* God," [in the plural] but "I am the Lord *thy* God (Exod. 20:2), [in the singular].

R. Yose bar R. Hanina said: The Divine Word spoke to each and every person according to his particular capacity [Hebrew: *koho*; literally, "his strength"]. And do not be surprised at this idea. For when manna came down for Israel, each and every person tasted it in keeping with his own capacity—infants in keeping with their capacity, young men in keeping with their capacity, and the elderly in keeping with their capacity. Thus, for the infants—in keeping with their capacity—the manna tasted like mothers' milk. For it is said "its taste was like the taste of rich cream" (Num. 11:8); young men according to their capacity for it is said "my bread also which I gave you, bread and oil and honey" (Ezek. 16:19); and old men according to their capacity for it is said "the taste of it was like wafers made with honey" (Exod. 16:31).

Now what was true about the manna—that each and every person tasted it according to his own particular capacity—was equally true about the Divine Word. Each and every person heard it according to his own particular capacity. Thus David said "The voice of the Lord is in strength" (Ps. 29:4)—not "The voice of the Lord in His strength" [as we might expect from standard Hebrew pronoun usage], but the voice of the Lord is in the strength and capacity of each and every person. Therefore the Holy One said: Do not be misled because you hear many voices. Know ye that I am He who is one and the same: *I am the Lord thy God.*

(Pesikta de Rav Kahana 12:25)

It is often said that whereas the Bible fought a battle against idolatry and therefore expunged from its pages, as best as it was able to, mythological references—rabbinic literature, perhaps because the fight against idolatry was long over, almost delights in raising those very mythological matters. Thus, unlike the Bible, midrash will tell us about the activities of God and the angels before the time of creation and will use metaphors for God that the Bible might have viewed as blasphemous. There is no better example than in the text before us, in which God is compared quite literally to an idol! For the Hebrew word used here is *ikonin,* a loan word from Greek which we recognize from our English use of icon (as in "iconoclast," literally "one who smashes idols").

98

Although the use of the metaphor of the statue with many faces here is surprising, it is meant to communicate one specific idea: God is viewed as addressing each individual so directly that standing at Sinai one might have said, "The Divine Word is addressing *me*." This reading, as we often see in midrash, turns upon an attempt to find a hidden meaning in the Bible's particular use of language, here the singular pronoun of Exodus 20:2, "*thy* God."

An interesting dimension of this text is the way in which the phrase "the Divine Word" seems to refer simultaneously both to God and to God's message. That is, when the midrash says "the Divine Word is addressing *me*," does it mean to say God is addressing me or the words of the Ten Commandments are addressing me? Either reading is possible and to my mind this ambiguity reflects a theological point—God and God's Torah are inextricably bound up with one another, identified with one another. As we have seen previously, in Judaism to study God's word means to confront God. In our text Rabbi Levi's teaching in the first paragraph appears to lean in the direction of focusing on God while Yose bar Hanina's talks more about the "Word," the content of the message. But both fit nicely together. Indeed, R. Yose's remarks seem to be an explanatory expansion of what Levi has said. Don't be surprised at Levi's idea, Yose says, after all we know from the example of the manna—and here he is alluding to another midrashic tradition about the variegated taste of the manna [14]—that divine miracles can have a very "individualized" quality.

Thus, our midrash is built as a metaphor (God is like a statue with faces on every side) that is explained by means of another metaphor or analogy (the experience at Sinai was like the experience the Israelites later had with the manna).

Of course, it is precisely that orientation toward the individualized dimension of the giving of the Torah that makes this midrash so fascinating. In a sense, such a reading flies in the face of the conventional understanding of the revelation at Sinai as it is described in the Bible. Our natural assumption from reading the biblical text is that Sinai was seen as essentially a communal experience—the tense is in the plural, as it were: *all* the people say,

"We will do and we will obey" (Exod. 24:7); all the people are warned about coming too close to the mountain (Exod. 19:23). And yet our midrash here moves in the opposite direction. Sinai, according to both Levi and Yose, was the individual experience of each Israelite, seen through the lens of the individual's eyes: "The Divine Word is addressing *me*."

Yose's analogy of the manna takes the idea one step further. He is attempting to explain what such an individualized experience of the "Divine Word" might mean. It was not only, as Levi saw it, a revelation to each person, as I might feel the Mona Lisa's eyes staring directly at me in the presence of the painting; it was a revelation appropriate "to each and every person according to his particular *capacity*." In other words, the *content* of the revelation was specifically appropriate to each individual.

Or at any rate to each class of individuals. Yose's analogy of the manna is built around certain types of persons, here arranged according to various ages: infants, young people, the elderly. If we push the analogy a little further, however, we could argue that "capacity" is only part of what is being discussed. One could say that equally significant is the matter of taste or preference. True, the infant is only capable of consuming a food such as mother's milk, but it is also what the infant *wants* to eat. And certainly the young people—since health is not an issue for them—could eat whatever they choose. The midrash weaves together a set of three verses, each of which is taken to refer to the appropriate taste or nature of the manna for the three different age groups.

Thus, I think it is not too big a leap to infer that this midrash suggests some kind of relationship between one's personal incli-nation (i.e., taste or preference) and the kind of connection to God that one might experience. Each of us, in other words, is going to experience God in his or her own way, a way that emanates from who we are and what we want or expect from that confron-tation with God. In addition, that experience is connected to what we are capable of understanding—it is connected to the compe-tencies, whether they be of mind or of heart, that we bring to it. That is, if even at Sinai revelation was individualized, certainly in ordinary human life the experience of God is rooted in who we are ourselves. It is hard and perhaps even inappropriate, therefore, for anyone to make generalized statements about the nature of God, because each of us has a different "capacity" or inclination for understanding God.

We have been talking about "capacity," a translation of the Hebrew word *koah,* literally "strength." It is around *koah* that the midrash turns, as we see from the twist given later to the verse from Psalm 29 that again ties into the same word. In typical midrashic fashion the rabbis look for the slight oddity in the biblical text (here a minor point in the Hebrew usage—the pronominal suffix is "missing" in Psalm 29's use of *koah*) that allows them to find biblical authority for the reading they have suggested for the nature of individualized revelation.

Of course, in saying "capacity" (and for this word I have stayed with the standard English translation of William Braude),[15] inevitably we have interpreted as well as translated. It is true that rabbinic Hebrew (and later Hebrew as well) does make use of the word in the sense of ability or capacity, and it is also true that saying "capacity" makes reasonable sense out of this midrash, but we must always be aware of the danger when translating of moving away from the plain sense of the original language. In other words, we should consider if *koah* translated as "strength" adds something to our understanding of the text that "capacity" may not.

Here it seems to me that "strength" has an interesting added connotation: People experienced the revelation, not only through their preference or through their competence, but also at the level at which they could *bear* it. Experience of God is not an easy matter. Indeed, the Bible shows that such experiences can be dangerous. Hence the prohibition against coming too close to the mountain, and hence the terrible story of Aaron's sons Nadav and Avihu who are destroyed when offering up a "strange fire before the Lord" (Lev. 10). In our times too we know about the stories of people whose journeys took them beyond that "boundary around the mountain"—burnt-out cases from the American spiritual supermarket and even worse, as the Jonestown horror of 1978 attests—and who destroyed themselves in the process. In that way the midrashic use of "strength" offers an additional facet to the same discussion.

Relationship to God, then, is connected to talent, inclination, and strength. But our text here suggests that it is also connected to something else—the place in the course of our lives where we are found at any particular time, what today psychologists such as Erik Erikson and Daniel Levinson would refer to as the developmental stages in a person's life.[16] This idea about the capacity and ability typical of different times in a person's life is shown even more clearly in a similar midrash about Sinai:

> Come and see how the Voice went forth—coming to each Israelite according to his individual strength—to the old, according to their strength; to the young according to their strength; to the children according to their strength; to the infants according to their strength, and to the women according to their strength; and even to Moses according to his strength, as it is said, "Moses spoke and the God answered him by a voice" (Exod. 19:19), that is, with a voice which he could endure.
>
> (Exodus Rabbah 5:9)

Once again the key word is *koah*, "strength" or "capacity." In this text the five different human types portrayed by the midrash —perhaps parallel to the five times the word *koah* appears in Psalm 29—range across both age and sex: the old, the young, children, infants, and women. It may be that women are seen as a kind of separate consciousness that cuts across all ages or it may be that the particular definitions of stages are rather loosely conceived by the midrash itself. More important for our purposes, however, is the sense that the midrash represents the experience of revelation, the perception of God, as differentiated according to the particularities of one's sex or certainly one's time in life.

The fact that one's stage in life necessarily affects one's views about God is something we too often overlook. As important as it is to understand that each person has a different "capacity" for understanding or relating to the idea of God, we should recall as well that the nature of the perception that each of us has will also change over time. Thus, it is impossible to expect that our views about God will remain constant throughout a lifetime—an idea which, I think, holds significant implications.

For one thing, it is important to recognize that the views we have about God are for many people a legacy from childhood which, like any inheritance from the past, is both a privilege and a burden. The privilege is the aura of powerful sentiment that such an idea will carry. Such ideas are connected to the past and it is comforting to hold on to such connections. But the disadvantages here are equally powerful. Thinking about God as the Old Man in the Sky, as the parental figure who is all-wise, means being stuck with a child's understanding of God. None of us thinks about any serious idea in the same way we did when we were children—our views about politics, art, music, and even food have grown as we have. Otherwise, we would all believe that the government can do no wrong and that chocolate cake is at the heart of a balanced diet. Of course, that doesn't mean we wouldn't *like* to believe either of these two notions—who would not want a righteous government and an uninhibited diet? But maturity simply will not allow us to hold on to those fantasies.

The nostalgia for untainted, uncomplicated beliefs is part of the allure of holding on to our childhood ideas about God. But isn't it appropriate to grant to the idea of God the same level of seriousness that we grant to any other important thinking that has changed as we have matured? The ideas of our youth are just not going to work for us as adults, and the image we hold of God should change and grow as well.

Aside from that, however, is another unalterable fact: No individual lives in a vacuum. The changes in the perception of God that occur in an individual's life are complicated by another significant point, the historical age in which one lives:

> Because the Holy One appeared to Israel at the Red Sea as a mighty man waging war, and appeared to them at Sinai as an educator teaching Torah and appeared to them in the days of Daniel as an elder teaching Torah, and in the days of Solomon appeared to them as a young man—the Holy One said to Israel: Even though you see Me in many different images, I am the same. I am He who is with you at Sinai: "I am the Lord your God" (Exod. 20:2).

> R. Hiyya bar Abba said: He appeared to them in an image appro-
> priate to each and every place and time. At the Red Sea he appeared
> to them as a mighty man waging war, at Sinai as an educator who
> stands in awe when teaching Torah; in the days of Daniel as an elder
> teaching Torah, for the Torah is best when it comes from the
> mouths of the old; and in the days of Solomon He appeared to them
> as a young man in keeping with the deeds of that generation. . . .
>
> (Pesikta de Rav Kahana 12:24)

This midrash explores a classic theological difficulty raised by
the matters we have been discussing: If God is always perceived
in different images, does that mean that there is more than one
God? No, the first section of the text answers, although the guises
may change, "I am He" underneath them all.

Still, what is of greater interest here is an unstated question that
remains beneath the surface—why does God assume all these
guises? Thus R. Hiyya bar Abba gives an answer: The images of
God held at different times in history are "appropriate to each and
every place and time." In other words, each age finds the understanding of God appropriate to its needs and circumstances. The
Israelites at the Red Sea sought the warrior image; the time of
Daniel required an elder teaching Torah; and so forth.

The historical circumstances in which we live are something as
much beyond our control as the stage of life we are in or the
"capacity" or inclinations that make up our characters. We cannot
go back in time even if we wanted to. We cannot change the fact
that we live in the latter part of the twentieth century with all that
that implies. Our views about God—indeed even about having a
view about God!—are part and parcel of the world of the present.
And perhaps most significantly that means that we cannot with
great ease reconstruct the images of earlier historical ages.

And yet, what are we to make of those images? My own sense
is that aside from being a commentary about the influence of our
time in history on our views about God, the midrash above holds
a personal dimension as well. Finding the images of God "appropriate to each and every place and time," as R. Hiyya bar Abba
put it, is a statement about our own lives and personal history
too. There is within the traditional language of Judaism a vast

reservoir of metaphorical representations of what we have been calling here essentially an unknowable mystery—the nature of God. Certainly these images include God the Father and King, the most common image of our childhood, as I have mentioned before. But there is also God the Mothering Presence, who shelters us under Her wings. And there is God the lover or husband of Israel, as we see in the midrashic explication of the biblical Song of Songs. And there is, in the language of the rabbinic literature, *Hamakom,* literally "the Place," an image that for me suggests some kind of storehouse or repository of values. And there is the austere God of Maimonides unknowable in its mystery. And there is the God of medieval Kabbalah. There we see a host of images in an attempt to understand the ultimately unknowable God (the mysterious *Ein Sof,* the "Without End"). According to Kabbalah, what we can attempt to grasp are aspects of the multilayered *Sefirot,* the divine emanations by which we can know God as well as human beings can. And there are Hasidic texts that represent God as "the lights within the holy letters."

And many others as well. In fact, we almost have an overabundance of images. To think of God as the "Without End" or as "the Place" is very different from thinking about the Father or the Mother; to think about the Elder teaching Torah is different from looking at God the Young Warrior.

What I am suggesting here is that the images of God that reside in the classic texts of Judaism are first and foremost more varied than we tend to realize, a fact that can aid our own adult perception of God. Secondly, that in accepting the changing nature of our own selves, we must also accept the idea that no one image of God will ever be appropriate for each time and place in our own histories. The images that make sense for us will change— certainly over time and even sometimes from day to day. The way to make sense out of this abundance is to recognize that searching for the one true explanation for God that will work for each of us and for all time is a futile enterprise. There are times when the image of God that leaps to mind will be God the Father. One may even say in one's rational mind, "I don't really think I *believe* this," yet it will be what speaks to me today.

To some this may seem problematic—how can I feel close to an image of God that in fact I really don't "believe"? But I wonder if this is such a difficulty. What I am suggesting is that all of us will find the image of God that works for us in the moment. And certainly at times *no* image will work. But that too should not be a difficulty if we recognize that we are likely to change once again, that we are likely to grow back toward a connection with God.

No one image can ever work all the time. In fact, one of the theological traps we seem to have fallen into over time is accepting a logician's view of the nature of speculations about God. At the heart of Judaism is something very different, something we could call a "poetic theology," not a theology of rational proofs but a theology of images and metaphors. This is not what we usually mean when we say "theology"—as seen in the classics of Christian theology or in the writings of the Medieval Jewish theologians by and large—but it *is* the heart of the theology of classic rabbinic Judaism and its offspring Kabbalah.[17]

These poetic images are not mere quaint curiosities or decorative flourishes. They speak to us with a power deeper than a rational proof or a well-reasoned argument. The language of images, after all, is the way our unconscious speaks to us too: it is the language of dreams. No one dreams a philosophical syllogism; deep within ourselves we are touched by metaphor. Nor will translating these images into explanatory statements allow them to retain their power. As the British educator Peter Abbs puts it:

> There is one last point to be made about metaphor. It cannot be converted into the language of discursive symbolism and retain its transforming energy. . . . Metaphor is not a clumsy or archaic or precious way of stating a truth that could be expressed more simply through a series of propositions. Metaphor is, on the contrary, a unique and enduring and irreplaceable way of embodying the truths of our inward lives.[18]

The same point can be made about the images for God found throughout Jewish religious literature. But aside from the *power* of metaphor, there is another advantage to the theological perspective offered by these texts. One of the great difficulties of the religious writing about God for contemporary people has been its overemphasis—in the language of philosophy—on the ontological at the expense of the phenomenological. In other words, in focusing on issues of "ontology"—namely, does God *exist*? What is God's nature?—we have ignored the actual way people *experience* ("phenomenology") their lives, which is to say, less through well-developed theological propositions than through the passing and changeable images of God that make sense for us in the encounter of the moment.

In explaining the nature of rabbinic literature we often say that despite the fact the rabbis did not write in the language of classic theology, it doesn't mean that they did not have a theology. Rather, they expressed it through interpretations of Torah rather than through logical statements and proofs. But we need to take this one step further: the lack of "consistency" in rabbinic theology is not only a descriptive characteristic, but for us today it may also be a gift and a blessing. That is, it is not only difficult, perhaps even inappropriate on scholarly grounds, to construct such a consistent picture of the rabbis' theology,[19] but, even more important, I would argue that the *very fact of the multiplicity of theological statements in rabbinic literature is a kind of theological position in and of itself.* Namely, in rabbinic Judaism there is no one theological case to be made: there is instead the ever-changing human perspective in which varied images speak to each individual in the moment in which they make sense. There are times in which God will speak to me as Judge or Father or Friend, as the midrash on Psalm 118 puts it—"Do you not recognize Him?" At other times God will be beyond all human images. God will be Light or Place or Fire, all classic images as well.

In the great prayer the Hymn of Glory (often known by its opening words, Anim Zemirot, "Sweet Melodies"), attributed to Judah HeHasid (d. 1217)—a prayer considered by many rabbinic authorities so sacred that it was limited to recitation only on holy days or the Sabbath—we hear a powerful version of this same sentiment:

> Sweet melodies and songs I sing
> Because my soul thirsts for You.
> My soul longs for the shadow of Your hand
> To know every secret of Your mystery.

The poet goes on to chart the record of his praises for God and his attempts to capture some hint of that which is beyond him:

> I will tell of Your glory
> Though I have not seen You.
> I will use images and names
> But I will not know You.

The images overwhelm him and the poet knows his task is impossible; indeed, the poem ends as it began, with the words "my soul thirsts for You." But in the course of his search he comes to see that the multiplicity of images is part of the human attempt to know the unknowable. That mystery, like the message of the Shema, is the oneness of God:

> Portrayed in countless forms,
> Beneath all these images, You remain one.

This chapter began with a consideration of the idea of mystery. To begin thinking about God, we suggested, is to understand that there are things that we can never understand. We moved from there to consider the idea of the self, the "soul" in classic rabbinic language, as an intimation of the reality of a world of meaning that cannot be seen. But seeing the world in that fashion, we suggested, is not today a matter of immutable fact. Rather, it is something we can choose to do. Nor is there one "choice," one understanding of God that will work for all people. Each person guided by temperament and one's place in life and one's culture and world—each person will by necessity find a different path to understanding God.

And not only *a* path. Relationship with God in each individual life is a matter of continual change and redefinition. For all of us the tradition offers a storehouse of images, each with its own valence. Some will appeal through reason and some through sentiment. Indeed, there are times, we have suggested, that we will surprise ourselves with the metaphors that speak to us at any given moment, some which we do not even "believe" if we applied the test of reason. Relationship with God is something that includes reason—but more as well. Entering the world of Jewish texts about God, we enter a world of constantly shifting images. In that palace of metaphors each of us can find a place.

We began this chapter thinking about God, and we finished it, quite naturally, talking about a prayer. For it is in prayer that the varied images of God are closest to the heart. Looking at the ways in which prayer might speak to the experience of individuals today will be our concern in the chapter that follows.

FIVE

THE HEART'S WORK

Prayer, we like to hope, is a moment of true speaking. At that instant we become the words we say: There is no deception, no ego to defend, no manufactured self. We speak from the heart. It is a plea for help, to be sure, but it is also a leap of joy, the expression of thanks for our very existence. We trivialize prayer if we think of it as a shopping list of requests. Prayer is carved-out time, the moments in which we allow ourselves to step out of ourselves, to look at the world not as an unending chain of little trials and triumphs, but to see as *largely* as we can. The time of prayer is when we say, "*This* is what matters to me the most."

It is not so difficult to accept this notion of prayer when the words we speak are the ones that leap from the mouth unbidden, when we say "Please!" or "Thanks!" spontaneously. But what about prayers written by someone else? What about the written liturgy, the prayer book? Is this also "true" speech? To think about Jewish prayer without also dealing with the prayer book, the siddur,[1] is an impossibility. But a liturgy also raises a whole set of complex issues at the heart of which is a simple question: What is my own relationship to the words that I pray?

Thus, one persistent problem is the every-present danger in a religion such as Judaism—with its emphasis on legislated behavior

110

in ritual life—that one's liturgical prayers would become so routinized that worship itself might turn into something virtually
mechanical. The discussion of this problem, which Abraham
Joshua Heschel aptly termed "religious behaviorism"[2]—plays an
important role in rabbinic literature. One passage in the Talmud
tries to explore the issue in more detail:

> *Mishnah*   R. Eliezer said: One who makes his prayer a fixed routine
> (*keva*)—that prayer is no plea.
>
> *Gemara*   What is *keva*? R. Jacob ben Idi said in the name of R. Os-
> haiah: Anyone whose prayer is like a heavy burden on him. The
> Sages say: Whoever does not say it in the manner of a plea. Rava and
> R. Joseph both say: Whoever is not able to insert something fresh in
> it. R. Zera said: I can insert something fresh in it, but I am afraid to
> do so lest I become confused.
>
> (Talmud, *Berakhot* 29b)

In typical fashion the Mishnah presents a short, unelaborated
statement and the Gemara tries to mine the passage for its many
meanings. Thus, we have four attempts at interpreting Rabbi Eliezer's view about *keva,* the term commonly used for a fixed
routine[3] in prayer. First, there is the view of R. Jacob ben Idi
quoting R. Oshaiah. The emphasis here is on the psychological
attitude one brings to the *act* of prayer. Hence, according to
R. Jacob, if you feel that the obligation of prayer is a burden, it
will be hard to pray with intensity and concentration.

A different view is then presented by the Sages (that is, this
tradition is attributed to a group of rabbis; no one particular person seems to be identified specifically with the interpretation).
They also address the psychological dimension of the prayer experience. But they are less concerned with the attitude one brings
to prayer than with the style of utterance within prayer itself. One
who says the prayers in a mechanical—and perhaps they mean in
an unemotional—way, is not really praying, according to this
point of view.

More demanding is the next perspective, the joint position of
Rava and R. Joseph. They are concerned with the need for inno-

vation in prayer. Even, one could argue, if you are successful in praying *without* a sense of burden and even if you *do* pray "in the manner of a plea," Rava and R. Joseph still require something more to avoid the charge of *keva*: You must creatively insert something new into your prayers.

The final comment in the passage reacts to the difficulties inherent in Rava and R. Joseph's argument. Here R. Zera appears to reject their view as overly radical. R. Zera asserts that indeed he has the ability to innovate in prayer, as Rava and R. Joseph desire, but he is concerned that focusing on innovation may distract him from prayer itself. The demand to innovate may inhibit one's ability to focus on the liturgy, thus, ironically, damaging that very concentration which one needs in an attempt to eliminate the problems of *keva*! And what about those people who do not have the religious genius that may be required to innovate? Is their prayer to be denigrated?

The quality of concentration that concerns R. Zera is called by the rabbinic literature *kavvanah*—being "directed"—and it is an idea that has a long and complicated history throughout Jewish religious life.[4] At its heart is the attempt to safeguard religious seriousness while retaining liturgical prayer. The question is, when we pray, what kind of relationship should we have to the words that we say, the words of a liturgy that are not of our own composition?

In one of the most important Jewish ethical and devotional works of the Middle Ages, *Duties of the Heart,* the writer, Bahya ibn Pakuda, addressed this specific matter:

> [The person at prayer should] consider to whom it is that his prayers are directed and what he intends to ask and what he intends to speak in the presence of his Creator, pondering the words of the prayers and their meaning. Know that so far as the language of prayer is concerned, the words themselves are like the husk while reflection on the meaning of the words is like the kernel. The prayer itself is like the body while reflection on its meaning is like the spirit so that, if someone merely utters the words of the prayer with his heart concerned with matters other than prayer, then his prayer is like a

> body without a spirit and a husk without a kernel, because while the
> body is present when he prays, his heart is absent. . . .
> (Bahya ibn Pakuda, *Duties of the Heart,*
> Chapter 8, "Self-Evaluation," Section 3:9)

Kavvanah, from Bahya's point of view, seems to come down to knowing that you are standing before the Divine Presence, combined with a strong emphasis on understanding the meaning of the words you are saying. Bahya too is concerned with the problem of *keva;* he is worried about the phenomenon of people merely mouthing the words of prayer without being aware of what they are saying. After all, "the words themselves are like the husk while reflection on the meaning of the words is like the kernel."

But, of course, for most people, at least most people today, focusing on the meaning of the prayers does not really solve the problem of prayer. The bilingual siddur—and in some cases the use of the vernacular in prayer itself—has pretty much eliminated the difficulty that the worshiper would not know what the words mean. In fact, knowing what the prayers mean may be the *source* of problems about prayer! Particularly when we look at the understanding of prayer found in the passage from Bahya above. For here the author focuses on the idea most commonly associated with the word "prayer." As he says, the worshiper should concentrate upon "what he intends to ask" from God. It is the "asking" side of prayer that most often comes to mind when people think about prayer and it is precisely that petitionary act that troubles them.

Looking at the Jewish liturgy, it has often been pointed out, we can see two other dimensions of prayer in addition to the prayers of petition: prayers that thank God and, closely related, prayers that praise God. At times the prayers of thanksgiving overlap with the prayers of praise. When one says, "Blessed be You, O Lord our God, King of the universe, who supplies my every need," is that a prayer of thanksgiving or praise? Generally, the distinction seems to be that prayers of thanksgiving tend to be specified—that is, God is thanked for a specific act—and prayers of praise are more generalized, such as "May His great name be praised throughout all eternity."

But knowing that there are three different kinds of prayer in the liturgy does little to help us in our own attempts at praying. Indeed, for people today all three types of prayer seem to be problematic and their difficulties are inherently connected to some of the theological issues that we have discussed in the last two chapters. To ask for something from God assumes the reality of a God who answers such requests. To thank God assumes that events that have occurred owe their existence to God's actions. To praise God is similarly to assert the reality of God's presence. But in a world without such theological certainties, prayer is bound to be difficult. And understanding the meaning of the words cannot help alleviate the problem; it can even exacerbate it. As someone once said, "I prefer not to read the libretto when I go to the opera. Then I might know what they mean with all that beautiful singing and it would ruin my entire evening!"

The classic Jewish sources were not unaware of the difficulties of prayer, as we have seen even in the texts above that deal with *kavvanah* and *keva*. And petitionary prayer raised other problems the rabbis tried to deal with, in particular the question of whether all petitions are legitimate. Thus, the Mishnah teaches:

> If someone cries out to God over what is past, this prayer is in vain. How? If a man's wife is pregnant and he were to say, "May it be Your will that my wife shall bear a male child," this prayer is in vain. If someone is walking along and hears cries coming from the city and prays, "May it be Your will that those cries are not coming from my family," this prayer is in vain.
>
> (Mishnah, *Berakhot* 9:3)

One can only pray for what is possible. Facts cannot be changed. History cannot be reversed. Petitionary prayer must make sense in a world of reason.

Praise and thanksgiving also presented difficulties for the classic sources, but we should remember that there are clear differences between their difficulties and our own. For us the problem of

114

praise and thanksgiving comes out of the doubt and theological uncertainty that are characteristic of modernity. For the rabbis the problem seems almost precisely the opposite: their belief in God's power, their lack of doubt, led them to question their own human adequacy to speak before the Ruler of the universe.

Nowhere is this more clearly seen than in one of the central hymns of the Sabbath and Festival Morning Service, the prayer called Nishmat Kol Hai ("The Breath of Every Living Thing"). This prayer is one of the masterpieces of Jewish liturgy. Joseph Heinemann, an important scholar in this field, characterized the prayer as "the most exalted and eloquent prayer in the hymnic style to be found in the statutory liturgy."[5]

In a certain sense the underlying theme of the prayer seems to challenge the very idea of liturgy—how is it possible for human beings to praise God? It begins with an assumption about the nature of reality:

> The breath of every living thing
> shall praise your name, O Lord our God,
> and every mortal being
> shall ever glorify and exalt your deeds, O our
> King. From eternity to eternity
> You are our God.
> And we have no one but You as our King,
> our Redeemer, our Savior, our Deliverer
> in every time of trouble and distress.
> God of first things and of last things,
> Lord of all creatures, Master of all generations,
> You are endlessly praised.

The very fact of God's existence, the fact that God is "Master of all generations," makes it appropriate for Him to be "endlessly praised."

Yet there is something troubling here. The prayer is facing up to a difficult situation—a God who is endlessly praised, who is eternal and infinitely powerful, is a difficult standard for anyone to approach. God, after all, is a master of words Himself. It is through words that God created the universe: "Let there be

light." The worshiper is caught in the awkward situation of need-
ing to use the medium of language, which is so closely associated
with God, in order to praise God.

And God is more than a master of language; God is the source
of language. How can a human being, so dependent on God—
"our King, our Redeemer, our Savior, our Deliverer in every time
of trouble and distress"—find an adequate way to praise the "God
of first things and of last things, Lord of all creatures?"

In the second section of the prayer, this task of praise seems to
overwhelm the worshiper:

> If our mouths were filled with song
> as the sea,
> and our tongue with joyful praise
> as the roaring waves;
> were our lips full of adoration
> as the wide expanse of heaven,
> and our eyes sparkling
> like the sun or moon;
> were our hands spread out in prayer
> as the eagles in the sky,
> and our feet swift as the deer—
> we should still be unable to thank You
> and bless Your name,
> Lord our God.

The sense of inadequacy is immense. Implied perhaps is an even
more oppressive ignominy. It seems that the animals, the sea, all
natural things *do* praise God. They praise simply by being—flow-
ing or roaring or shining. But human beings feel their own voice
to be weak. We do not have the words to respond to God's
reality.

The prayer then turns to list God's great kindnesses throughout
Jewish history. God liberated us from the bondage of Egypt and
nourished us in times of famine and helped us in times of plenty
and rescued us from sword and disease. All these acts are cata-
logued by the prayer and yet it is through the process of recounting God's deeds that the prayer finds its resolution. The worshiper
realizes that we have no choice but to praise God, despite our

sense of inadequacy. In the same way that God's power makes us feel small, it inescapably compels and inspires us to make the effort to praise. Thus the prayer continues:

> Therefore
> the limbs which You have given us
> and the spirit and soul
> which You have breathed into our nostrils
> and the tongue which You have placed in our
> mouths—all will join in giving thanks
> and in praising Your name, O our King.

What is interesting here is that the transition from the historical recounting—that very striking "therefore" in the text—leads to the knowledge that indeed we can praise God. Why? Because it is God who has given us the very ability to pray. The prayer Nishmat suggests that by redefining our sense of our own selves, our own bodies, we can accept the burden of praise and make the attempt to speak. It is no longer merely "*our* tongue," as we had thought, but the tongue "which *You* have placed in our mouths." Thus, Nishmat becomes a kind of journey of self-discovery. We learn our place and our powers, and in doing so we learn how to praise. It is a prayer of praise, but it is also a prayer about the act of praising. We can pray, Nishmat argues, because it is God who is the source of prayer.

Nishmat, then, is well positioned in the structure of the liturgy. Appearing at the beginning of the Morning Service on Sabbath and Festivals, Nishmat leads the worshiper into the heart of the service itself, the Shema and the Amidah. Once one has said Nishmat Kol Hai and understood its meaning, lived through its process, the service is ready to begin.

This prayer, as I said at the outset, tries to deal with the problem of human inadequacy, a problem the rabbis felt was inherent in prayers of praise and thanksgiving. But what is our reaction today to its message that "we can pray because it is God who is the source of prayer"? For us this statement of "fact" is considerably more problematic, or at any rate a good deal less rooted in certainty.

What I have tried to do here is to walk through the meaning of the prayer, to focus on the words, as Bahya recommended, looking at the "kernel beneath the husk." But, as I have said above, focusing on the meaning will not solve our problems with prayer. To actually *pray* a liturgical piece that asserts the message of Nishmat ("we can pray because it is God who is the source of prayer") is different from analyzing a text that comes to the same conclusion. Unlike study, mustn't prayer involve the assent of the worshiper? In *studying* materials from the past we can look at the texts with distance; even if the texts speak to us only in part, we can edit out, so to speak, those sections with which we cannot connect. But praying reflects a more intimate relationship between person and text; in prayer, as I've said above, the text literally becomes *our* words. And how is distance possible in that case?

Of course, we have to consider how much we really "mean" the words when we say them. Is that what the prayer experience is all about? To focus on the meaning of the words, as Bahya recommends, means focusing on the straightforward, denotative meaning of the words, but such a view makes prayer a considerably more intellectual experience—closer to study, in other words —than in fact it actually is. First and foremost, as Bahya himself argues, prayer is standing before God. That is, prayer is essentially an *experience,* the experience of feeling oneself face to face with the holy. My understanding of the passage in the Talmud requiring that one's prayer be a "plea" is that it is another way of focusing on the emotional or nonrational aspect of prayer. Of course, as we have seen, there are differences in opinion over what constitutes a plea, but there is no debate about the primacy of the supplicatory nature of prayer.

In that case, how should we view the words of the liturgy? To begin with, it is clear from a historical point of view that the Jewish liturgy itself is a kind of "second-order" language. Like an autobiography "ghosted" by another, the liturgy represents those words we might want to say if we had the talent to compose them ourselves. It is language, in other words, written to deal with the inabilities we all have in standing before the Divine. And of course the traditional Jewish liturgy also was designed to ensure that the statutory requirements of prayer—the times of prayer, the number and content of blessings, the order of the service—as developed by the rabbis, would be fulfilled.

Scholars of rabbinic Judaism believe that prayer originally was meant to be the spontaneous outpouring of the individual worshiper, but the content of that verbal expression was to be based on a set of fixed topics said in a certain order. Thus, how the individual's own words would express the topic like "God's Kingship" would vary according to the individual's own perception and ability. Eventually, a fixed liturgy emerged, although this was a slow process and the innovative, personal side of the prayers remained present for many years. In fact, we have in ancient sources different versions of particular prayers, existing side by side, each representing personalized efforts to fulfill the specified liturgical requirements.[6]

The history of the liturgy offers a kind of insight into how we ourselves might think about prayer. I do *not* mean to argue that we should abandon the traditional liturgy so that we can return to spontaneous prayer (although it's good to remember—as we often do not—that spontaneity in prayer is not something rejected by classical Jewish practice). Such a step would not solve our problems with prayer and it is likely that the same human inadequacies that led to the creation of a liturgy in the first place have not changed for the better over the centuries. Indeed, given the uncertainties about belief characteristic of modernity, we today would probably have more difficulty than our ancestors in creating our own personal prayers.

Rather, the "second-order" nature of the traditional language suggests a kind of *relationship* that we might adopt in connection to that liturgy. These are not, after all, our own words that we are speaking. Therefore, although they are words that can help us or guide us, our relationship to that language is different from our relationship to words of our own choosing. What we seek to develop, then, is a more flexible stance in our personal connection to the words of the prayers. The liturgy, in other words, is there to assist us; rather than letting our difficulties with the words hinder us, our goal should be to attain the ability to go *beyond* the words while at the same time taking advantage of what they have to offer us. Most of us do not have the religious genius to compose poetic prayers, but the liturgy provides a different alternative: the basic skeleton that we ourselves fill out. The tradition provides the melody, so to speak, but our own personal improvisation upon that melody varies it, changes it, makes it different perhaps from its original intention, but it makes the song our own. What we need to consider next is how that improvising can occur.

Improvisation is always happening in prayer because we are constantly "editing" the words as we say them. Of course, in non-Orthodox versions of Judaism, this editing of the liturgy has occurred quite literally as certain phrases deemed "objectionable"—such as the concept of the chosen people in the Reconstructionist prayer book or some of the prayers for the restoration of the Temple sacrifices in the Conservative prayer book—have simply been eliminated or rewritten.[7] But my point is that even without such radical steps, during prayer all of us are *mentally* editing the liturgy as we walk through the prayers. We do it by simply tuning out the noise of those phrases that don't touch us or that we disagree with or even by establishing our own silent dialogue with the text as we speak the words. In that way, as I will try to show below, we create a kind of "countertext" to the liturgy, which is to say we mentally adjust the literal content of what we are saying to conform to our own beliefs and values. To put it another way, we think the words we *mean* to be saying as we are saying the words printed on the page. Perhaps it's not even "thinking" these alternative words; it may be more of a kind of "leaning" toward them, like whispers in the back of the mind.

Of course, one could say in response: "Why do you need all this mental editing—if particular words bother you so much, why not just eliminate them?" But as artificial as this strategy may sound, there may be reasons why it is worthwhile to retain those difficult phrases, and not just for the predictable reasons of sentiment or "tradition," though these too should not be underestimated. What I am suggesting here is that keeping the traditional language means creating moments of tension between ourselves and the liturgy, and there is something in that very process that keeps prayer active and alive. The traditional liturgy throws down a kind of challenge to us; it forces us to assert who we are and what we stand for, even in "opposition" to the liturgy itself.

In a curious fashion the liturgy itself provides examples of this very tension in the way that it has adopted certain biblical verses into its own language. Of course, the siddur is filled with biblical allusion and the actual language of the prayers has often been taken from the Bible. Thus, large sections of the Book of Psalms, to take the most obvious example, have been incorporated directly into the liturgy.

But the tension that I have been alluding to can be seen in a more subtle example. At the center of the Morning Service is the following blessing: "Blessed are You, O Lord our God, King of the universe, who forms light and creates darkness, makes peace and creates all." Yet the language of this blessing represents a kind of hidden midrash, for it is a direct allusion to a passage in Isaiah (45:5–7):

> I am the Lord and there is none else;
> Beside Me there is no god.
> I engird you, though you have not known Me,
> So that they may know, from east to west,
> that there is none but Me.
> I am the Lord and there is none else,
> I form light and create darkness,
> I make peace and create evil.

The last two lines were incorporated verbatim into the Morning Service with one significant change—the last word, "evil" (Hebrew: *rah*) was changed in its liturgical setting to "all" (*ha-kol*).[8] Of course, this is no small change, and it is obvious that the composers of the liturgy felt that to say in prayer each morning that God was creator of evil might have been more than any individual could bear in starting the day. But the *fact* of this adaptation (something that has often been noted in studies of the liturgy) is far less important than the *effect* of this change on the person who prays these words.

121

For the person who hears the "midrash"—that is, the change from the context in Isaiah to its use in the service—there is an inevitable tension that is created and a kind of "mental editing" forced upon us, in this case by the text of the prayer book itself. That is, every time one says the statement "God creates all" in the Morning Service, one is reminded in this tiny way that "creating all" means "creating evil" as well. We may not say the words out loud, but the tension between the hope for peace and the existence of evil (parallel here to the world of "light" and the world of "darkness" in the phrase directly before it) resonates in our minds. Here the change was made in the liturgy itself, but the active participation of the worshiper is engaged by just that tension.[9] Of course, "hearing the midrash" within the prayer assumes that one knows enough Bible to appreciate the subtle changes the liturgy has introduced. And because of that it is clear that *studying* the prayer book as a text can serve the purpose of enhancing the quality of one's worship.

It might be asked: Does a time ever come in which the liturgy itself should *actually* be edited or rewritten? I have suggested that the "tension" between the liturgical language and one's own thoughts is a healthy one, but there may come a point at which the tension is too great and the gap too deep between the liturgy and one's perception of reality. For each individual this gap may occur at a different point. In fact, in chapter 3 we discussed a midrash from the Talmud (*Yoma* 69b) that dealt with precisely this point—Jeremiah and Daniel change the actual text of Moses' prayer because they cannot bear the tension between the words, which assert God's power, and the reality of the alien conquest of the land that the two prophets had witnessed. As R. Eleazar said: "Since they knew that the Holy One, blessed be He, insists on truth, they were unable to say any false things about Him." It is only Ezra and the Men of the Great Assembly who were able to restore the original prayer of Moses *by creating their own midrash on the original words,* in other words, by "mentally editing" the text. Thus, they asserted that when Moses' prayer talked about God's "might" it meant that God was so mighty that He suppressed His anger against the nations.

Since it is impractical for each person to carry around his or her own printed prayer book (although I have suggested that in essence we do this in our heads), we tend to rely on the institutions with which we identify to do the editing for us. Thus, there are certain Orthodox synagogues that will not say the Prayer for the State of Israel, while most Orthodox congregations do say it. And of course examples from non-Orthodox Judaism have been mentioned before. If you walk into a particular synagogue, you are likely to know (or find out very quickly!) where it stands on various issues concerning the liturgy.

The issue of an unbridgeable gap between text and self can be coupled with the traditional liturgical weight of the prayers in question. There are certain sections of the liturgy (for example, the Shema or the Amidah) whose liturgical status according to tradition is higher than others (for example, the introductory morning Psalms). By the traditional standard, then, making a change in the Shema would be very different from changing or eliminating one of those Psalms. The question then is: How do we balance the standards of the tradition with the values of today? But this is precisely the primary challenge of religion in a modern age. Liturgy in that sense is no different from any other area that one can address, although it may be somewhat more visible, since the prayer service has such a public function.

Of course, no liturgy could work if it simply functioned as a standard of *disagreement* and most of the experience of Jewish prayer, it seems to me, is not of the conflictive sort that I have been describing above under the rubric of "mental editing." More often than not the liturgy serves as an affirmative statement of what we *do* indeed believe, but the problem lies elsewhere: in the fact that the affirmation is stated in a specifically theological language with which we may not always be comfortable.

There is little doubt that the composers of the liturgy did believe the literal content of what they had written (although the midrash about Ezra and the Men of the Great Assembly makes the matter somewhat more complex than it might at first seem), but if we follow the prescription suggested earlier, that the liturgy is a second-order language that is ours to reinterpret, we can look at the formulae of the prayer book in a different fashion. We can look at the siddur as a way of *focusing* who we are, both in our tension with it, as I've suggested above, but even more clearly in our *connection* to the values of the liturgy. We may, in other words, take the theological language of the liturgy simply as a linguistic style, a kind of conventional structured framework, while we orient ourselves instead to the underlying values expressed by those words.

Look, for example, at some of the blessings that appear at the beginning of the traditional Morning Service:

> Blessed be You, O Lord our God, King of the universe,
>   who clothes the naked.
> Blessed be You, O Lord our God, King of the universe,
>   who releases those who are bound.
> Blessed be You, O Lord our God, King of the universe,
>   who supplies my every need.

To look at the liturgy as a way of focusing means to say to oneself in repeating these blessings: Each morning I assert a set of basic values. I believe that it is crucial "to clothe the naked," which is to say, to try to take care of the poor and homeless; I believe that it is essential to work for "the release of those who are bound," which means to help people in need and those who desire to be free; I believe that "my every need is supplied"—in other words, I should remember to think more carefully about my "need" to buy something and to be satisfied by that which I have; and so forth.

Now of course each person will read the "values" of the prayer book in a slightly different way—for some, the phrase "releases those who are bound" may cause them to think about captives of war; for some, "supplies my every need" may make them think about the need to preserve the ecological balance in nature. But in every case the liturgy becomes a meeting place for the classic values of Judaism and the things we ourselves believe in and care about, but which we may often let slip from our minds. The existence of the liturgy ensures that each time we pray, we come face-to-face with the deepest values of our lives. Prayer, then, becomes an opportunity for renewal. Like mental editing, "focusing" is a personal, individual process, but here it is a matter of how one interprets in a positive way the assertions and values of the liturgy. And these matters are not fixed in stone; indeed, each day you may read the same words in a different way and with a different understanding.

Focusing too is a kind of editing. What it does is place the weight of prayer on what we ourselves value (or want to value) rather than on what we might expect from God. These blessings from the Morning Service are written as statements about God. They are prayers of praise. In essence, I have suggested here that we put the emphasis in each line on the closing words "who clothes the naked" rather than on the "Blessed be You, O Lord our God, King of the universe, who . . ." There is no reason, certainly, why one cannot do both simultaneously—people can praise God *and* assert those values that matter most in their lives. But for many the theological difficulties of these assertions (that is, does God *really* clothe the naked?) make the words difficult to say. My point is that the reinterpretation of the words in this case is a shift of emphasis from the first to the latter sections of blessings such as these. Like Jeremiah and Daniel, we try to speak truth.

I have said above that each day we may see the values of the prayer book in a different light. Clearly, this will depend upon the facts of one's own life at any particular time. Thus, if I go to sleep with news about the homeless in my ears, I may find myself thinking about that issue when I say "clothes the naked" in the morning prayers. And this phenomenon—the effect of one's own personal situation at any given time on the way the prayers are understood—leads me to another way of experiencing the traditional liturgy.

Up to this point I have focused on the issue of the content of the prayers—both how we might approach liturgical language we disagree with and how we can approach words whose values we do agree with, but whose theological formulations present difficulties. I have tried to look at the experience of praying and the reality of what it means to pray through use of a liturgy. But the experience of prayer can also involve another relationship to the words of the liturgy, something beyond concentrating on their content. Prayer also gives us an opportunity for a more reflective or meditative experience and hence a different kind of connection to the words we say. I would call this latter experience prayer as "associative reverie." Let me try to explain what I mean in more detail.

Liturgical prayer is a meeting point between the community and the individual. For the individual this is most obvious when sitting in a synagogue, feeling oneself to be part of the community that surrounds one, but even when a person prays alone, as long as he or she is using the siddur, community—as represented by the book one is holding—is present. Of course, there are always varying degrees of distance and connection between the worshiper and the expressed values of the community, depending upon the words one is saying and the relationship one has to the content of those words.

But there are times in which the words of the prayer book can do something else: they can serve as a kind of catalyst for personal reflection. In those times the "individual" side of the individual-community continuum moves high up on the scale. The people around you matter very little; indeed, the denotative *content*—that is, the plain meaning—of the prayer book's words becomes secondary. What matters is the moment of reflection, the reverie, that occurs in prayer. Reverie is not without content; it lies somewhere between a daydream and a thought. I call this "associative reverie" because the moment of reflection is touched off by a *personal association* that one has with the words one is praying.

This sense of connection to the liturgy is something difficult to communicate to another person because the thread of association is too complex and too subtle to express easily in words. More often than not, this personal association is not really like a daydream (which tends to be elaborate and lengthy), but is rather a quick associative thought that flashes through the mind as one moves on to the next word on the page.

And these associations are bound to vary from day to day.

Indeed, it may be that very fact that keeps prayer from being routinized, as one sees in the following text:

> Faith is the basis of all worship;
> > only the truly faithful can pray each day.
> And what is the basis of faith?
> > "He renews each day the work of Creation."
> The faithful one sees
> > that every day is a new Creation,
> > that all the worlds are new,
> > that we ourselves have just been born.
> How could we not want to sing
> > the praise of the Creator?
>
> If we do not have the faith
> > that God creates anew each day,
> > prayer becomes an old, unwanted habit.
> How difficult it is to say
> > the same words day after day!
> Thus scripture says: "Cast us not into old age!"
> May the word never become old for us.
> > > > *(Degel Mahane Ephraim)* [10]

Of all the various movements within the history of Judaism, none placed a greater emphasis on prayer than Hasidism in the late eighteenth century. Here the author of the text, Rabbi Moses Hayim Ephraim of Sudylkov, stresses the need to feel oneself renewed each day in prayer. He bases his interpretation on a line from the morning liturgy quoted in the text above, "He renews each day the work of Creation," but he stresses here—in midrashic fashion—a reading of a verse from Psalms, "Cast us not into old age." The understanding of the verse is not its obvious meaning—the plea not to be abandoned in one's old age—but rather the desire that the words of prayer not become "old" and meaningless. But how does one do this work of renewing prayer? Through the personal associations that come to mind during prayer the dangers of *keva* can be overcome. Each day is new and thus necessarily each prayer is to be new as well.

If we return to our earlier example of blessings from the daily

Morning Service, we can imagine associative reveries that can occur when each of those blessings touches off images in my mind. I think about "clothing the naked" and my mind reflects, perhaps, on an encounter I had with a beggar on the street. I do not turn this reflection into a statement of belief or values, but that encounter with the beggar, the *experience* itself—and it can be either good or bad or neither—is what comes to mind. The blessing that ends "supplies my every need" may mean on one morning a thought about my own life and what my needs are; another morning I may reflect upon the world of nature and my connection to it. I may think about an incident from my life or a promise that I made or an experience that this blessing helps me put into perspective. And all of this may—like most passing associations—dart through my mind in an instant.

When I say the blessing about God as Creator of light, the word "light" may cause me to think about the light I see outside this morning and how it differs or resembles the light I see on other mornings. Or I may think of "light" as something symbolic of truth, and thus on *that* morning the blessing has nothing to do with light in its prosaic sense, while on the next morning it may lead me to reflect on sunlight itself. Or the blessing for "a new light to shine upon Zion" may on one day connect to something I read in the newspaper about contemporary Israel (I may think about issues concerning prospects for peace in the Middle East), while on another day it may have a completely different association. Thus, the liturgy—through the associative power of the worshiper's own mind—is constantly changing.

The distinction between the associations that come to mind under the rubric of "focusing," which I discussed earlier, and those I am referring to now has a good deal to do with the state of mind involved: here I am speaking of images or fragments of thoughts, a kind of dreamlike quality at times. "Focusing" was concerned with intellectual propositions, ideas, values that I ascribe to.

In a way, of course, the two are closely related. But the point I want to emphasize in making the distinction is that prayer is *not only* a matter of affirming intellectual beliefs. Most discussions of prayer tend to emphasize the "belief" side of prayer and the denotative content of the words. But prayer has a strong nonrational component as well. Associative reverie is an experience that Heschel described as "the imaginative projection of our consciousness into the meaning of the words."[11] Of course, it is hard to put this associative mode of prayer into words and for each person these associations will be different, but without this element one of the most important dimensions of prayer will be ignored or lost.

The early Hasidic writers also saw the potential danger in associative prayer. There was always the possibility that personal reflections could move a person *away* from prayer into a kind of banality. Thus, there is a considerable literature in these sources about the problems of *mahshava zara,* "alien thoughts," distractions in prayer that take the worshiper away from the task at hand. One should be careful not to forget that prayer is meant to be "sacred time" and not time for reflection on the stock market or the errands one has to do in the afternoon. Thus, in one text we are told:

> When a distracting thought comes to you in prayer,
>   hold fast to God and break through
>   to redeem the sacred spark
>   that dwells within that thought. . . .
>   *(Likkutim Yekarim)*[12]

And in another:

> As you stand before God in prayer,
>   you should feel that you stand alone—
>   in all the world only you and God exist.
> Then there can be no distractions;
> Nothing can disturb such a prayer.
>   *(Ben Porat Yosef)*[13]

Looking at the words of the liturgy in an associative manner means trying to find the "sacred spark that dwells within," which to my mind means seeing the words as an opportunity to reflect seriously upon one's life in a sacred context. When you see yourself as standing "alone" before God, the text implies, there are no distracting thoughts because you are facing up to your deepest sense of yourself.

Associative prayer is still very much focused on the words of the liturgy, though in an open-ended fashion. But there is another dimension of prayer that takes the experience one step further— prayer that seems to be *beyond* the words themselves. Here we enter a side of prayer that verges on the mystical, and yet it is an aspect of prayer that is not as unfamiliar as it may first appear. For many people have had experiences in prayer that have little to do with the words one is saying, times in which one is simply being swept up in the power of the moment. These experiences, which for lack of a better term I will simply call "beyond the words," are described by Hasidic texts in the following manner:

> When you focus all your thought
> on the power of the words,
> you may begin to see the sparks of light
> that shine within them.
> The sacred letters are the chambers
> into which God pours His flowing light.
> The lights within each letter, as they touch,
> ignite one another,
> and new lights are born.
> It of this the Psalmist says:
> "Light is sown for the righteous,
> and joy for the upright in heart" (Ps. 97:11).
> *(Keter Shem Tov)*[14]

It is clear in this text that the author is speaking of a very special type of prayer experience. And perhaps a special type of ability in the person who prays. The meaning of the individual words is insignificant; rather it is the "lights" one sees *within* the letters— in some way an aspect of the mysterious God—that one seeks to find. Values, associations, meanings seem very insignificant in such an understanding of prayer.

For most of us this kind of prayer seems impossible to attain.

But I want to focus upon the emotional aspect of prayer—the side of prayer that has no "content"—that the text above is advocating. Even without seeing "lights within the letters," a similar kind of purely emotional experience in prayer may in fact be something that we can encounter in our lives too.

Another text makes the point even more clearly:

> Do not think that the words of prayer
> as you say them
> go up to God.
> It is not the words themselves that ascend;
> it is rather the burning desire of your heart
> that rises like smoke toward heaven.
> If your prayer consists only of words and letters
> and does not contain your heart's desire—
> how can it rise up to God?
>
> *(Or Ha-Meir)* [15]

The "burning desire of your heart" is the side of prayer we often ignore. But prayer is as much that as it is the beliefs that we hold. When I said before that people are less unfamiliar with this side of prayer than they might think, I was thinking of one specific example (although there surely are others as well): namely, the kind of connection to *music* that seems to speak very directly to many people in a prayer service.

Some may have found this connection in the sound of singing during certain parts of the service—their own singing mixed with that of their fellow worshipers. Others experience it in the singing voice of the leader of the service, and for others it might be found in a choir or in musical instruments. Of course, music is only one example of the experience of being "beyond the words" in prayer. One of the strongest memories from my childhood of being swept up emotionally in synagogue is not so much of the power of singing, but of feeling the sheer numbers of people around me on the holiday evening of Simhat Torah.

We might wonder if such experiences can be "programmed" in advance. Is it possible to create such "beyond the words" time in one's prayer? In that light consider the following text:

131

There are times when you are praying
   in an ordinary state of mind
   and you feel that you cannot draw near to God.
But then in an instant
   the light of your soul will be kindled
   and you will go up to the highest worlds.

You are like one who has been given a ladder:
The light that shines in you is a gift from above.
                              (Likkutim Yekarim)[16]

As this text points out, these experiences of being "beyond the words" probably cannot be orchestrated (to continue my musical metaphor for a bit); more often than not, they come upon us in an instant. We can be singing in a congregation on Yom Kippur or we can be saying the morning prayers silently and alone while looking out the window. And suddenly, if not to "the highest worlds," we have at least gone beyond ourselves, no longer connected to the liturgy or even to any thoughts at all.

One of the curious aspects of contemporary Jewish religious life has been its lack of emphasis, its virtual antagonism, to fostering any nonverbal aspects of prayer, aside perhaps, from the performance side of synagogue music—the role of the cantor or the choir. This has been particularly true in the world of non-Orthodox synagogues. In general, the large suburban synagogues of the post–World War II era, have emphasized the communal dimension of the service at the expense of the individual side. That is, the focus of the service has been "to the front," so to speak, on the rabbi, the cantor, and the ceremony. But liturgical prayer, as I have tried to argue, is a complex balance between the communal and the individual poles. In what way, just to take one example, does the institution of the public "responsive reading" within the service foster the inwardness required for mental editing or associating (not to speak of being "beyond the words") in prayer? Very little, it seems to me.

In contrast, the style of prayer in a traditional setting—and here I do not mean the words but the way that the service is conducted —has helped create opportunities for that balance of the individual and the communal. In the Ashkenazic service the leader will say the opening words of a particular prayer, after which the entire congregation continues saying the prayer, each person to himself, in a kind of half-chant, half-mumble undertone. The leader will then repeat the last line of the prayer, or the blessing with which it concludes. During that middle period—between the opening line and the closing phrase—the individual is free to focus on the liturgy in whatever way he or she desires. Thus, the communal and the individual are blended within each prayer.[17] The Sephardic rite is somewhat different, and there one finds a good deal of communal chanting. The entire congregation sings together, with the leader taking more of a pacing role. Nonetheless, the chant creates a kind of communal hum that still leaves room for individual reflection.

Nor can we underestimate the power of the Hebrew language as an evocative factor in such settings. Of course, ideally everyone in the congregation would understand the Hebrew of the prayers. Personal association, for instance, can only work when at least a modicum of linguistic knowledge is present. But even when the comprehension of the language is weak, Hebrew may invoke a kind of magical quality for the worshiper. One feels a sense of connection to the ancient words of the Jewish people and, at least in the realm of "beyond the words," this has the potential to make a compelling spiritual effect on the worshiper.

This is not to say that nontraditional models of prayer cannot work. What I want to suggest, however, is that those new approaches that might be developed try to take into account the reasons why the traditional style of prayer has been so powerful. One might consider, for example, the ways that associative reverie might be attempted using the English translation of the siddur, or the ways that music or communal chanting could be introduced into the synagogue service. The key point is to begin with the insights of tradition and then reshape them to contemporary circumstance.

Of course, the traditional style of prayer has its own problems, most of which can be found in the hurried pace of the service, which often leaves little time for the individual's own thoughts, as one simply tries to keep up with the leader's pace. And in addition the sheer number of prayers can be overwhelming. But the concept of individual and communal interaction is what matters, even if the specific execution is not ideal in many congregations.

I began this chapter with a discussion of prayer and the issues that one faces in harmonizing the personal and emotional side of prayer (*kavvanah*) with the challenges of a fixed liturgy (*keva*). I have described four different stances, four ways of approaching the language of the traditional prayer book: "mental editing," which tries to deal with discontinuity between the worshiper and the liturgy; "focusing," which tries to center on the values embodied in the liturgy, irrespective of the theological language in which they are framed; "associative reverie," which sees the liturgy as an opportunity for one's own personal reflections and connections and experiences; and "beyond the words," which looks at those times in prayer when one is swept away by the emotional side of the experience.

In delineating these four stances, I do not mean to imply that there is a ladder of values here, that "beyond the words," for example, is a "higher stage" of prayer than mental editing (although I think it is fair to say that the Hasidic sources quoted before *would* make such a statement). These are points of relationship to liturgy, not steps to attain. And indeed throughout any service one is likely to float back and forth among all four of these points of relationship. Or, as the Hasidic literature is well aware, one might not be able to find any relationship to a particular service on a given day. "Alien thoughts" might rule.

But there is one final way of looking at the liturgy that I would also like to suggest. I am speaking of those times in which one is completely in harmony with both the sentiment and the language of the siddur, so much so that the liturgy requires no mental editing at all and the words one says are a simple "plea" from the heart. The four stances I have developed above are in some ways reactions to a sense of disconnection from prayer or the prayer book. But now I am speaking about the opposite phenomenon—

when we experience the language of the prayers as literally "our own."

This experience, to my mind, is connected to an idea mentioned in the last chapter: times when we relate to statements about God in their most elemental way, as literal fact, even though we know that is not what we "believe." In a similar fashion there are times that the liturgy will seem completely "true." Our theology will matter very little. We might say "Cast us not into old age" during a Yom Kippur service, and each word will ring true as a call toward a God who answers prayers in the most direct fashion imaginable. And it won't matter that our own rational beliefs about God are far more complex or far more full of reservations and qualifying statements than the prayer seems to imply. The experience may not be rational and will certainly not remain constant every time we pray, but at times the words and we are in harmony. And that too is an experience of prayer.

SIX

THE CIRCLE OF COMMUNITY

Our rabbis taught: The pious ones of earlier generations used to hide their thorns and broken glass in the midst of their fields at a depth of three handbreadths below the surface so that the plough would not be hindered by them. R. Sheshet used to throw them into the fire. Rav threw them into the Tigris. R. Judah said: He who wishes to be pious must fulfill the laws in *Seder Nezikin*. But Rava said: The matters dealt with in the Tractate *Avot*. Still others said: Matters dealt with in the Tractate *Berakhot*.

(Talmud, *Bava Kamma* 30a)

What does it mean to lead a holy life? The Talmud, in the passage above, tries to address the question by looking at the exemplary behavior of the "pious ones of earlier generations," what we might call the religious "role models" from the past. The context of this passage is a discussion of liabilities for damages that a person can incur through irresponsible actions. If someone is hurt by my carelessness, to what extent am I responsible? In the midst of that discussion the passage above appears. Here we are given three examples of the way one might avoid causing damages: The pious ones used to bury discarded thorns and broken glass to keep them out of harm's way, R. Sheshet used to throw them into the fire, and Rav used to throw them into the river.

Following the description of those actions, R. Judah makes a

136

more general statement that seems to be inspired by the discussion that has just taken place. Those who want to be "pious," that is, those who want to live a holy life, should fulfill the laws defined by *"Seder Nezikin,"* meaning that section of the Talmud that deals with laws concerning damages. (The Talmud is composed of six topical orders—Hebrew: *seder*—or divisions. Each order consists of a number of tractates.) Thus, R. Judah believes that the way to piety is defined by one's care—exemplified by the opinions concerning glass and thorns quoted directly before—in dealing with property damages.

Rava, however, has a different view. To his mind the key to holiness is to be found in the Tractate *Avot,* the section of the Mishnah that in an aphoristic way discusses ethical and spiritual behavior. Finally, "others" take yet another view: the way to holiness is to be found in the Tractate *Berakhot,* the section of the Talmud that deals mainly with matters of prayer.

These three contrasting views represent different visions of the nature of the religious life. Up to now in this book we have been talking about the dimension of Judaism that deals most directly with the individual and his or her own personal religious experience, matters addressed, we might say, by the Tractate *Berakhot* (and to a lesser extent by *Avot*). This is the inner life of religion, the place where a person confronts questions of meaning and one's relationship to tradition, to God, and to prayer. Within the tradition itself this aspect of Judaism is usually called *mitzvot bein adam l'makom,* literally, "commandments between human beings and 'the Place,' " the latter term, as we have mentioned in chapter 4, being one of the many appellations for God used in the classical sources.

But Judaism has always asserted a broader self-definition than one limited to concerns of the inner life alone. As R. Judah and Rava argue in our passage above, the world of *mitzvot bein adam l'makom* represents only one aspect of a larger picture, one side of the coin of tradition. Of equal weight are the commandments that deal with relationships between the self and others, known as *mitzvot bein adam l'havero,* which are explored in *Seder Nezikin* and through the greater part of the tractate *Avot.* Indeed, if we were to tally the number of topics and pages, it is likely that the greater part of the Talmud, at least in its "practical" dimension[1] (to take the most important example of classical Jewish literature) is more concerned with this latter category of mitzvot in all its many ramifications than with the commandments between human beings and God. How should a Jew deal with business concerns, with marital life, with divorce, with property? All of this lies within the scope of *mitzvot bein adam l'havero.*

But the realm of interpersonal relationships was not understood by the tradition as being a "secular" domain. There is a close connection, according to the rabbis, between one's individual religious life and the social fabric of community. *Both* are aspects of the holy, a connection indicated in the following statement from the Mishnah dealing with the holiest day of the year:

> Yom Kippur atones for transgressions between human beings and God [Hebrew: *bein adam l'makom*]; but Yom Kippur will not atone for transgressions between a person and others [Hebrew: *bein adam l'havero*] until one makes peace with one's fellow.
>
> (Mishnah, *Yoma* 8:9)

The transgressions you may have done in ignoring your relationship to God—in prayer or in ritual, let's say—these can be repaired by the Day of Atonement. But in the realm of interpersonal relationships, you must first find those individuals you have hurt and gain their forgiveness or make restitution to them for what you have done before the prayers of Yom Kippur can be effective.

At one level this text is rooted in the commonsense wisdom of ordinary human psychology. It is difficult for anyone to concentrate upon the issues of self-evaluation and renewal that are the great themes of Yom Kippur while one's mind is still occupied by the damage you have caused others. One must first clear the air and be settled in one's social milieu before you can turn to God. And of course there is something hypocritical about asking for divine forgiveness while one is still caught up in the interpersonal conflict that may exist between people.

But beyond the psychological dimension, something else is proposed by the text as well. The two realms of interpersonal and divine concerns are indivisibly intertwined. The text does *not* assert that you need to get forgiveness from other people for your personal transgressions and get forgiveness from God for your "religious" sins, and the two matters are unconnected. Rather it says that once the interpersonal pardoning has occurred, *then* Yom Kippur can atone for the *interpersonal* sins. (And of course the transgressions in the realm of *mitzvot bein adam l'makom* are a separate matter and must also be resolved.) Now of course we could still argue that the text suggests that the interpersonal peace-making is the key point; it is that act which allows God to forgive. But even so, the idea that these texts always come back to is that God is involved in the interpersonal too. After all, they are called mitzvot, commandments, and are therefore as binding and as sacred as any commandment about prayer or Shabbat.

The world of "religion," in other words, is as much concerned with our lives in relation to other people as it is with our ritual behavior. Both are aspects of the holy. And yet when we think about Judaism, why are the *mitzvot bein adam l'makom,* the "God-oriented" commandments, the ones that first leap to mind, the ones that seem to be what Judaism is all about? Indeed, one of the critiques lodged against contemporary traditional Judaism has been its almost single-minded focus on the God-oriented commandments at the expense of *mitzvot bein adam l'havero.* In other words, why do we hear outcries from the traditional Jewish community about the tiniest details of keeping kosher or, in Israel, protests about matters such as movies being shown on the Sabbath and we hear nothing about the plight of the homeless or about insider trading scandals on Wall Street?

There is no denying the weight of this question. Indeed, in a subtle way it may indicate something about the way that Jews have assimilated the values of the larger non-Jewish community. By focusing on *mitzvot bein adam l'makom* at the expense of *mitzvot bein adam l'havero,* Judaism today has unwittingly bought into a kind of non-Jewish "spiritualization" of religion that does not represent the tradition at its best. That is, the spiritual concerns of Judaism (the *mitzvot bein adam l'makom*) have always been viewed as only half of the picture. To see these today as the heart of

Judaism redefines the tradition in an alien vocabulary which says that religion is only what happens within carefully delineated "sacred" boundaries and is not concerned with the broad dimensions of ordinary human life, in essence making a kind of dichotomy between "church" and "state."

Of course, it is not difficult to see why this has occurred. As we have said previously in this book, all of us are the products of modernity and Western culture. And since the values of that culture and at least some of the values of Judaism in the realm of ethical values certainly overlap, it would be hard for any of us to say that we know stealing is wrong *because* Judaism tells us this is so, rather than because it is the general rule of law in Western society. And to point out the obvious fact that the ethical values of Western culture itself owe a great deal to Jewish sources, especially to the Bible, does little to change the way we perceive the matter. Indeed, it is precisely the essential harmony between *mitzvot bein adam l'havero* and modern Western ethical values that allows Jews to feel so at ease within the culture in which they live. As Jews we would have a much more difficult time living in a society with laws that sanctioned murder or which believed that the punishment should not fit the crime.

And more than that, the tendency to define Judaism by its God-centered commandments is clearly related to the fact that many of the interpersonal mitzvot, the *mitzvot bein adam l'havero,* reflect a rationality that simply seems "obvious." To learn that stealing is wrong or that we should not hurt other people surprises no one. Reason and our knowledge about human nature makes it clear that such rules of behavior must obtain in any organized society. By contrast, the realm of ritual behavior, the *mitzvot bein adam l'makom,* is particularly intriguing simply because those practices do *not* conform to reason or at any rate do not seem *necessary* to help a community function. In other words, any reasonable society needs a rule about not stealing, but we do not really need the ritual of lulav and etrog to live in a workable community.

The distinction between the commandments that seem rational and those that do not is certainly not a new one: Some talmudic sources interpret the biblical term *hukkim* ("statutes") to refer to those laws that seem to be unconnected to ordinary reason.[2] In the Middle Ages Maimonides summed up the distinction between the two types of commandments by saying that the *hukkim* were those commandments whose causes are hidden from us because of our incapacities, and the *mishpatim* ("laws") were those "commandments whose utility is clear to the multitude," such as the prohibition of killing and stealing.[3]

For us today this distinction also makes sense, but we tend to take the matter one step further. It is precisely the ritual aspects of Judaism—some of which are "rational" or can be seen to be rational and some of which are not—which seem to us to be the essence of Judaism. The *mitzvot bein adam l'havero* are relegated to the realm of "ethics" or to the norms of our general society. In contemporary Israel this issue is seen in clear relief when we look at the attempts to create a Jewish state that is also part of Western democratic modernity. In what ways, it can be asked, are the laws or norms of Israel "Jewish" and in what way are they simply examples of the "Western democratic" tradition?[4]

In the past, before the integration of Jews into Western culture, the *mitzvot bein adam l'havero* formed the inner vocabulary of Jewish behavior. When a person acted in an ethical manner, even the terms used to describe those actions were expressed by traditional language. Rather than say "Yes, this is the reasonable way to behave—one should not gossip about another person," the traditional Jew would say or think, "We are forbidden by the Torah to engage in acts of *lashon ha-rah*," literally, "bad speech" about another. Now, of course, as we know from the seriousness of the ethical literature within Judaism, not all of our ancestors were saints. They too struggled to act morally and they did not always succeed. But my point here is that even the language and terminology used to understand their actions indicated that they saw their behavior as an integral part of traditional Jewish life. For us, however, the world of "religion" and the world of interpersonal behavior often seems quite distinct.

Nonetheless, it is clear that the "reasonableness" of ethical behavior has always presented a certain kind of problem, even within the traditional Jewish society of the past. The ethical writers within the Jewish tradition[5] worried, as might we today, about the danger of the *banality* of such discussions. Thus Rabbi Moshe Hayim Luzzatto, the eighteenth-century author of one of the most influential ethical tracts in the history of Judaism, *Mesilat Yesharim (The Path of the Upright),* begins his book with these words:

> I have not written this book to teach people anything they do not know. Rather it is my aim to remind them of that which they know already and which is generally accepted. For you will find in most of my words things that most people know and do not doubt at all. But to the same extent that they are well known and clear to all, so are they overlooked and greatly forgotten. Therefore, the benefit from this book will not come from reading it once, since after one reading the reader will find few new things which he did not know already. Rather the benefit will come from rereading and struggling with it. Then he will remember the things people usually forget and take seriously the obligations which one usually tries to avoid.
>
> (*Mesilat Yesharim,* Introduction, p. 1)[6]

Luzzatto's book deals with both *mitzvot bein adam l'makom* and *mitzvot bein adam l'havero* as he seeks to explore the path toward *hasidut,* a holy life. Since these matters are so obvious, so rational, so well known to everyone, Luzzatto argues in the passage above, they are issues that people easily ignore. Indeed, the more we think we know about these matters, the easier it seems to forget them. Ethical behavior in particular is the kind of issue that is virtually impossible to talk about. Since we all know how important and how essential it is, it bores us to talk about it:

> It is not because these matters are unimportant to people [that they ignore them]. If you were to ask them, everybody would reply that they are essential and that one cannot be considered wise without clearly understanding all these things. But the reason they don't devote themselves to studying these areas is that the issues are so well known and commonplace that studying them does not seem to demand much time.
>
> (*Mesilat Yesharim,* Introduction, p. 2)

Indeed, Luzzatto goes on to say, these areas of study are not considered appropriate for "fine minds" and are therefore left to those with limited intellectual talent. And, as he says to the reader, if you were found dealing with these matters, you too might be considered one of those lesser individuals! Thus, he articulates a very telling idea: within sophisticated societies there is a kind of subtle social pressure that relegates those who concern themselves with ethical behavior to a lower rung of intellectual achievement. After all, why bother to spend your time thinking about the obvious, belaboring the rules of moral behavior that everyone already knows?

Of course, as Luzzatto well understood, it is precisely because of this danger that one needs to spend time thinking about these matters. And we today are no different in that regard from Luzzatto's readers. It is because of the "obviousness" of the ethical that we have to find ways of getting inside of the issues. But how to go about it is the question.

One possible route is to look back at the Bible, focusing on the prophetic dimension of Judaism. The call of an Amos or an Isaiah can still stir us today. When we look around us at a world of immense wealth in which many are still hungry and homeless, the words of Jeremiah can penetrate our society's self-satisfaction:

> He who builds his house with unfairness
> And his upper chamber with injustice,
> Who makes his fellow man work without pay
> And does not give him his wages,
> Who thinks: I will build me a vast palace
> With spacious upper chambers,
> Provided with windows,
> Paneled in cedar,
> Painted with vermilion!
> Do you think you are more a king
> Because you compete in cedar?
> Your father ate and drank
> And dispensed justice and equity—
> Then all went well with him.
> He upheld the rights of the poor and needy—
> Then all was well.
> That is truly heeding Me.
>   —Declares the Lord.
> But your eyes and your mind are only
> On ill-gotten gains,

On shedding the blood of the innocent,
On committing fraud and violence. . . .
                    (Jeremiah 22:13–17)

But as much as the poetry of the prophets is compelling, in leaping back in history to the Bible we should be careful not to ignore the particular contribution of rabbinic literature in dealing with the issues of an ethical life. The rabbis tended to speak with less rhetorical power than the Bible, but they nonetheless tried to work on these same issues, focusing on the small details of ethical behavior, trying to tease out the complexities of implementing the vision of the prophets into normal human existence.

For the rabbis there was one essential underlying question: What does it mean to lead a holy life? Since they saw God's hand in all matters, they wished to determine what God wanted from human beings in all dimensions of behavior—in ritual practice *and* in interpersonal relationships. Thus, the intricate, complex, sometimes frustrating discussions in rabbinic legal literature have at their heart this all-encompassing enterprise; not so much to establish *what* is "the good" but rather *how to actualize* "the good" in ordinary human life. The rabbis wanted to explore what it means, in the Bible's phrase, to be "a kingdom of priests and a holy nation"?

There is no doubt that Luzzatto's warning about the difficulties of exploring issues "so well known and commonplace" is not to be taken lightly, and so we should ask ourselves what in particular the study of rabbinic sources about ethical behavior can offer a reader today? To begin with, we can say that, like the study of Jewish texts about other issues, the exploration of these *mitzvot bein adam l'havero* offers the same sense of rootedness in tradition, the same weight of history, that has been discussed previously in this book. But there are two other matters that can be added as well.

First and most simply, there are times when we can argue that Judaism offers a perspective on a particular issue that differs from that normally found in Western culture. In doing so, Judaism offers a kind of critique of the way we think we should behave.

One could look, for example, at classical texts about gossip, about business ethics, or about the return of lost objects to see the way that Jewish ethical principles may have something striking to teach us.[7]

But even in those cases in which the values of contemporary Western thought and those of Judaism are fairly congruent, rabbinic sources have a contribution to make as well: in the *process* of ethical exploration that lies at the heart of these texts. Rabbinic texts, as we have said, begin with an assumption. Their job is to actualize in an unperfected world the realities of ethical behavior.

Perhaps this grew out of the history of the Jewish people—the need of a community small in numbers to find ways to survive. Or perhaps it was inherent in the nature of the biblical teachings themselves. But no matter the origins, the implementation was quite clear. Rabbinic considerations of ethical issues are rarely lists of desired behaviors—ideal or idealized standards—stated baldly and without elaboration. Instead, we have something else: the process of debate and deliberation, accommodation to human frailties and the realities of real life, disagreements—some without a hard and fast resolution—exemplary tales to indicate proper behavior and counterexamples that present the other side.

There is in all of this an acceptance of how real human life works, how communities grow and sustain themselves, how imperfect our knowledge about moral action actually is. And it is precisely that sense of open deliberation, that process of discussion without easy answers, that can speak to us now and give us something to learn. The rabbis seem to have understood that coming out with the simple conclusion, the uncomplicated prescription, would never persuade those who listened to their teachings. In reading the rabbinic discussions we sense the process of hard thought and moral struggle behind the words, and that is what provides this literature with its power to touch one's life.

Of course, in this vast literature there are comments about belief and desired behavior stated without elaboration and dialectic. But even the bold directness of the teachings in *Pirkei Avot* are elusive and cryptic, appearing at times to be a kind of Eastern wisdom that conceals more than it reveals. Thus, with the ambig-

145

uous circuitry of a Zen master, Rabban Gamaliel used to say: "Make His will your will so that He will make your will His will. Set aside your will before His will so that He will set aside the will of others before your will" (*Avot* 2:4). Or, in the best-known of these comments, Hillel used to say, "If I am not for myself, who will be for me? But if I am only for myself, what am I? And if not now, when?" (*Avot* 1:14).

And here too there are disagreements. Shimon the Just tells us that the world resides on three foundations: Torah, divine service, and acts of kindness (*Avot* 1:2), and just a few lines later Rabbi Shimon ben Gamaliel asserts: "The world rests on three foundations—truth, justice, and peace" (*Avot* 1:18). Are both correct? It often seems that these blunt statements of fact are really only pared-down summations of life experience, the wisdom of those who have seen much and have come—each of them—to slightly different conclusions.

And finally there is another point that must be added. I have said earlier that one of the essential functions of this literature was to provide a vocabulary of human behavior rooted in a sense of mitzvah. It is important in our world to think about the implications of living in such a way, for to live with these ethical matters as *commandments* is something different from what most of us are used to.

The idea that the deeds we do in our relations with others are commandments is something that seems to go against our essential Western commitment to the value of individual freedom. Isn't it better, isn't it a "higher" level of behavior, we tend to think, to perform actions that are freely chosen, which emanate out of our principles and which are unbridled by any sense of "have to," any authority making us do them? Indeed, when we look at the work of contemporary thinkers about ethical behavior, we can find such a tendency. In particular, the work of recent developmental and educational psychologists who try to study the stages of growth in ethical behavior point in that direction. For example, in the "stage theory" of Lawrence Kohlberg, the most influential of these thinkers, a person who is in stage six of Kohlberg's six stages of moral development—the highest level of behavior—will act based on "self-chosen ethical principles. . . . When laws violate these principles, one acts in accordance with the principle." While at stage one, the person does what is right in order to "avoid breaking rules backed by punishment" and "obedience is for its own sake."[8]

But despite our modern predilections for the value of freedom (as exemplified by Kohlberg's work), we should not underestimate the power of seeing one's life in the light of "obedience," as a set of commandments that one fulfills. Indeed, the rabbis saw a high stage of morality in *freely choosing to obey*. Thus, we find the following statement:

> Rabban Gamaliel said: A person should not say, "It is impossible for me to eat milk and meat together; it is impossible for me to wear garments of mixed kinds [forbidden in Lev. 19:19]; it is impossible for me to have a forbidden sexual relationship. But one should say, "It is quite possible for me, but what can I do if my Father in Heaven has commanded me not to do it!"
>
> (Sifra on Leviticus 20:26)

We should also be aware that the inclination our culture feels toward valuing acts performed because one "wants to" rather than because one "has to" also emanates to a certain extent out of the influence that classical Christian doctrine—beginning with Paul's critique of the mitzvot—has had on Western consciousness. In the sense that Western culture is "Christian," it is influenced by Paul's notion that "those who rely on obedience to the law are under a curse" (Gal. 3:10).

The Christian notion of "charity," for example, is very different from the Jewish concept of *tzedakah*. Charity evolves from the Latin *caritas,* meaning an act of love (as in the English "caring"); *tzedakah* (usually translated as "charity," thereby missing the point) evolves from the Hebrew word for "justice." When we feed the hungry, we do not do it because we want to, because we feel like it, according to classical Judaism, but because God demands justice. God demands that we do right, even if we don't feel like it.

Thus, seeing one's actions as fulfilling the demands of the mitzvot has the advantage of institutionalizing ethical behavior as a given fact of life in the community in the way that relying on acts of love may very well not. And more than the societal function of such a system, seeing ethical behavior as mitzvah gives the individual a kind of defining rootedness that lets one see the discrete experiences of one's life as acts of serving God. One is not simply helping someone else, one also is doing what the Creator demands. Thus, one's actions are integrated into a personal commitment to doing what's right.

To see the *mitzvot bein adam l'havero* as commandments means to assert my own individual desire to act rightly *not* when I happen to feel like it, but to act rightly because I am essentially *committed* to it. Viewing these actions as commandments means I can do no other.

Of course, I am still left with the issue of what is "the right" to which I am committed? It is here that we enter the exploration of ethical issues in the classical Jewish sources. But I want to reiterate something said earlier. At the heart of this literature is the process of discussion that is spun out around these issues and the awareness of how difficult "doing right" actually is. And there is something else as well. By engaging these texts, by entering the debates that they open, we the readers are thrust directly into the life of such ethical debates ourselves. The study of these materials is not only for the purpose of learning how to act, but the process of study itself is a heuristic device, an educational tool. It too is part of what it means to be an ethical person: We are required not simply to do the good as a passive recipient of a set of rules of behavior, but to struggle in an active way with the subtle complexity of these issues.

I want to turn to some texts that will exemplify what I have been talking about here, and the issues I want to focus on first are those that deal directly with the small community of an individual's friends and acquaintances. The way that Jewish sources might or might not be relevant to larger political questions involving right and wrong is a matter I wish to take up in the next two chapters, since it involves other considerations that also need to be explored. But first I want to look at those areas of life that are a good deal more within our control—what happens in the relationships we have with those who are near to us.

There are numerous issues explored in the classic sources that deal directly with areas of interpersonal relationships. There are texts that deal with gossip or envy or dealings between employers and employees, and many others as well. In each of these areas, the typical method of discussion is the talmudic or midrashic debate, which centers on biblical verses and tries to tease out the various possible ways of behavior in any given situation. Behind the deliberation remains the pressing question: What does it mean to do right? And recognizing the complexity of human life, the rabbis try to look at all sides of the issue: Is gossip ever permitted? Might envy not be a positive virtue in certain cases?

I want to illustrate what I mean by looking at one example in detail. My goal here is to demonstrate the nature of rabbinic debate on ethical matters, but I also want to address a matter that strikes me as one very relevant to the way we live today. Namely, how do we deal with conflict, with a breakdown in the community of friends? What does it mean, therefore, to rebuke another person, a friend or relative, who has done something wrong? For most people that kind of expression of anger is terribly difficult, but as the rabbinic sources well knew, for a community to function, such means of confrontation had to be found. But how? And under what circumstances? These are the questions I wish to explore now.

The issue of confrontation begins with a famous biblical verse:

> You shall not hate your kinsman in your heart. You shall surely rebuke your neighbor, and not bear sin because of him. You shall not take vengeance or bear a grudge against your kinsfolk. Love your neighbor as yourself: I am the Lord.
>
> (Leviticus 19:17–18)

Every community must deal with issues of disharmony among its members. What happens when a person has violated the norms of the society? Or what happens when there is conflict between two individuals? Chapter 19 of Leviticus tries to deal with numerous issues that might occur within a communal context.

It is clear that among its other concerns the Bible wished to avoid the dangers of the kind of festering hatred that can occur when someone nurses a grudge by hating his neighbor "in his heart." But the biblical passage leaves the precise nature of what human beings are supposed to do somewhat murky. In the same way that rabbinic interpretation tries to tease out the implications of biblical narratives, explication of legal passages from the Bible was also a significant concern. Indeed, one could say, even *more* significant because the implementation of biblical law was essential to the day-to-day functioning of Jewish communities. The laconic style of the Bible—the way the Bible tells both its stories and its laws in very few words and therefore needs to be explicated—necessitated developing a legal midrash to clarify the fine points of the law in the same way that it led to a midrash on narratives that "filled in" the details of the stories.[9]

Thus, in looking at our passage above, later commentators were perplexed in particular by the relationship between the two parts of verse 17: What is the connection between "You shall surely rebuke your neighbor" and "not bear sin because of him." The confusion about the inner meaning of the verse is indicated by the fact that the leading contemporary scholarly translation of the Bible (Jewish Publication Society, 1985) renders the verse like this: "Reprove your neighbor, but [Hebrew: *ve*] incur no guilt because of him," taking the *ve* for "but," where the older translation, as we have quoted it above, uses the equally acceptable "and." Indeed, the new JPS translation gives a footnote explaining that the "exact force" of the *ve* is "uncertain."

The differences between the two translations are subtle but significant. The "and" reading seems to suggest that the second half of the verse offers an explanation of the first that would go something like this: Rebuke your neighbor, for if you don't, you yourself will bear sin (or as the New JPS puts it, incur guilt); meaning, as the twelfth-century Spanish commentator Ibn Ezra puts it: "If you do not correct him, you might be punished on his account." In other words, there is something in the very nature of a holy community that requires each member to take responsibility for the transgressions of others. If you do not rebuke the other person, it is almost as if you yourself are guilty for what the person did.

Ibn Ezra's view is a demanding one. It suggests that people are bound up with one another in a community of profound connection. But is this a community that we could see ourselves being part of? To the modern ear there is something here that smacks of Big Brother, too much attention to what one's neighbor is doing. But much as we may have difficulty with such a perspective, we should not overlook what motivates Ibn Ezra's point of view. It is the attempt to live a life in accordance with God's will. And unlike the society of Orwell's *1984,* we are not talking about reporting your neighbor to the authorities, but rather actually confronting the person face-to-face. Perhaps it is *that* level of honesty or clarity about one's own ethical point of view that makes us feel uncomfortable.

But Ibn Ezra's concern goes beyond the guilt one may bring upon oneself by *not* rebuking the neighbor. He sees the motivation for confrontation as twofold. First and foremost is the need to make sure that the enmity you bear within your heart is based on the truth:

> Perhaps you hate someone because you suspect him of something which never happened; therefore "you shall surely rebuke your neighbor." On the other hand, perhaps he actually did something which calls for reproof. In that case, "do not bear sin because of him"—if you do not correct him, you might be punished on his account.
>
> **(Ibn Ezra, Commentary on Leviticus 19)**

Ibn Ezra suggests that the Bible has instituted the practice of interpersonal reproof (in the vocabulary of traditional Jewish ethics the term is *hokheah tokhiah*: "You shall surely rebuke") in order to make sure that you do not resent someone without cause. He imagines a very real scenario: Perhaps you have heard that someone has said something about you or has done something disreputable. Ibn Ezra recognizes the natural human tendency to believe the worst about someone else and therefore he sees *hokheah tokhiah* as the tool by which we can discover the real facts. It is only once one discovers the truth that the second side of confrontation comes into play—if you learn that indeed the facts are as you had suspected, then you must reprove the other.

It is interesting that neither the Bible nor Ibn Ezra's commentary clarifies the nature of the other person's wrongdoing, but it is our natural tendency to think that the case applies to interpersonal tension between two individuals ("you" and the "neighbor") rather than to a more general wrong that your kinsman may have committed. It makes sense to think that "hatred in the heart" would emanate from a wrong done (or inaccurately *perceived* to have been done) by your neighbor to *you,* rather than a transgression against the community, the law, or God.

Of course, from the text of the Bible we cannot be sure, but that tendency in interpretation is borne out by the commentary of the early rabbinic midrash Sifra on the same verses in Leviticus. Sifra—in a passage that later became well known through being quoted by the eleventh-century commentator Rashi[10]—looks at the next verse in our biblical passage and explains it with an example out of the ordinary human interaction of neighbors. "You shall not take vengeance or bear a grudge against your kinsfolk" refers to the following situation:

> If one says to another "Lend me your sickle," and the other replies, "No!" and the next day the neighbor in turn comes to him and says "Lend me your hatchet," and he replies, "I am not going to lend it to you, because you refused to lend me your sickle"—that is what the Torah means by "taking vengeance."
>
> And what is "bearing a grudge"? If one says to another, "Lend me your hatchet," and he replies, "No!" and on the next day the neighbor in turn comes to him and says, "Lend me your sickle" and he replies, "Here it is. I am not, like you, a person who would not lend someone else a hatchet!" This is called "bearing a grudge" because he retains enmity in his heart even though he did not actually avenge himself.
>
> (Sifra on Leviticus 19; also quoted by Rashi)[11]

There is a homey, almost prosaic quality to these situations as Sifra portrays them. These are moments of interpersonal conflict between two ordinary people, fights over sickles and hatchets, not matters with larger religious or communal implications.

When we turn to Rashi's comment on our particular question —What is the nature of *hokheah tokhiah,* reproof and confrontation?—we see something different from Ibn Ezra's understanding of the verse. Rashi views the second part of Leviticus 19:17 not as an answer to *why* we should rebuke the other, but as an indication of *how* that rebuke should be effected:

> Though rebuking him, you should not publicly embarrass him [Hebrew: *malbin panim,* literally "make his face grow pale"], in which case you will bear sin on account of him.
>
> (Rashi, Commentary on Leviticus 19; a similar view is found in Sifra)

To return to a point made earlier, Rashi, in a sense, supports the "but" reading of the verse from Exodus: "Reprove your neighbor, but incur no guilt because of him." In other words, you should confront your neighbor, *but* reprove the neighbor in an appropriate way, in a manner that will bring no blame upon you. The key issue from Rashi's point of view is *malbin panim,* publicly embarrassing another person, an ethical violation that was viewed with great seriousness by rabbinic sources. Thus, the Talmud states in dramatic, almost hyperbolic, terms:

> He who publicly shames his neighbor is as though he shed blood. . . . Rabbah bar Bar Hanah said in Rabbi Yohanan's name: It is better for a man to cohabit with a woman whose divorce is in doubt than to publicly shame his neighbor. . . . Rabbi Yohanan on authority of Rabbi Shimon bar Yohai said: It is better that a person throw himself into a fiery furnace than publicly to shame his neighbor.
>
> (Talmud, *Bava Metzia* 58b–59a)

But obviously in real life *hokheah tokhiah* is a complicated matter. When we confront another individual, how far are we allowed to go in expressing our anger? When, precisely, does that moment of public embarrassment occur? Is there a distinction between a wrong done to us personally and a wrong done to someone else which we might be aware of? The Talmud tries to address some of these issues in an interesting passage:

> How do we know that if a person sees something reprehensible in his neighbor, he is obliged to reprove him? Because it is said: "You

shall surely rebuke." If he rebuked him and he did not accept it, how do we know that he must rebuke him again? The text states: "surely rebuke"—that is, in all cases. One might assume this to be obligatory even to the point of his face changing color, therefore the text states: "You shall not bear sin because of him. . . . "

(Talmud, *Arakhin* 16b)

This passage raises an issue we have not dealt with up to this point. What happens if your rebuke of the other goes unheeded? Indeed, what does it mean to go unheeded? The rabbis understood the emphatic verbal form[12] of the biblical Hebrew *hokheah tokhiah* (in English: "surely rebuke") as a message: Even if your reproof has been ignored, you must repeat it. Surely, then, they expect the confrontation to produce some kind of *result*.

The biblical passage itself does not say anything about results, beyond that of expressing one's anger, of not nursing resentment in one's heart. In the biblical context, it seems that the purpose of the confrontation was to give the angry person a chance to express his own inner disturbance. What that confrontation does for the other, the person who receives the rebuke, is not made clear at all. But here in the Talmud the emphasis has shifted. In confronting your neighbor, you are trying to reform him, and if you do not succeed at first, you must repeat the efforts, as is indicated in another passage from the Talmud:

One of the rabbis said to Rava: Perhaps *hokheah* means to rebuke the other once and *tokhiah* means to rebuke the other twice. He answers: *Hokheah* means to rebuke him even a hundred times! As for *tokhiah*, I only know that the master must rebuke the student. Where do we know that the student must rebuke the master? From *hokheah to-khiah*, implying under all circumstances.

(Talmud, *Bava Metzia* 31a)

The question here is how to interpret the repetition of the verbal form from *hokheah tokhiah*. One of the rabbis comes to Rava and suggests that the specific language of the text signifies a person's need to *repeat* his rebuke of the wrongdoer. After two tries, you have fulfilled your own obligation. But Rava rejects this view. For him the stark command of *hokheah* is sufficient. A person is obliged to try to change his neighbor, even if it takes an enormous effort to do so, indeed a hundred confrontations! Rava's view of the emphatic verbal form is that it indicates the need for confrontation "under all circumstances," even with those, like one's teachers, whose status is higher than one's own.

Still, even this kind of confrontation has its limits. To return to our earlier talmudic text (*Arakhin* 16b) we can see that the teaching clearly states that the second half of Leviticus 19:17 is to be read as a corrective concerning the nature of that rebuking. You can only go so far, the Talmud warns. Be careful not to embarrass publicly the person you wish to rebuke. Of course, publicly embarrassing another is a wrong in itself, but Ibn Ezra's warning mentioned earlier is also relevant here: It may be that your information is wrong and you have rebuked someone for something that they have not even done.

The same talmudic passage continues, and the issue of how to confront is explored in more general terms:

> . . . It was taught: R. Tarfon said, I wonder if there is anyone in this generation who knows how to accept reproof, for if one says to another: Remove the chip of wood from between your eyes, he would answer: Remove the beam from between *your* eyes!
>
> R. Eleazar ben Azariah said: I wonder if there is anyone in this generation who knows how to give reproof.
>
> (Talmud, *Arakhin* 16b)

Rabbi Tarfon points out something well known to all of us: When we come to tell another of his or her errors, we are likely to receive an even greater indictment of ourselves in return! Few of us know how to receive reproof, but Rabbi Eleazar ben Azariah points out that just as few of us know how to be the one who *gives* reproof. What would it mean to give reproof to another in a humane way?

Many years after our talmudic discussion it is a question that Maimonides tries to address in his great law code, the Mishneh Torah. Here he summarizes and interprets the rabbinic legal tradition and turns to the appropriate *method* of the rebuke:

> He who rebukes another whether for offences against the rebuker himself or for sins against God, should administer the rebuke in private, speak to the offender gently and tenderly and point out that

155

> he is only speaking for the wrongdoer's own good, to secure for him
> life in the world to come. If the latter accepts the rebuke, that is fine.
> If not, he should be rebuked a second and a third time. One is bound
> to continue the admonitions till the other strikes the rebuker and
> says to him, "I refuse to listen."
> (Mishneh Torah, *Hilkhot Deot* ["Laws of Moral Qualities"] 6:7)

Maimonides gives some very specific advice here that appears
to be his attempt to deal with R. Eleazar ben Azariah's complaint
that there is no one in this generation who knows how to admin-
ister reproof. Maimonides is trying to find the best way to insure
both that the reproof will be accepted and that the danger of
public embarrassment will be avoided.

What would happen if we were to take Maimonides' directives
quite seriously? We, after all, live in a time in which "expressing
one's anger" is seen to be a positive value. But Maimonides points
out that the confrontation itself is not the point. What we hope to
do through the means of *hokheah tokhiah* is not to vent our own
hostility, but to effect change in the other. By "speaking to the
offender harshly so as to put him to shame," we are more likely
to get the response that R. Tarfon worries about ("Remove the
beam from between *your* eyes!") than any movement toward reconciliation. The confrontation is, in the end, for the benefit of the
other, not for one's own self-satisfaction, not for venting one's
own anger. As expressed in the language of Maimonides' world,
"He is only speaking for the wrongdoer's own good, to secure
for him life in the world to come."

In addition to thinking about the nature of the confrontation,
we might also want to reflect upon the possibility that there are
times when it is appropriate to avoid confrontation by simply
ignoring the wrong done to us and moving on. The essence of
the biblical precept is to avoid hating one's fellow in one's heart.
Isn't it possible to get over those hurts or insults *without* a confrontation? At first this might seem like a coward's way out.
Don't we all need to clear the air when such tensions occur? But
in fact it may be that there are other options:

> R. Ilea stated in the name of R. Eleazar son of R. Shimon: As one is
> commanded to say that which will be heard, so one is commanded

not to say that which will not be heard. As it is written, "Do not rebuke a scoffer, for he will hate you; reprove a wise man and he will love you" (Prov. 9:8).

(Talmud, *Yevamot* 65b)

A rabbinic principle is articulated here which states that it is inappropriate to tell someone to do something if you know from the outset that the other will not obey you. Thus, there are times that *hokheah tokhiah* is an irrelevant practice: We all know that there are people who simply will not change, and if we are certain of that, an act of confrontation and rebuke with such people does not make sense. Of course, in real life the difficult part is *knowing* that the other cannot change. The question we always have to ask ourselves is if our "certainty" ("Why bother to talk about it? I'll never get him to change!") is merely an excuse to avoid the unpleasantness of confrontation.

Maimonides raises yet another situation in which confrontation might best be avoided:

> If one who has been wronged by another, and does not wish to rebuke or speak at all to the offender because the latter is a very common person or mentally incompetent, and if he has sincerely forgiven him, and neither bears him ill will nor rebukes him—he acts according to the standard of holy people [Hebrew: *hasidim*]. All that the Torah objects to is harboring ill will.
>
> (Mishneh Torah, *Hilkhot Deot* 6:9)

Maimonides suggests that there is a high level of ethical behavior, that practiced by very righteous people (*hasidim*), in which one does *not* confront the other. These are the cases in which it is clear that the confrontation will do no good because of the character or abilities of the one being rebuked. Thus, we do not confront mentally incompetent people because the encounter will produce no results and may even do more harm than good. Similarly, we can understand "common" (or "boorish"; Hebrew: *hediot*) as referring to people who would only react to one's rebuke with anger or scorn. The key, however, is that the injured person truly accept the reality of the situation, forgiving the other even without a confrontation. Perhaps Maimonides is led to call such

157

people "holy" because they have such an advanced level of ethical consciousness.

We have seen in this chapter an important ethical practice as it was explored by the traditional Jewish texts. Confrontation with others also holds the possibility of being an essential dimension in the relationships we forge with people today. And to my mind it makes a good deal of sense to think about the circumstances in which it might be appropriate and the ways it can be effected. Taking this practice seriously means looking at all the complex matters raised by these texts: issues of public embarrassment, of determining the truth behind supposed facts, of the manner of speech we use in rebuking others, of the times that confrontation simply doesn't make sense, of the times that we try to hide from the confrontations we really should have, of the way we give rebuke and the way we accept it too.

Finally, we might look at one other issue in a bit more detail: What is the nature of the "wrong" that the other person has done? Is this a crime against the community—do we confront our neighbors for dumping their garbage in an offensive manner? Is it against the laws of the state—do we reprove them for cheating on their income tax? Is it a ritual infraction—do we rebuke them for violating the Sabbath? There are clearly distinctions that can be drawn.

In the Mishneh Torah, after warning that "one should be careful not to publicly shame anyone, whether young or old," Maimonides then raises an issue relevant to the questions above by making a point we have not seen in the discussions up to now:

> . . . All this [concern about public embarrassment] applies to matters between human beings, but in the area of obligations between human beings and God, if an individual, after being privately rebuked, does not repent, he *should* be shamed in public; his sin should be openly declared; he is to be reviled, affronted and cursed until he returns to the proper path. This was the method followed by the prophets of Israel.
>
> (Mishneh Torah, *Hilkhot Deot* 6:8)

Suddenly, the terms have been changed. According to Maimonides—in a view that has not been specifically stated in the central rabbinic texts quoted before—we must make a distinction between transgressions in the human realm of *mitzvot bein adam l'havero* and those in the category of *mitzvot bein adam l'makom.* In the case of the latter (commandments between God and human beings), we *are* allowed to embarrass the other, if no other course has been effective. His justification is an interesting one, for here Maimonides looks back at the ancient biblical prophets and asserts that the reason they were able to publicly embarrass Israel with their enumeration of the people's sins and their calls to repentance was because these transgressions were strictly in the realm of the God-centered commandments.[13]

But for us perhaps, the story may be different. It is hard for us to imagine today publicly criticizing one's neighbor for violating the Sabbath. Indeed, one of our difficulties with the ultra-Orthodox, particularly in Israel, is that they rebuke secular people for their transgressions of the *mitzvot bein adam l'makom,* such as driving on Shabbat. In a way, our own inclinations may move in a different direction. As the children of modernity, we may be prepared to let each person choose his or her own way of relating to God; but in matters of the pain that might occur between people, we too can see the power of rebuke and confrontation.

The case of *hokheah tokhiah* was intended to illustrate the process by which the classical Jewish sources address an issue of ethical concern as it affects the life of people in their own communities—living with friends and relatives. We often think about religious traditions in the larger sense of their global missions, their attempts to deal with the big questions of society, but my intention here was to show that in the more mundane experiences of our lives, these writings also have something to say to us. As I have said earlier, other examples of a similar sort could easily be found, but what I wish to do now is leave the small arena of interpersonal concerns and look at the way that Jewish ethical texts might have something to say about an issue with far broader scope. Jewish texts and the question of justice will be our concern in the next chapter.

SEVEN

A WORLD OF JUSTICE

... R. Aha said in the name of R. Tanhum, son of R. Hiyya: Though a person has learned Torah and taught it, observed and performed it, yet if one was able to protest against wrongdoing and did not protest, or was able to maintain scholars and did not maintain them, he is considered "cursed" hence it is written "Cursed be he who will not uphold [Hebrew: *yakim*] the terms of this Torah" (Deut. 27:26). R. Jeremiah said in the name of R. Hiyya: If a person has not learned Torah and has neither performed, observed nor taught it to others, but though he did not have the means to maintain scholars, yet did maintain them and though he was not strong enough to protest yet protested, he is on this account considered blessed.

(Leviticus Rabbah 25:1)

The text above comes at the end of a complex discussion that deals with the nature of a person's obligations concerning Torah. This midrash wants to explore the question "How can people fulfill the requirement to *study* Torah when it is clear that most people do not have the time to devote themselves fully to study?" In the section of the midrash preceding that quoted above, the text focuses on a verse from Deuteronomy and remarks that given our failings in regard to Torah study, it is fortunate that the Bible proclaims "Cursed be he who will not uphold the terms of this Torah" (Deut. 27:26) instead of "Cursed by he who will not *learn* Torah"!

By understanding the Bible's Hebrew term for "uphold" (*yakim*) in its rabbinic sense of "support or maintain scholars," the midrash reasons that it is possible for us to fulfill our study obligations by donating money to support others who apply themselves to study in an intensive fashion.[1]

After exploring that idea in more detail, the midrashic section concludes with the lines quoted above. Obviously, the connection to the previous discussion is found in our text's concern with people who were "able to *maintain* scholars and did not maintain them." But a different element is also introduced here: "If one was able to protest against wrongdoing and did not protest," such a person—like the person who ignored the needs of scholars—is to be considered "cursed."

Two versions of a similar sentiment, both ultimately connected to R. Hiyya (either directly or through his son R. Tanhum), are given in our text. The first states that even if you have learned Torah and taught Torah and observed all the commandments properly, you still have two other obligations—to protest against wrongdoing and to maintain other scholars. By stating this, the text seems to move into a new direction, beyond the concerns of the opening section of the midrash. There the concern was "How can I fulfill my obligations to study? How can I avoid being 'cursed' when I have little time for study?" The answer was simple: "Financially support the work of the scholars."

Here there is a move outward—to support scholars not just because the supporter himself does not have the opportunity to study. The person who is being discussed in this section of the midrash has been identified as one who *has* "learned Torah and taught it, observed and performed it." Such a person is not in need of a surrogate scholar who will devote the time to study that the other doesn't have. Rather, the midrash is interested in the obligations we have in general to that which is *beyond* ourselves— the need to support scholarship as a value in and of itself, the need, without any selfish motivation, to let others have the chance to learn. And more than that, the text then leaves the realm of study completely: Out of nowhere it seems, without the usual linguistic association we tend to find in midrash (the wordplay, the pun), the text adds another dimension—the requirement to protest against wrongdoing.

This new element is surprising, but I think the logic of the text is clear. It is another expression, like the obligation to maintain scholars, of a person's need to take responsibility for others. To the rabbis the world of "religion"[2] is not limited to an individual's concerns with prayer or ritual celebrations or even one's life in the small circle of community made up of one's friends and acquaintances. Religion—or, to put it in the traditional terminology, mitzvah, doing what God requires of us—is also concerned with what we owe to others, to people we may not even know at all.

R. Jeremiah's formulation of the obligation is put in even stronger terms than R. Aha's: Even if one has ignored essential aspects of Jewish tradition—performing, observing, and teaching Torah to others—one is still considered "blessed" if "he did not have the means to maintain scholars, yet did maintain them and though he was not strong enough to protest yet protested." The essential distinguishing mark of this type of "blessed" individual, according to R. Jeremiah, is that quality of going beyond one's self, that sense of sacrifice for others. You did not have the means, but you still gave money to support others; you did not have the "strength," but you still protested against wrongdoing.

It is that latter idea that interests me here: protesting against wrong even though one is not, perhaps, such a courageous person. In the rabbinic view the concern for righting wrong, for looking beyond oneself, is a holy enterprise rooted in the nature of the relationship between God and humanity:

> R. Hama, the son of R. Hanina, taught: What is the meaning of "Follow none but the Lord your God . . . and hold fast to Him" (Deut. 13:5)? How can a human being follow and hold fast to God of whom it is said He is "a consuming fire" (Deut. 4:24)? "Following the Lord and holding fast to Him" must mean, therefore, imitating his qualities.
>
> He clothes the naked, as it is said "And the Lord God made garments of skin for Adam and his wife and clothed them" (Gen. 3:21). You too should clothe the naked.
>
> The Holy One, blessed be He, visits the sick [as we learn from the

story in Genesis 18 when God appears to Abraham soon after Abraham's circumcision]. . . . You too should visit the sick. . . .

(Talmud, *Sotah* 14a)

And the text continues with other biblical cases of God's acts of kindness, all of which are seen as moral examples for human behavior. Even for those who are uncomfortable with the personal, almost anthropomorphic aspect of God presented by this midrash, it is clear that the rabbinic notion of God as a kind of ultimate standard for human action, a repository of "the good" in ethical situations, is one that is not difficult to comprehend.

Rabbinic literature is filled with examples of discussion about the acts of kindness that God requires from human beings, but none is more central than the concern with *tzedakah,* the support of those who are in need. There are even rabbinic statements that seem to place the obligation to do *tzedakah* at a higher level than other ritual requirements.[3] It is significant also that in the Middle Ages when Maimonides attempted to codify previous Jewish law, he stated that

it is our duty to be more careful in the performance of the commandment of *tzedakah* than in that of any of the other positive commandments, for *tzedakah* is the mark of the righteous person who is of the seed of our father Abraham. . . . The throne of Israel cannot be established, nor true faith made to stand up except through *tzedakah* . . . nor will Israel be redeemed except through the practice of *tzedakah.*

(Mishneh Torah, *Hilkhot Matanot Aniyim* ["Gifts to the Poor"] 10:1)

In other words, of all the mitzvot which we might name—the Sabbath, the various holidays, the prayers, the wedding rituals, *whatever*—of all those, it is *tzedakah* that the greatest sage of the Middle Ages sees as the practice about which we should be most punctilious.

For Maimonides the fundamental and characteristic way of being Jewish (and that practice which according to the text above will lead to the messianic redemption) is concern for acts of charity. Thus, looking at the vast network of contemporary Jewish philanthropy—even where the contributors are not motivated by the ostensibly "religious" sense of divine commandment—we can see the expression of a very old and legitimate Jewish consciousness, albeit one that has been "secularized" in its philosophical underpinnings and in the style of its practical implementation.

The importance of giving *tzedakah* was so great that, as Maimonides stated, "He who refuses to give *tzedakah* or gives less than is proper for him, must be compelled by the court to comply, and must be flogged for disobedience until he gives as much as the court estimates that he should give"![4]

The rabbis saw the obligation to the poor as one that went beyond one's own personal comfort. The midrashic text Esther Rabbah, to choose just one example, tells the story of a man named Barbuhin who gave a bushel of coins to charity, while his family would eat only exceptionally simple food. When asked by the rabbis about this disparity, Barbuhin replied, "With myself I am stingy, but with the commandments of my Creator I cannot be" (Esther Rabbah 2:3). "Commandments" is a key word here, for giving charity according to the classical rabbinic view is a matter of mitzvah, command. God demands that we help those in need.

Of course, no one was so naive as to suppose that every person could be relied upon to fulfill this obligation, nor would everyone fulfill the commandment with the selflessness of a Barbuhin. In the Middle Ages, in fact, Maimonides delineated eight levels of *tzedakah* as a way of showing the variety of responses engendered by this commandment. The notion of "eight levels" is instructive in and of itself because it shows how the same basic requirement can be understood, amplified, and interpreted in many different ways. As Maimonides shows, one can, for example, give charity grudgingly or one can take pains to protect the feelings of the person in need; one can give one's gift in the form of secret, anonymous charity or one can give it publicly.[5] Maimonides tries to spell out the interweaving of kindness and self-interest in giving to others, and the issues are subtle and more complex than simply acknowledging that it's good to give *tzedakah* to the poor.

Today, sad to say, the issue of the poor and the specter of

poverty continue to haunt us, and the rabbinic admonitions are as alive as they were fifteen hundred years ago. In fact, I wonder if we might now be *more* indifferent to that suffering because we find it so, shall we say, inconvenient, or just plain messy. Our ancestors probably saw a good deal more poverty eye-to-eye than most of us do today, and though one might suppose that that exposure to misery would have made them callous, it seems to have had a different effect. Helping alleviate poverty became a kind of sacred mission.

At times one finds in rabbinic writing about poverty a kind of passion and pathos, as if the details of the reality cannot be pushed from one's mind:

> When R. Joshua ben Levi went to Rome, he saw marble pillars there which had been carefully covered with wrappings to keep them from cracking during the heat and freezing in the cold. At the same time he saw a poor man who had no more than a reed mat under him and a reed mat over him to protect him from the elements.
>
> (Pesikta d'Rav Kahana 9:1)

It's a picture that makes one think of the urban poor today, sleeping over subway grates in the richest cities in the world.

Such scenes can also push one to see poverty as a kind of irresolvable dilemma. We feel overwhelmed and overmatched by it. But one of the most noticeable aspects of rabbinic writing about *tzedakah* is the interest in *activism* that characterizes it. Look, for example, at the following text that tries to contrast Job and Abraham:

> When that great calamity came upon Job, he said to the Holy One, blessed be He: "Master of the universe, did I not feed the hungry and give drink to the thirsty . . . ? And did I not clothe the naked?"
>
> Nevertheless the Holy One, blessed be He, said to Job: "Job, you have not yet reached even half the measure of Abraham. You sit and stay in your house and the wayfarers come in to you. To him who is accustomed to eat wheat bread, you give wheat bread to eat; to him who is accustomed to eat meat, you give meat to eat; to him who is accustomed to drink wine, you give wine to drink. But Abraham did not act in this way. Instead he would go out and around everywhere,

165

and when he found wayfarers, he brought them into his house. To him who was unaccustomed to eat wheat bread, he gave wheat bread to eat; to him who was unaccustomed to eat meat, he gave meat to eat; to him who was unaccustomed to drink wine, he gave wine to drink. And more than that, he arose and built large mansions on the highways and left food and drink there, and every passerby ate and drank and blessed Heaven. That is why delight of spirit was given to him.

(Avot d'Rabbi Natan, Chapter 7)

Job, for rabbinic literature, is a perplexing biblical character. One interpretive concern is the attempt to place Job in some kind of "historical" context, and the comparison to Abraham in the text above may result from the prevalent rabbinic conception that Job lived in the time of Abraham. Of course, even more significant is the discussion of Job's tragic story—why was Job afflicted and what was the meaning of the biblical tale?

Our text above seems to suggest that Job's sufferings are linked to failings of character. When he complains about his affliction to God, pointing out all the good deeds he had done in his life, God replies, in essence, "You think you've been good? Look at Abraham!" Thus, the text becomes a kind of double-sided coin. On the one hand, it explains Job's "calamity" in the light of the inadequacy of his acts of *tzedakah*; and on the other hand it tries to elucidate true *tzedakah* by referring to the example of Abraham.

What characterized Abraham's approach to *tzedakah*? Two qualities in particular are mentioned by the text. First, where Job sat and waited for the poor, Abraham "would go out and around everywhere," and Abraham "arose and built large mansions on the highways and left food and drink there." In other words, Abraham sought out the poor and made efforts on their behalf. Second, Abraham went beyond restoring the poor to their former state—the way that Job would feed meat to those "accustomed to eat meat," etc. Abraham would *improve* their lot over what it was before: "To him who was unaccustomed to eat wheat bread, he gave wheat bread to eat," and so forth.

It is a remarkable portrait of a man of *tzedakah*. But there is something troubling here, for the text cannot help but leave the reader with an uneasy feeling too. To blame Job's sufferings on a lack of charity seems too harsh. It is not as if the text claims that Job *ignored* the suffering of the poor; if that were the case, we might understand his afflictions as punishment. But instead he is shown to be one who reacted to them with compassion. His only failing was in not being Abraham! Job in this text becomes a kind of literary foil that enables the rabbinic interpreters a chance to point up the accomplishments of Abraham. Yet it is clear that Abraham, as presented here, belongs to another category entirely. He has gone beyond the law, *lifnim mishurat ha-din,*[6] as it is called in the rabbinic texts, and no one can be held to the standards of saints. Indeed, if we look at a later Jewish text for illumination here, we can see that Maimonides, in delineating the requirements for giving *tzedakah,* seems to require precisely the level of piety exemplified by Job, as portrayed in the midrash above! It was Job who, according to the midrash, helped people return to what they were "accustomed," exactly what Mainmonides expects all of us to do:

> You are commanded to give the poor person according to what he lacks. If he has no clothing, he should be clothed. If he has no house furnishings, they should be bought for him. If he has no wife, he should be helped to marry. If it is a woman, she should be given in marriage. Even if it had been his custom to ride a horse with a manservant running in front of him, and he has now become poor and has lost his possessions, one must buy him a horse to ride and a manservant to run before him, as it is said "Sufficient for whatever he needs" (Deut. 15:8). You are obligated to fill his want; you are not, however, obligated to restore his wealth.
>
> (Mishneh Torah, *Hilkhot Matanot Aniyim* 7:3)[7]

But despite the extraordinary—extralegal, one can say—nature of Abraham's example, it seems nonetheless to be a model of behavior that has something powerful to say to us today. To begin with, that quality of activism, of going to seek out those who are in need, is something that seems particularly appropriate to a time in which our connection to the downtrodden of society tends to be so passive: We receive solicitations for *tzedakah* through computerized mailing lists, and the realities of middle-class American life rarely present the poor on our doorstep (and when they do, we find it a terrifying aberration). For us, taking on that same activist challenge—Abraham's commitment to "to go out and around everywhere"—would be a statement of concern that we might do well to emulate.

And it also seems right to consider the implications of Abraham's standard of action: "To him who was unaccustomed to eat wheat bread, he gave wheat bread to eat; to him who was unaccustomed to eat meat, he gave meat to eat; to him who was unaccustomed to drink wine, he gave wine to drink." Job fed the poor at the level to which they were accustomed. But what do we do in the case of the poor who have fallen not from a comfortable state into poverty, but who have *never* gone without hunger, who have never had what they need? As Maimonides reminds us, we are not talking about making the poor wealthy; we are simply trying to do *tzedakah* in the literal sense of the word, that which is *just*—"You are obligated to fill his want." And that means a level of commitment—personal and national—which says that none of us should feel satisfied if there are any around us who are not satisfied.

Our level of responsibility for the poor, rabbinic literature asserts, goes beyond the obvious. We are responsible even if their fate is determined indirectly:

> There once was a poor woman who dwelt in the neighborhood of a landowner. Her two sons went out to gather gleanings, but the landowner did not let them take any. Their mother kept saying: "When will my sons come back from the field; perhaps I shall find that they have brought something to eat." And they kept saying: "When shall we go back to our mother; perhaps we shall discover that she has found something to eat."
>
> She found that they had nothing and they found that she had nothing to eat. So they laid their heads on their mother's lap and the three of them died in one day.
>
> Said the Holy One, blessed be He: "Their very existence you take away from them. By your life! I shall make you, too, pay for it with your very existence."
>
> And so indeed it says, *Rob not the weak, because he is weak, neither*

crush the poor in the gate; for the Lord will plead their cause, and despoil of life those that despoil them (Prov. 22:22f.).

(Avot d'Rabbi Natan, Chapter 38)[8]

This is a story of pathos, a miniature tragedy evoked in a few simple lines. With its depiction of the quiet death of the mother and her two sons, with the dashed hopes of their search— " 'When will my sons come back from the field; perhaps I shall find that they have brought something to eat' "—it is hard not to be moved.

The situation is based on the biblical (and later rabbinic elucidation)[9] of the stricture in Leviticus 19:9–10 that "when you reap the harvest of your land, you shall not reap all the way to the edges of your field or gather the gleanings of your harvest . . . you shall leave them for the poor and the stranger: I am the Lord your God." The landowner in the midrashic story forbade that which was expressly required by the Torah.

One of the striking things about this text is how little background and detail we are given here. We don't hear the dialogue between the landowner and the two sons; we don't know if he was nasty or merely indifferent; we don't know why he said no and we don't know if "they would have died anyway" from their weakened state. But on the main point the text is very clear, very uncompromising: If you could have helped and you didn't, if you didn't do your obligation to help the poor, you are responsible.

And the moral force of the text is enhanced by the ambiguity of referent in God's words of rebuke. To whom are these words addressed (" 'Their very existence you take away from them. By your life! I shall make you, too, pay for it with your very existence' ")? To the landlord, or to us? The generalized quality of the quotation from Proverbs seems to suggest that the whole midrash is being directed as much at the reader as at the landowner. And the sudden shift into the present tense (" 'Their very existence you *take* away from them' ") reinforces the contemporaneity of the text, that quality of direct rebuke to the listener. This is not a story about something that once occurred a long time ago, the text seems to say, it is something that is happening right now.

For us today, in other words, to look at the situation of the poor and say "What can I do?" or "I'm not to blame," or "What happens to them is outside of my control or responsibility" is an attitude that a text such as this one rejects in the strongest possible way.

Of course, the classical sources also recognize how complicated such matters are in real life; and the pages of rabbinic literature are filled with discussion about the complexities inherent in the practice of *tzedakah*. What, for example, do we do about a person who pretends to be in need of *tzedakah* when he really is not (what in our terminology might be called a "welfare cheat"). Certainly, we don't want to be so gullible as to be taken advantage of, and the rabbinic texts are well aware of such a possibility:

> R. Hanina had a poor man to whom he regularly sent four zuz every Sabbath Eve. One day he sent that sum through his wife, who came back and told him that the man was in no need of it.
> R. Hanina asked, "What did you see?"
> She answered: "I heard the 'poor man' being asked: 'On what will you dine tonight, the silver-colored cloths or the gold-colored cloths?' "
> It is because of such cases, said R. Hanina, that R. Eleazar taught: Come let us be grateful to the deceivers, for were it not for them we would have been sinning every day, for it says in the Torah "And he [your needy kinsman] will cry out to the Lord against you and you will incur guilt." (Deut. 15:9).
>
> (Talmud, *Ketubot* 67b–68a)

It is R. Hanina's wife who figures out that the poor man has been tricking her husband all this time, but as is typical with these tales, some of the most interesting details are not given: How long had this been going on? And what motivated R. Hanina to send his wife on this particular day? Is it possible that she had suspicions about a fraud and she asked him to let her check it out for herself? Most intriguing of all is the question of R. Hanina's attitude toward his wife's discovery. Doesn't he seem remarkably calm about her news? Perhaps, in fact, he suspected all along that he was being had; perhaps he preferred to play along with the "poor man" rather than confront him; or perhaps he worried about the possibility that his suspicions might be unfounded. What would happen if he accused the poor man and then found out that in fact the man *was* in need? Would they ever be able to look at one another again? To R. Hanina it might not have been worth the risk.

Of course, I have sympathy for R. Hanina's wife too. I remember dropping some money once into the outstretched arms of a legless beggar on the street, only to discover, when I looked back, that the man was packing up his things and strolling away! I remember how annoyed I was, how I felt like such a fool. And we all know stories of phony "accident" victims taking advantage of those who turn to give them some help. R. Hanina's wife may have felt similarly taken advantage of; and she just wasn't going to take it anymore. Or maybe she was tired of watching her softhearted husband being duped. Or perhaps it was all an accident: She too thought she was giving money to a deserving poor man; imagine her surprise when she discovered what fools both she and her husband had been.

Giving *tzedakah* is certainly as complicated as receiving it. It is equally filled with questions about one's own attitudes or one's self-esteem or pride. And—as in the case above—no one wants to be deceived; you don't want to feel as if your own better nature has caused you to be taken in.

At the end of the text R. Hanina quotes R. Eleazar, making the following point: Since it is clear from the Torah that all of us are required to help the needy and since it is also true that none of us is sufficiently attentive to the needy all around us, that indeed "every day" we ignore those who are in need, one could argue that we are constantly sinning (as the biblical verse puts it, "you will incur guilt"). Thus, R. Eleazar notes that we should be grateful for the "deceivers," people like the "poor man" in our story, whose trickery justifies the fact that we do not respond to every request for *tzedakah*: Knowing that there are those who falsely ask for charity, we can honestly ignore some of the appeals that we get on the grounds that they may be phony.

Of course, this idea suggests that any time we do ignore a

request for *tzedakah,* it should come out of a careful, good-faith evaluation of each appeal. But to me it often seems that the decision to ignore a request, let's say from a beggar on the street, has less to do with a sincere consideration of the person's true need than it does with our own laziness or discomfort. Usually, we just don't want to bother. R. Eleazar's directive demands that we do not say no out of mere inconvenience.

But there is another problem recognized by the text. In choosing to reject some appeals, it is likely that people truly in need will also be overlooked. Our evaluation of the request may simply be mistaken. This text at any rate is prepared to accept such a possibility. We do not all "incur guilt" each day as we walk down the street. Our ignoring of some of the needy comes out of an honest mistake, since we are allowed to protect ourselves from those who might be out to cheat us.

And yet that too takes a toll. Are we really prepared to evaluate each case so carefully as it comes before us? Perhaps that is why R. Hanina seems so calm in our story here. He is prepared to accept a certain level of "*tzedakah* fraud" because that will ensure that the honest appeals will not be rejected. When the truth about the deception is discovered, he accepts it, but in the meanwhile he is prepared *not* to look too carefully at those who ask for help.

The complexity of the matter is illuminated further by a very similar story told a few pages later in the same talmudic tractate:

> Mar Ukva had a poor man in his neighborhood to whom he regularly sent four hundred zuz on the Eve of every Yom Kippur. One time he sent them through his son, who came back and said to him, "He does not need your help."
>
> "What have you seen?" his father asked.
>
> "I saw that they were spraying old wine before him." [Probably as a perfume for the room.]
>
> "Is he so delicate?" the father said, and doubling the amount, he sent it back to him.
>
> (Talmud, *Ketubot* 67b)

Is Mar Ukva simply a gullible fool? The structure of this story resembles the story of R. Hanina, but in the first text the rabbi was prepared to accept as truth what his wife reported. Here Mar Ukva discounts what his son reports. Of course, it's possible that Mar Ukva doesn't credit his son's judgment, his son's ability to distinguish between fraud and true need, while R. Hanina respected his wife's evaluation of the situation. But I think the issue is more subtle than that.

Mar Ukva reads the incident of the poor man's wine not as deception but as a different kind of need. "Is he so delicate," Mar Ukva asks, that he needs his room to be filled with perfumed fragrance? Thus, at one level the text is arguing that there is more than one way to read the facts of the case, indeed any case, concerning *tzedakah*. We can imagine that if Mar Ukva had heard the report R. Hanina's wife had given to her husband, he might have taken a different reading of those facts too. R. Hanina, unlike Mar Ukva, was not prepared to offer an alternative possibility. Of course, such an understanding of the tale may still present Mar Ukva as something of a dupe. But perhaps the story suggests something else as well.

Mar Ukva, who was a man of considerable means, seems to be telling his son that we should be careful about judging the "needs" of the poor. Perhaps the poor man could have got along without the wine, but Mar Ukva may be saying, why should we ask the poor man to live at a standard of living which is "merely adequate"; if we appreciate the perfume of "old wine," if luxury of that sort is something that we want, why is it illegitimate for the poor to want that too?[10]

And finally there is another possibility too: In this reading we can see Mar Ukva as no fool. He understood that the poor man was deceiving him, but as one who practiced the mitzvah of *tzedakah,* Mar Ukva was prepared to accept that risk. He was prepared to give his charity without careful investigating because unlike R. Hanina, he was not willing to reject the needy accidentally in an attempt to weed out the cheaters. It just wasn't worth it to him. He felt that giving the benefit of the doubt to everyone was better than hurting by mistake those who might truly be in need. Perhaps Mar Ukva believed that punishing the deceivers was not his business but should be left in the hands of heaven, a

position expressed by the following Talmudic dictum found a
page or so later in the tractate:

> If a man pretends to have a blind eye, a swollen belly or a shrunken
> leg [possible reading: "a hump"], he will not pass out from this
> world before actually coming into such a condition. If a man accepts
> charity and is not in need of it, he will not pass out of the world
> before he comes to such a condition.
>
> (Talmud, *Ketubot* 68a)

If, in other words, you pretend to be disabled in order to gain
tzedakah, you will be punished with that very disability as a kind
of divine retribution.

But divine punishment or not, Mar Ukva, it appears, was more
concerned about the dangerous implications of deciding *not* to
give. He was worried less about his own pride and his own self-
image than about the poor that he might overlook in his attempt
to be careful. Perhaps Mar Ukva is too generous or too meticu-
lous in this matter for our taste. After all, it was Mar Ukva who
willed on his death bed that half of his wealth should be given to
the needy.[11] But even so, it is instructive to see what Maimonides
did, many years after the discussions in the Talmud, when he
tried to set a normative practice for Jewish life in regard to matters
of charity. In particular, consider how he deals with the question
of what to do about the problem of *tzedakah* cheaters:

> If a poor man unknown to anyone comes forth and says, "I am
> hungry; give me something to eat," he should not be examined as to
> whether he might be deceiving—he should be fed immediately. If,
> however, he is naked and says "Clothe me," he should be examined
> as to possible fraud. If he is known, he should be clothed immedi-
> ately according to his dignity, without any further inquiry.
>
> (Mishneh Torah, *Hilkhot Matanot Aniyim* 7:6)

Maimonides' decision alludes to a debate in the Talmud[12] over
the question of who should be examined as to possible *tzedakah*
fraud—the person who asks for food or the person who asks for
clothes. In the Mishneh Torah Maimonides takes the view attrib-

uted in the Talmud to R. Judah, who says, among other things, that the person without food is in actual danger of dying while the other is merely suffering from humiliation (the assumption being that the "naked" person is not in danger of actually dying from exposure); thus, we should immediately feed the hungry beggar, but examine the one asking for clothes as to his truthfulness.

This is the case with an anonymous supplicant. But one who is known to you deserves to be clothed "according to his dignity" without any questioning. It is unclear from the text if Maimonides understands the reasoning to be that the person known to you would, of course, not be able to dissemble—that is, the truth of his situation would be familiar to everyone—or because being without clothes in front of someone you know is too great a humiliation in and of itself to require that the person be put through the further indignity of an examination concerning his honesty. Even if you are being deceived, one might argue, the request of a "naked" acquaintance must be answered. Or, to look at the case from another perspective: No one would humiliate his personal dignity by feigning nakedness in front of someone he knows.

The key point in the text above, to my mind, is that Maimonides tries to walk a line between the remarkable openness of Mar Ukva and the genuine human concern about being exploited, such as we see in the story of R. Hanina's wife. And perhaps that kind of middle path may be the one most appropriate for our own concerns about this issue today. None of us wants to be taken advantage of, but we also want to balance that worry with the danger of ignoring those who might truly be in need, whose requests we might unwittingly reject. Maimonides suggests the following: When the person seeking charity is unknown to you, the decision you take should be influenced by what they are requesting. The beggar asking for food is in too precarious a state for us to "examine" him; but the person asking for something beyond that basic necessity (like the person who approaches you asking for twenty dollars to get his car fixed) can be looked at more closely. The beggars on the streets of our cities, the homeless, the hungry—those whose very lives may be in danger—deserve a level of compassion, in other words, that puts our skeptical standards of judgment on the back burner for a while.

Indeed, the standard of Mar Ukva may also be worth remembering: perhaps it would be good for *us* to put our critical faculties on hold sometimes. Perhaps the very fact that someone will stoop to begging is a sign that he should be helped. After all, who are we to judge what another may really "need"? In that sense I like to keep in mind Mar Ukva's response to his son. And though we may not believe, as the Talmud apparently did, in direct divine retribution for those who deceive, do we really want to be the judges? In stating that heaven will punish the deceivers, the Talmud in its own way may be suggesting that it is best that we put such matters aside; perhaps a little fakery that gets rewarded is better for *our* souls than the quality of cynicism that infects us, leading us to see every needy person as one who is out to cheat us.

Up to this point in the chapter I have focused on the issue of *tzedakah* and poverty because the matter seems so pressing in our time. We see the poor all around us and we wish to find some kind of response within the Jewish tradition to this terrible reality. But I think it is important also to consider the significance of the very search for a connection between a contemporary social problem such as poverty and traditional religious texts such as those explored earlier in this chapter. In other words, this enterprise itself—seeking a relationship between the social and political issues of today and the literature of the past—raises a set of questions that we ought to explore in more detail. What does a traditional literature have to say to a contemporary society? How do we read the texts that explore such issues? And what, if anything, are the limits of the relationship between the traditional sources and the issues of today?

We can begin with a midrashic statement that expresses the orientation behind any such investigation of the classical sources:

> **Why was the Torah given in the wilderness? It was done to teach you that if a person does not search himself as a wilderness, he would**

not merit the words of the Torah. Just as the wilderness has no limit,
so the words of the Torah have no limit. As it is said: "It is longer
than the earth in measure and wider than the sea" (Job 11:9).
                                          (Pesikta d'Rav Kahana 12:20)

The text above is an attempt to understand the significance of
the geographic setting of the Sinai revelation. Why does God
choose to give the Torah in the wilderness, in such a remote and
lonely place? The midrash here gives two answers. The first, a
rather cryptic and illusive passage, seems to be saying that in the
same way that a wilderness requires exploration and investigation,
so the human being must "search himself" in order to merit receiving the Torah. Self-reflection—in some fashion not entirely
clear in the comparison to the wilderness—is at the heart of a
person's relationship to Torah.

It is the second comparison in the text, however, which is
relevant to our concern here: "Just as the wilderness has no limit,
so the words of the Torah have no limit." That is, the Torah is
relevant to any situation that we might encounter. The Torah,
this position would assert, is as relevant to a social issue such as
poverty in the twentieth century, as it is to matters of prayer or
ritual. And this text is not alone in asserting such a view.
Throughout the classical literature there is a strong inclination to
see the ever-present, ongoing reality of Torah's message.

But such a view is not without its difficulties and dangers. How
far are we to take the "relevance" of Torah and how specifically
are we to enact its suggestions or policies? The interpretation of
the Torah in the light of contemporary social issues (or perhaps
one should say, the interpretation of contemporary social issues
in the light of the Torah) is a position that was also not without
controversy throughout Jewish history. The question was raised
in particular during the Middle Ages in regard to the proper function of the sermons preached by rabbis and itinerant preachers.
Was it the job of the preacher to relate the Torah to contemporary
issues, or should he focus on ethical problems without connecting
that message to the Torah itself? Or was his role primarily to
bring inventive interpretations of Torah before the congregation
without being concerned about ethical matters at all? These are

some of the questions that the intellectual leaders of the time raised.

Within Judaism there is a long sermonic tradition which, aside from those preserved in the Talmud and midrashic works (and the published sermons of some twentieth-century rabbis), has essentially remained unexplored and unknown, even among scholars. Indeed, many of these sermons (as well as works *about* the role of the sermon) remained in unpublished manuscripts or in books long out of print. Fortunately, a recent anthology in English makes a fine selection of this material available, providing at the same time excellent commentaries on the material and an important introductory essay on the role of this literature in Judaism.[13] One of the issues that Marc Saperstein, the scholar who edited and translated the collection, discusses is the debate over the issue of contemporary relevance and the worries and frustrations felt by the preachers of the time:

> The task of the preacher was fraught with paradox. If he admonished the people for their behavior and they ignored his warning, he would actually increase their sinfulness by making them conscious transgressors instead of ignorant ones. The effect of his striving would be the opposite of what he had intended. . . .
>
> Finally, if people did not mend their ways, what was the preacher to do next? Those who came to a sermon wanted to hear something original, not just the same old litany of complaints. Preachers were expected to base their rebukes on novel interpretations of biblical verses or rabbinic statements. But the constant demand for ingenuity and originality risked alienating people who realized that the simple meaning of a passage had nothing to do with the preacher's point. The choice between being implausible and boring was not a happy one.[14]

For the preachers of the past and for us today as well, at the heart of any explication of Torah aimed at ethical change is the question of effectiveness. Does listening (or reading) really bring about personal change? As Saperstein puts it,

> For the true preacher it was not enough to establish a reputation for preaching ability. He wanted to change people in a lasting way. The

most important thing, as one put it, was not the impression made during the sermon but what was left afterward. Not a few confessed their doubts about the efficacy of their labors.[15]

Can people be changed by Torah? We can see sermons that in their time attempted to do just that. There is, to choose one outstanding example, a sermon of Rabbi Saul ha-Levi Morteira, a seventeenth-century preacher in Amsterdam, who took a verse from the first chapter of Exodus (1:7—"The Israelites were fertile and prolific; they multiplied and increased very greatly, so that the land was filled with them") as a text upon which to build an ingenious condemnation of the ostentatious high-living Dutch Jews who were his congregants. Like the ancient Israelites who became Pharaoh's slaves, Morteira argues, the Jews of the present day would be punished for their materialistic, selfish ways. In the words of the sermon:

> Then the Torah says, *The Israelites were fertile,* after the death of their parents. Then, having reproduced abundantly, they were no longer content to live in their original space. They refused to endure crowded conditions and to remain content with little, so as to avoid the hostile glares of their enemies. Rather, *wa-yishresu,* meaning that they spread out [that is, they moved into larger-than-appropriate living quarters, as he explains]. . . .
>
> This is inappropriate for those who live in exile. They should be prepared to endure hardship; happy are those who have what they need and no more. But such a contented disposition is not what we see today. A man who is alone with his wife, or even a single man, lives in a large house with unnecessarily spacious rooms. Such people waste their money, which they may well need some day, by giving it to the Gentiles and receiving nothing of value in return. This is not befitting a people living outside its land, in the land of its enemies. . . .

Note how easily Morteira slips back and forth between biblical history and contemporary times. He rebukes the Israelites and explains the reasons for their enslavement and at the same time admonishes his seventeenth-century listeners:

179

> For when they accumulated wealth, it was not in order to preserve it
> for their children and to serve God in accordance with their means,
> but in order to enlarge their homes. One who at first lived in a single
> room became wealthy, began to think that even five rooms would
> not suffice, and spent his money for this foolish purpose; that is why
> God diminished it. . . . They choose houses not according to the
> number of their children, but according to their social class. All this
> is repugnant to God in a period of exile, while His House lies in
> ruins.[16]

The boundaries of past and present almost dissolve. We are the
Israelites and they are us. This is not interpretation for interpretation's sake. Morteira sees contemporary Jews directly in the light
of the Torah's mythic history. As Saperstein puts it, "Here we see
a preacher marshalling the ancient texts in order to address what
he considers to be a pressing problem of his time." [17]

Of course, we must consider the implications of utilizing such
an approach to Torah today, in an age considerably more skeptical
about the "truth" of the biblical text. But even in the past—in
what we sometimes, perhaps not with complete accuracy, picture
as a more pious age—this kind of exegesis could be seen as problematic. Rabbi Judah Low (often known by the Hebrew acronym
Maharal, which stands for "Our teacher, the Rabbi Low") of
Prague, one of the most important Jewish scholars of the sixteenth
century, was disturbed by the exegetical inventiveness of the
preachers he saw around him:

> They interpret biblical verses and rabbinic statements to mean some-
> thing never intended, something which never occurred to those who
> said them. They claim to be explaining the meaning of these state-
> ments, but the result is harmful. If they would just leave the words
> of the sages as they are, these statements, understood simply, would
> display great wisdom. . . . It would be better for them to preach in
> public about matters that have nothing to do with Torah than to
> preach the way they do! [18]

Maharal then raises the question of the personal ego involved
in such displays of wit and goes on to consider the danger of
relying on these kinds of interpretive fireworks:

This way of treating the words of the perfect Torah must be vigor-
ously protested, for a great religious duty is turned into fraud when
such interpretations are incorporated into public sermons. These
preachers want only to show off to people who do not know any
better, by pretending to discover novelties in the Torah. They may
reply, "If we do not do this, we say nothing new, only what others
already know." But how can they think that those whom they come
to rebuke will accept their message? They know that the point has
no basis in the rabbinic statement the preachers have cited, the only
reason they tie their message to a novel interpretation of a talmudic
statement being their assumption that otherwise they will have done
nothing original—for everyone knows the simple meaning of the
statement—and that therefore their sermon will be worthless, and
they might as well remain silent.[19]

Of course, the preachers themselves *do* have a problem: how
do you bring an ethical message to people who know it all already? How do you bring about change within an ethically jaded
public? But the preachers' solution—to clothe their rebuke in inventive interpretations of the Torah—is no way out of this difficulty, according to Maharal. In his view the preachers are not
only using their interpretive creativity for the unworthy purpose
of showing off for the crowds, but they are also bringing dishonor
to the Torah itself. For the congregants know well that the "novelties" taught by the preachers are far from the simple meaning of
the biblical and rabbinic texts the preachers purport to be interpreting:

Will anyone accept these totally groundless lies? People will say
rather that the sermons contain not wisdom but merely one individual's fabrication. It would be better if they would speak their piece
without any talmudic statement at all, for people would then say,
"these are the words of a preacher of ethical rebuke." Although this
is not entirely proper, for the words of the sages are certainly worthy
of being taught and used to rebuke the congregation, it would still
be better to eliminate them entirely. But now that they take someone
else's thoughts and peg them onto rabbinic statements that everyone
knows have nothing at all to do with the subject being discussed and
provide no true basis for their point, how can they think their sermons are beneficial?[20]

According to Maharal, it is better to eliminate the fanciful interpretation than to misuse the words of the sages in a foolish quest for novelty. The kind of preaching that Maharal rejects is doubly problematic: On the one hand, it leads people to scoff at Torah, since it is clear that the outlandish interpretation proposed by the preacher could not possibly be correct, and on the other hand it fails to accomplish its supposed purpose anyway, to bring people toward ethical change.

It seems from Maharal's remarks that preachers are driven to seek inventive interpretation because the simple message will not be heeded. Thus, the preachers believe, better an inventive sermon that doesn't "work" (that is, it doesn't produce ethical change) than a straightforward one that is equally ineffective. At least in the former case the preacher's own reputation will be enhanced! The real problem of the times, Maharal declares later in his sermon, is that no one will listen to *any* kind of ethical rebuke:

> Furthermore, we find today that if someone comes from afar to rebuke others for behavior scandalous in any Jew . . . the members of the community say, "Are not all of us holy, are not God and His Torah in our midst? We will not heed or accept ethical instruction from another."[21]

Certainly, our situation today differs from the Jewish community of Maharal's time, but the task of the ethical "preacher" is still similarly problematic. We too are stuck in the situation in which it is easier to talk about "what is right" than to do it. Maharal tries to offer a solution to the preachers' dilemma: In constructing their sermons they should try to find ways to mix both aggadic and halakhic materials in their remarks:

> It was [in the past] inconceivable not to include such halakhic material within the aggadah, and it was wise to preach on a halakhic subject in the context of aggadah. For it is through aggadah that people become enamored of Torah. When, in the middle of an aggadic sermon, the preacher admonishes the congregation with words of Torah, the message penetrates to the listeners' hearts. They accept it, and it remains with them, affecting their future behavior.[22]

It is possible to say, of course, that in Maharal's community the power of halakhic demand was considerably stronger than it is among most Jews today. But even so, the mixture of inventive aggadah and the halakhic demand is worth keeping in mind. We too can easily find ourselves as the listeners whose reaction to a particularly creative bit of aggadic interpretation would be to say —and perhaps quite rightly—"this is a lot of foolishness." There is something refreshing in the hard and clear demand of an utterance from a Maimonides, especially in the context of a certain limited amount of aggadic fancy.

But what about the idea of the unlimited message of Torah? What about that line from the earlier midrash: "Just as the wilderness has no limit, so the words of the Torah have no limit"? Are we saying that Torah is not applicable to all times and to all situations? In responding to this question, I think we have to keep our eye less on every specific detail and more on the general outline of the *principles* of Torah. In other words, there is an ethical thrust within the history of Judaism that can speak directly to contemporary life. And such a notion implies that applying with exactitude biblical or rabbinic statements to a present-day problem is not going to work all the time. It is this, I imagine, that was troubling Maharal when he said of the preachers, "They take someone else's thoughts and peg them onto rabbinic statements that everyone knows have nothing at all to do with the subject being discussed and provide no true basis for their point." Knowing the answer in advance, in other words, one finds a clever way of "discovering" it within the text you choose to quote.

Dealing with the materials of another age necessitates interpretation, and certainly the history of Jewish interpretation—in particular legal interpretation—has been an attempt to translate the articulated principles of an agrarian or village society to the evolving social and economic realities of changing times. The society of ancient Israel, of Hellenistic Palestine, of fifth-century Babylonia, and so forth dealt with realities far different from those of twentieth-century Western culture. The job of *translation* is the key point. What does it mean to see talmudic utterances about poverty in the light of today's society, for example? What I have tried to show earlier in the chapter is that many of those principles are still effective reminders of what it means to live a life of justice.

In that sense it is clear that the traditional literature of Judaism is not dated. But its historical context must also not be ignored. The underlying principle—that, for example, we seek justice and compassion for the poor—is one that still operates. And the active working out of that principle in a real-life situation—such as in *tzedakah*—is also still relevant. But what also needs to be added is the context and reality of today, the cultural and political structures, for example, of a modern Western society and how they interact with the demands of the tradition. And because it is clear that our world and the world of the rabbinic past differ in significant and undeniable ways, not every policy decision about how to deal with social or political or ethical problems of today can be based in the *specifics* of tradition. We may find guidance there, we may find wisdom, we may find principles and useful analogies— but we also need to recognize that not every point of detail will be relevant to the realities and concerns of the present.

In addition, there is the danger articulated by Maharal above, of taking one's own political ideas and finding a way to "peg them onto rabbinic statements that everyone knows have nothing at all to do with the subject being discussed." Thus, it has been popular for a long time, at least in America, to identify the "position" of the classic Jewish sources as being coterminous with American liberal political policy. What Judaism believed about an issue such as racial justice or peace, in other words, was another version of New Deal–style liberalism.

But as we have said before, the trick is to find the right balance of respect for the historical context of the past on the one hand and legitimate interpretation for the times we live in today on the other. Perhaps the criterion should be something like this: At what point does our historical knowledge and self-consciousness so drown the text that they destroy its living power and turn it into *artifact*? And looking at the other side, at what point do our inventive interpretations stretch credibility so greatly that the text loses any power to speak with authority, creating, as Maharal puts

184

it, "no true basis for their point"? Somewhere between these two poles lies the effective reading, the interpretation that has the ability to move us or shake up our lives.

What the traditional texts surely can give us is a combination of the poetic utterance of aggadah, such as in the tale of Rabbi Hanina's wife or the story of Mar Ukva's generosity, with the clean line of halakhic demand—God demands justice and we must seek the means to realize it. We must recognize as well that like all the Jews of the past, we too live under the influence of contemporary values. Some of this contemporary worldview is debilitating and corrosive, to be sure, but other values of the general culture are a positive and compelling resource that we want to hold on to. None of us would want to give up the advantages and significance of democratically electing our government, of legal commitments to human rights, and of other such freedoms that we feel are part of the world we have inherited. Not all of these specific matters are to be found in the Jewish traditional texts and like the midrash about Moses' inability to understand Akiva's teachings, our ancestors would find some of the things we take for granted quite puzzling.

And yet in our enthusiasm for historical self-awareness and for the advantages of Western culture, we should not forget the other side of the coin: There are times when the Jewish tradition offers us wisdom of a very direct sort, even about matters rarely discussed in present-day Western culture. We can see it in the care that the tradition gives to an issue such as the "deceiver" seeking *tzedakah,* especially when we compare that attitude to remarks of elected officials of our times who berate citizens for giving handouts to the poor!

Such concern can be seen in more dramatic issues as well. To my mind no better example of this aspect of looking at traditional sources can be seen than that exemplified by the Kahan Commission report in Israel, which tried to assess the extent of Israeli responsibility in the massacre of Palestinian refugees by Christian Falangists in the Sabra and Shatila refugee camps in West Beirut during September 1982.

The commission's report was an interesting model of the way

that a terrible contemporary event could be seen both in the light of Western law and morality and in the light of Jewish sources. Even though Israeli military forces were not involved in the actual massacre itself, the commission felt compelled to explore the issue of *indirect* responsibility and it looked at four perspectives on the case: the rules of international law, the generally accepted rules of behavior expected of a "civilized" society, the lessons of Jewish history, and the classical texts of the Jewish tradition. The commission found that even though the rules of international law and the ethical demands of civilized nations were in fact *not* clear in regard to the question of responsibility in the case at hand, the demands of both Jewish history[23] and the texts of the Jewish tradition *did* call for accepting indirect responsibility for what happened. Thus, in placing blame on a number of government and military figures, the commission asserted that Jewish tradition demanded a higher standard of ethical behavior in looking at this contemporary case.[24]

Beyond the conclusions, however, was the *method* of the commission. It assumed that Jews living in the modern world must understand that two demands could equally apply to the case at hand: both the traditions of the Jewish past and the traditions of Western law and morality. Living in that tension between both poles is the fate of anyone who wants to find a way to embrace modernity and tradition simultaneously.

It is not surprising that our final example comes from the contemporary reality of the State of Israel. Because of its history, its founding, indeed its very existence, it is in Israel that the balance between tradition and modernity is most apparent and most dynamic, both for good and for ill. In the next chapter we will try to reflect more on Israel and the way the traditional Jewish sources might relate to the reality of Israel in our times.

HOLY LAND

In the last chapter I tried to explore the relationship between classical texts and contemporary social and political issues. I wished to indicate ways that traditional Jewish sources might relate to an issue such as poverty and the need for charity, and I also wanted to discuss the legitimate reservations one might raise—indeed reservations that *have* been raised by figures such as the Maharal of Prague—about finding a connection between the texts of the past and the concerns of today. The chapter concluded with remarks about the Kahan Commission and its approach to dealing with a particular contemporary event and the way that the Jewish tradition could relate to such an occurrence.

It was not accidental that the chapter ended with a reference to events connected to the State of Israel, for there is no arena in which the relevance of tradition to the concerns of modernity is more obvious and more challenging than in the life of Israel today. No book that tries to address the concerns of a contemporary vision of Judaism can ignore the significance of Israel. It is the central fact of contemporary Jewish life.

One cannot turn off its reality; it lives with us in the newspapers and on television, in popular novels and in raging political debates. That very "presentness" of Israel is in itself something of a mystery. Why, the argument goes, should a nation the size of

New Jersey, with a total population about half that of New York City, be so much in the news? Who ever hears about Malawi (twice the population of Israel) in the news? How often does Portugal make the front page of the local newspaper? Why don't the journalists write about some place else for a change?

One is tempted to view the weight of Israel in the press either as, on the one hand, conspiratorial in some way or another (expressed by lines such as "Everyone is out to get the Jews" or "The media focus on Israel because of all those Jews in the media") or, on the other hand, as merely politically pragmatic—"After all, the Middle East is a major hot spot in the world" or "The Arab-Israeli conflict is connected to U.S.-Soviet competition around their 'client states.' "

Looking at the issue of Israel, that is, the land itself—Eretz Yisrael as it is called in Hebrew—from the perspective of Jewish tradition makes the issue somewhat more complex. Judaism has been bound up with the specific place of Eretz Yisrael ever since its biblical origins, and dreams of a "return" to the land have influenced Jewish messianic speculation for almost two thousand years.[1] As we shall see, one only need open the pages of the prayer book to see how real that dream has been in every liturgical context. True, there have been thinkers or even movements within traditional Jewish life that turned "Eretz Yisrael" into metaphor,[2] but for most Jews Israel, at least the idealized dream of the land, was a powerful force throughout the generations.

Jews today who live outside Eretz Yisrael seem to be caught between two almost contradictory inclinations in regard to these matters. First, there is the definition of Judaism that has most suited the needs of life in the world of modernity, at least in the West: Judaism is seen as a "religion"; like Catholicism, Protestantism, Islam, and Greek Orthodoxy, Judaism is a faith to which one subscribes. This point of view is captured by the three balanced elements in the title of Will Herberg's influential book of the early 1950s, *Protestant-Catholic-Jew*.[3]

Such a perspective has been advantageous in a number of different ways. It helped fit Judaism nicely into the niche of American society in the years following the Second World War; it allayed fears of "dual loyalty" and it allowed Jews also to feel part of the general American connection to religion. But it presented serious difficulties as well.

For what it did *not* do was explain significant details of Jewish consciousness, such as the Jewish opposition to intermarriage and its recognition of "nonreligious" Jews as still being Jewish. Thus, a person cannot be a "lapsed Jew," in the way that one can choose to leave the Church. Nor need you pledge your faith to stay within the fold—if you're *born* a Jew, you remain one. Judaism is a community of blood lines, rather than a community of "faith" in the Christian sense of the term. It resembles, therefore, being part of a family: You have to be born into it or, one might say, "marry" into it through the ritual called conversion. Such a notion of Judaism suggests a much broader definition than that of "religion."

And finally the focus on religion did very little to explain the matter with which we began: the Jewish connection to Eretz Yisrael. For why does a religion, at least in the modern understanding of the concept, need a *land*? Catholics remain Catholics without any deep connection to a specific geographical locality called Rome. Why should the Jews—*if Judaism is a religion*—need a place, even a state, of their own?

Of course, in ancient times these matters were considerably different. The split between religion and peoplehood or nationhood was almost inconceivable. To be an Israelite meant that you were part of the people of Israel who lived in the Land of Israel and worshiped using the practices delineated in the sacred scripture of Israel. Indeed, certain aspects of that ritual—such as agricultural and sacrificial law—was predicated on the fact that the people dwelled in its land. It was only after the destruction of the First Temple (587–586 B.C.E.) and the subsequent exile of a portion of the population to Babylonia that a new idea was born— religion in exile, a religion of the Diaspora, the dispersed. But the longing to return to the land was intimately tied to a sense that only there, only in the land itself, as a nation like other nations, yet more than other nations—a kingdom of priests, after all—could the people of Israel do the will of its God in its fullness. As Abraham Joshua Heschel has put it:

> Exile from the land was conceived as an interruption, as a prelude to return, never as an abandonment or detachment. Bonds of hope tied us to the land. To abandon these bonds was to deny our identity.[4]

Judaism survived well in the Diaspora, however. Its features were adapted to deal with those changed circumstances; rituals tied to the land itself were put on hold; other rituals were symbolized and allegorized.[5] Memory—often of a place never actually experienced, but memory nonetheless—substituted for place. But the Jews continued throughout to see themselves as a "people," not just a religion.

I have said earlier that Jews today seem to find themselves caught between two contradictory trends of self-understanding. The first, as we have seen, is the concept of Judaism as religion, the view of Judaism that seems most in harmony with the post-Enlightenment world and one that blends in comfortably with a life in the Diaspora, a landless condition. The second is a more recent development, but one which fits more easily with that other aspect of Judaism—peoplehood and land—that we've been looking at above: Namely, Judaism can be seen in the context of a general awareness today of what we usually call "ethnicity." In contemporary America much of this has resulted from the focus on ethnic self-consciousness within the black community that emerged in America on the heels of the 1960s civil rights movement and its assertion of "black pride." Instead of the ideal of the "melting pot," people began to see the importance of preserving and applauding the unique strengths and particularities of various ethnic groups.

Thus, there has been a tendency for Jews also to focus upon their own ethnic self-identification. Some of this inclination has emanated from the general temper of the times, particularly in America, but one cannot ignore two other key factors that have influenced Jewish self-understanding in the last forty years. The first is the importance of the Holocaust in Jewish consciousness, and in the context of our current discussion I am referring to the terrible and obvious fact that Jews were murdered during the Holocaust *not* because of Judaism, that is, because of their *religious* beliefs and practices, but simply because they were Jews. Thus, assimilated Jews, even Jewish converts to Christianity, were killed by the Nazis because of the *people* to which they belonged, not because of their religious ideas.

And of course the second factor that has also stimulated a sense of Jewish ethnic identification in recent history has been the creation of the State of Israel. For here once again we see the people-hood—in this case even the *nationhood*—rather than the religion of the Jews as the central identifying factor. Indeed, whenever I try to reflect on what I consider to be essentially an impossible task, namely, finding some connection between the destruction wrought by the Holocaust and the rise of the State of Israel, in a hazy and mysterious way one thing does speak to me: The Jews, who had no land or place or nation, destroyed because they were a *people,* found some kind of response—certainly not recompense, but at least a response—in the emergence of Israel as a nation, as a people's land.

Certainly, as I have said earlier, the importance of Israel throughout the history of Judaism is hard to overestimate, but before we turn to some rabbinic texts that deal with this issue, I should reiterate a point raised in the last chapter as well. Whenever we try to find the connection between the texts of the past and the issues of today, we should tread with considerable caution. In particular, this is true when we consider a topic that raises issues as politically charged as those surrounding contemporary Israel. No specific political *program* should emerge from such a discussion, but such an exploration can raise ideals and concerns, powerful principles and fundamental values, which must be the background behind any political action or discussion.

Rabbinic literature is filled with discourse about the connection of the Jewish people to Eretz Yisrael.[6] It is a connection of history and religious obligation, certainly, but it is important to recall how filled with *sentiment* that connection is as well. In particular, we see this emotional attachment in the rabbinic writing that reacts to the destruction of the Second Temple. There, for example, God is depicted as weeping over the catastrophe, even though it is God who, the rabbis asserted, was the source of that very destruction.[7] In one text, for example, God is represented as saying, quite astoundingly: "Woe is Me that I have destroyed My house, burnt My tabernacle and exiled My children among the pagans"! (Sifra on Leviticus 20:22).

But even in texts that do not have the destruction of the Temple as their focus, we see the great emotional attachment to Eretz Yisrael. Thus, in one midrash the following parallel stories are recounted:

> It once happened that R. Judah ben Betherah, R. Mattiah ben Heresh, R. Hananiah ben Ahi, R. Joshua, and R. Jonathan were going abroad. When they reached Platana and remembered the Land of Israel, they raised their eyes [heavenward] and wept, rent their garments, and recited the verse, *And ye shall possess it and dwell therein, and ye shall observe to do all the statutes and the ordinances* (Deut. 11:31–32). They said: [The duty of] dwelling in the Land of Israel is equivalent to all the other commandments of the Torah put together. And another time R. Eleazar ben Shammu'a and R. Yohanan the Sandalmaker were going to Nisibis to study Torah under R. Judah ben Betherah. When they got to Sidon, they remembered the Land of Israel, raised their eyes [heavenward] letting their tears flow, rent their garments, and recited this same verse, *And ye shall possess it and dwell therein, and ye shall observe to do all the statutes and ordinances.* They said: [The duty of] dwelling in the Land of Israel is equivalent to all the other commandments of the Torah put together. Thereupon they returned to the Land of Israel.
>
> (Sifre Deuteronomy 80)[8]

It is hard to know how we should understand the statement that the commandment of "dwelling in the Land of Israel is equivalent to all the other commandments of the Torah put together." It may be an example of rabbinic hyperbole, exaggerated statements that abound in the Talmud and midrashic literature, such as those that claim that if it were not for such-and-such commandment a person would or would not merit the world to come.

But there may be something else here as well. The rabbinic view of the particular quality of the Land of Israel, its holiness, if you will, is what encourages these rabbis to speak in such an inflated fashion. It is only in Eretz Yisrael, they seem to be saying, that a Jewish religious life can be lived to its fullest.

But why is that true? Why would that act of living in the land have such religious import? One's first reaction is to assume that the land itself has a quality of holiness, almost a magical dimension. But, interestingly enough, it is another point—and a far less mystical one—that seems to be emphasized:

> R. Simlai taught: Why did Moses our teacher yearn to enter the Land of Israel? Did he need to eat of its fruits or satisfy himself from its bounty? Rather thus spoke Moses, "Many mitzvot were commanded to Israel which can only be fulfilled in the Land of Israel. I wish to enter the land so that they may be fulfilled by me." The Holy One, blessed be He, said to him, "Is it only to receive the reward [for obeying the commandments] that you ask to enter the land? I will count it as if you performed them."
>
> (Talmud, *Sotah* 14a)

The talmudic text here speaks almost with disdain, rejecting the possibility that Moses' view of Eretz Yisrael might be associated with particular, almost sensuous, aspects of the land itself. Moses did not wish to eat the fruit of the land for the sake of its pleasures, rather he wanted the opportunity to fulfill those commandments that can only be performed in the Land of Israel, such as the laws of the sabbatical and jubilee years enumerated in Leviticus 25 or the rules of tithes, mentioned in Deuteronomy 14:22ff., and many others. Thus, connection to Eretz Yisrael in these sources is related to the system of commandments that is at the heart of the rabbinic conception of Judaism.

Simply put, living in the land is a chance to perform mitzvot, which, like other commandments such as Shabbat or *tzedakah,* is the essence of a Jew's connection to the divine. This is not to deny the true emotional quality that one finds in texts such as the one from Sifre quoted above, but rather to see sentiment in the light of a larger context. And even in the Sifre passage we see the idea of mitzvot as the defining focus that occupies those scholars—when they talk of the land, they conceptualize it in relation to their fundamental touchstone of values, the commandments. Perhaps it is not accidental too that the talmudic passage is attributed to Rav Simlai, a man, it seems from the sources, who was born in Babylonia and chose to settle in Eretz Yisrael.

The logical step that follows upon this notion of the land and the mitzvot is the view that living in Eretz Yisrael should be a *requirement* for Jews. If the Land of Israel is the place where one can do God's will in its most elaborate and detailed form, then surely it is the place where a Jew must live:

> Our rabbis taught: One should always live in the Land of Israel, even in a town most of whose inhabitants are idolaters, but let no one live outside the Land, even in a town most of whose inhabitants are Israelites; for whoever lives in the Land of Israel may be considered to have a God, but whoever lives outside the Land may be regarded as one who has no God. For it is said in Scripture, "To give you the Land of Canaan, to be your God" (Lev. 25:38). Has he, then, who does not live in the "Land," no God?
>
> No, what the text wants to tell you is that whoever lives outside the Land may be regarded as one who worships idols. Similarly, it was said in Scripture in the story of David, "For they have driven me out this day that I should not cleave to the inheritance of the Lord, saying: Go, serve other gods" (1 Samuel 26:19). Now, whoever said to David, "Serve other gods"? No, the text intended to tell you that whoever lives outside the Land may be regarded as one who worships idols. . . .
>
> (Talmud, *Ketubot* 110b)

Of course, what is most striking about this text is its audacious assertion that "whoever dwells outside the Land of Israel is as one who has no God," a statement that seems to deny any possibility of Jewish existence in the Diaspora, for if a person living outside of Eretz Yisrael has no God, then how can a Jew possibly live in such circumstances? Indeed, this statement—as a reader might suspect—has occasioned a long history of interpretation, beginning in our talmudic passage above with the question "Has he, then, who does not live in the Land no God?" and the subsequent statement, "Whoever lives outside the Land may be regarded as one who worships idols."[9] Perhaps this latter rendering is intended to qualify the first comment; certainly it is no testament of praise, yet at least one could say that a person who worships idols does "have a God."[10] Still, the fact that idol worship was always considered one of the most heinous of sins leads one to wonder what kind of "qualification" is really being offered here.

It is Rashi's commentary in the margins of the page that offers the true reworking of the Talmud's assertion. Writing centuries after the talmudic passage and from the perspective of a medieval Frenchman firmly entrenched in the Diaspora, Rashi takes an historical perspective and claims that our text really means to refer to living outside the land "in the time of the Temple," thus exempting himself and the rest of Diaspora Jewry from the demands the Talmud expresses in this passage. Without the Temple, in other words, we no longer have the obligation to live in the land. But this is not the only talmudic statement that deals with the question of the obligation to live in the land. Thus we read:

> Our rabbis taught: One is not permitted to leave the Land of Israel unless two *se'ahs* of produce cost one *sela*. R. Shimon said: This applies only if he cannot find anything to buy, but if he is able to find something to buy he should not leave even if the cost is one *sela* per *se'ah*.
>
> (Talmud, *Bava Batra* 91a)

The passage refers to measures of produce (*se'ahs*) and amounts of money (*selas*) and the idea is simply this: You are not allowed to leave the Land unless food shortages are so great that produce reaches the high price of two *se'ahs* per *sela*. R. Shimon adds a more stringent requirement: Even at one *se'ah* per *sela* you have to stay if you can find anything around to buy. In other words, even with economic hardship you must remain in Eretz Yisrael.

Of course, we can return to Rashi's earlier point of view and ask, is such a view still applicable? Is it still a mitzvah to live in the land? The medieval talmudic commentators discussed this question in some detail as they tried to interpret the following passage, which raised the question of dwelling in the land:

> Our rabbis taught: If a husband desires to move to Eretz Yisrael and his wife refuses, she must be compelled to go up, and if she does not consent, she may be divorced without a marriage settlement. If she desires to go up and he refuses, he must be compelled to go up, and if he does not consent, he must divorce her and pay her marriage settlement.
>
> (Talmud, *Ketubot* 110a)

Does this passage still have legal validity, the medieval rabbis wished to know? In general, it was concluded that the principle should no longer be enforced.[11] For at the very least, holding on to this view would open up the possibility of blackmail—anyone who wanted a "free" divorce could simply threaten that he or she planned to move to Israel! But deeper questions about the validity of *aliyah* (moving—literally, "going up"—to Israel) as a principle in Jewish law were also raised. As the important talmudic commentary *Tosafot* puts it, "This law does not apply at the present time, because of the dangers of the journey."[12] And the general thrust of medieval halakhic opinion was in the direction of not enforcing the principle, either because of the dangers of the journey or because of the difficulties of economic conditions in Israel, or even because of the practical difficulty of fulfilling those very agricultural mitzvot that were at the heart of the tradition's interest in Eretz Yisrael.[13]

Even in the earlier writings, in the Talmud itself, we occasionally see a diffidence about denying the validity of life outside the Land of Israel, especially when we keep in mind the obvious fact that the Talmud was a product of Jewish life in Babylonia! Thus, we read, "Whoever lives in Babylon is accounted as though he lived in the Land of Israel" (*Ketubot* 111a).

And of course one finds the view, expressed by certain extreme religious factions in our own time as well, that aliyah should not be a human concern, but should be left to God's messianic wisdom. Thus, Rav Judah states, "Whoever goes up from Babylon to the Land of Israel transgresses a positive commandment, for it is said: 'they shall be brought to Babylon and there they shall remain until I take note of them—declares the Lord of Hosts—

and bring them up and restore them to this place' " (Jer. 27:22).[14] In other words, dispersion was God's plan and in God's good time redemption will occur too. Until the messianic age we should remain where we are.

Of course, in our time many of these texts take on a different hue. We live after the establishment of a state in Eretz Yisrael, thus "going up" to the land becomes a living possibility, and there are few of us willing to stand with the text we have just read, which says that settling the land must wait until the Messiah comes. And yet aliyah is certainly not an option that most Jews, at least most Jews in America, are likely to choose, certainly as long as life remains reasonably secure in North America. In a certain sense we have accepted Rashi's reading of the situation— historical realities have changed the way we view the "obligation" to live in the land.

And yet the actuality of the State of Israel gives this old debate a different edge. Israel's existence forces us to face the challenge of aliyah in a way that previous generations did not. Unlike previous generations, we could, if we desired, envision the possibility of living a life in Israel and that very fact changes our relationship to the land and to the state. Our involvement with Israel as a living reality forces a different kind of connection to Eretz Yisrael.

For one thing it adds a new dimension to the way we look at the role the Land of Israel plays in the familiar texts of Jewish religious life. In the daily prayer book, for example, the central liturgical prayer, the Amidah, is said standing and in silence three times a day. It is hard to ignore the insistent reminders of Eretz Yisrael that one finds in this prayer:

Gather the dispersed from the ends of the earth. Blessed are You, Lord who gathers the dispersed of His people Israel.

or

Have mercy, O Lord, and return to Jerusalem, Your city. Dwell there as You promised and build it now, in our days for all time. Reestablish quickly there the throne of David, Your servant. Blessed are You, Lord, who builds Jerusalem.

or

May we witness Your merciful return to Zion. Blesed are You, Lord, who restores His Presence to Jerusalem.

After eating, Jews are required to recite the Grace After Meals and here too the land is recalled with a blessing "for the land and for for food." The shorter Grace, recited after eating a meal without bread[15] even more dramatically states a connection to the Land of Israel.

Blessed are You, Lord our God, King of the universe, for the earth's bounty and for the pleasing, good and spacious land which You gave to our ancestors, that they might eat of its produce and be satisfied from its goodly yield. Have mercy, Lord our God, for Jerusalem Your city, for Zion the home of Your glory, and for the Temple. Build Jerusalem soon and in our day, bring us up rejoicing in its restoration to eat there of the land's good fruit in abundance and to bless You in holiness and purity.

Examples multiply: The traditional liturgy changes the wording of the service to reflect the seasonal cycle of Eretz Yisrael, praying for rain in the winter and dew in the summer. Indeed, special liturgical poems are recited twice a year to mark the point in the season that these daily prayers are changed. Prayers for rain and dew, like the other examples cited above, essentially move the worshiper out of his or her own specific geographical locality into another place—the Land of Israel, *not* as symbol or ideal, but as a living reality, a place where actual fruits grow, where dew or rain falls in a seasonal routine different from that which most of us experience in North America.

The fact that these texts appear in the siddur is also not insignificant. The prayer book is the text that, despite communal or denominational differences, actively unites the Jewish people, for it is a book that Jews *use* every day in places around the world.

And the constant reminder of the Land of Israel in these prayers puts it on both the personal and global agenda of the Jewish people. As we stated in the introduction of this book, the texts of Judaism are the books of a people and no theme resounds more insistently than the place of Eretz Yisrael in Jewish consciousness.

In our time, as I've said, these words speak with particular relevance because of the reality of Israel the nation. Thus, the challenge to live one's life in that very land is for us more serious and more urgent than it was for Rashi or for any Jew who lived in the Diaspora in the past nineteen hundred years. But what are we to do about this, especially given the likelihood, as I have suggested above, that aliyah will not be an option for most American Jews?

It seems to me that for any Jew who cares about the texts of the tradition, Israel and the question of living there will continue to be a fact of one's life. The simple act of opening up the siddur will guarantee that. That does not mean that aliyah will be the result, but that possibility and challenge is something that will constantly be with us.

And there is another point to consider too. When we look back at some of the texts quoted earlier in this chapter, we might consider *why* the rabbis considered living in the Land of Israel "equivalent to all the other commandments of the Torah put together" and so important that one was "considered to have a God"? What might that idea be saying to us? Israel is a challenge to us not only because it comes up so often as a theme in classical sources, but because, as these rabbinic texts suggest, living there changes the nature of one's religious life. Outside the land it is as if you "have no God"; inside the land one does.

I would like to push these texts a little beyond their own intention, perhaps, to suggest that what we are being told about here is the power of living the kind of life only possible in Eretz Yisrael. Only in Israel is the living reality of the text fully possible; only there do the words of the siddur—the rain and dew— actually come to life. As the rabbis pointed out, it is only in the land that one can fulfill all the mitzvot. To put it another way, it is only in Israel that being Jewish in its fullest sense is a real possibility. Because in Israel one's entire life—one's daily affairs, one's social reality, *and* one's spiritual life—is lived in a Jewish context.

And perhaps most of all, there is the factor of language. The religious texts of the tradition are by and large written in Hebrew; certainly Hebrew is the language of the siddur. In our time the fact that Hebrew has once again become the spoken language of the Jewish people in its land is a powerful reminder of the connection to traditional literature that one absorbs by living in Israel, a connection shared even by those people who are not traditional themselves. The novels and newspapers of modern Israel are written in the language of the Bible. To be sure, biblical Hebrew differs from modern Hebrew, but the essential language is the same. Living in Israel, one's voice is thrust quite literally into the world of the classical text. Words reverberate with double meanings because of their traditional overtones, and therefore even in one's speech another kind of link is made to the past.

All of this makes me think of a story a friend tells that has stayed with me a long time. My friend had spent two years studying in Israel, and a few weeks before returning to the United States, she met an old woman in the market and got into a conversation with her. "So you're returning to America?" the woman asked. "Yes, I am," my friend replied. And then without making any of the classic Zionist arguments, without ideology or debate, the old woman simply looked at her and said, "We've waited all these generations and now you're going back?" It was as if she spoke with the consciousness of all of Jewish history, and there was nothing my friend could say in response.

Of course, I do not want to romanticize the difficulties that the reality of the State of Israel also presents. One may speak of Israel as a place where an integrated Jewish life can be led, but Israel's existence has raised a set of wrenching problems as well as offering unprecedented opportunities. As long as the "return to Zion" was a phrase in the prayer book and nothing more, we could ignore the implications of what statehood might mean. But today the existence of Israel occasions debates on issues of survival, relations with Arabs, questions of peace and negotiation, geopolitical facts of life. And the whole enterprise of Israel is threatened as well by tensions from within, internal disputes inside the Jewish community itself.

It is in this realm in particular that certain powerful rabbinic texts come to mind, namely, those sources that deal with an earlier crisis in Jewish history, the destruction of the Second Temple. Here we see the rabbis wrestling with the question of internal divisiveness in the community and the terrible consequences it brings.

In the midrashic literature that followed the destruction in the year 70 C.E. (and the failure of the subsequent Bar Kokhba revolt against Rome in 132–35 C.E.), the rabbis tried to find explanations for this terrible tragedy. What is remarkable is the discussion of the internal causes behind these apparently "external" events:

> Abaye said: Jerusalem was destroyed only because the Sabbath was desecrated therein, as it is said, "and they have closed their eyes to My sabbaths, therefore I am profaned in their midst" (Ezek. 22:26).
>
> R. Abbahu said: Jerusalem was destroyed only because the reading of the Shema morning and evening was neglected. . . .
>
> R. Hamnuna said: Jerusalem was destroyed only because they neglected the education of school children; for it is said, "Pour it out [that is, God's wrath] because of the children in the street (Jer. 6:11): why pour it out? Because the children are in the street. [And not in school!]
>
> Ulla said: Jerusalem was destroyed only because they [its inhabitants] were not ashamed of each other, for it is written, "They have done abhorrent things—yet they do not feel shame, and they cannot be made to blush . . . therefore they shall fall" (Jer. 6:15).
>
> R. Isaac said: Jerusalem was destroyed only because the small and the great were made equal. . . . R. Amram son of R. Simeon b. Abba said in R. Simeon b. Abba's name a teaching of R. Hanina: Jerusalem was destroyed only because they did not rebuke each other: for it is said, "Her princes are become like stags that find no pasture" (Lam. 1:6): Just as the stag, the head of one is at the side of the other's tail, so Israel of that generation hid their faces in the earth, and did not rebuke each other.
>
> Rav Judah said: Jerusalem was destroyed only because scholars were despised therein. . . .
>
> (Talmud, *Shabbat* 119b)

Whether it was the desecration of the Sabbath or the neglect of Jewish education or the lack of interpersonal confrontation and rebuke, the rabbis saw the cause of Israel's political destruction rooted in the life and failings of the Jewish community itself. Of all these explanations none is as detailed as two stories brought in rabbinic literature to interpret the reasons behind the destruction. The first appears in the Talmud [16] and it tells of a personal conflict that led to national tragedy:

> The destruction of Jerusalem came through two men, one named Kamza and one named Bar Kamza: A certain man had a friend Kamza and an enemy Bar Kamza. He once made a party and said to his servant, "Go and bring Kamza." But the servant went and brought Bar Kamza instead.
>
> When the man who gave the party found Bar Kamza there, he said, "See, you tell tales about me; what are you doing here? Get out."
>
> Said Bar Kamza: "Since I am here, let me stay, and I will pay you for whatever I eat and drink."
>
> The host replied: "I won't."
>
> "Then let me give you half the cost of the party."
>
> "No," said the other.
>
> "Then let me pay for the whole party."
>
> The host still said "No," and he threw him out bodily.
>
> Said Bar Kamza, "Since the rabbis were sitting there and did not stop him, this shows that they agreed with him. I will go and inform against them to the Government."
>
> He went and said to the Emperor, "The Jews are rebelling against you."
>
> The Emperor said, "How can I tell?"
>
> He said to him: "Send them an offering and see whether they will offer it on the altar." So the Emperor sent a fine calf with Bar Kamza. While on the way Bar Kamza made a blemish on its upper lip, or as some say on the white of its eye, in a place where we Jews count it as a blemish but the Romans do not.
>
> The rabbis were inclined to offer it nonetheless in order not to offend the Government. But R. Zechariah ben Avkilus said to them: "If we offer it, people will say that blemished animals are offered on the altar." The rabbis then proposed to kill Bar Kamza so that he should not go and inform against them, but R. Zechariah ben Avki-

lus said to them, "Is one who makes a blemish on consecrated animals to be put to death?"

R. Yohanan thereupon remarked: "Through the scrupulousness of R. Zechariah ben Avkilus our House has been destroyed, our Temple burnt and we ourselves exiled from our land."

(Talmud, *Gittin* 55b–56a)

Although this story has a "historical" setting, it is clear from the presentation that, like other rabbinic tales, its purpose is moral or religious rather than a recounting of history in our sense of the term.[17] These instructive tales have an almost allegorical quality, and in this story in particular even the odd names of the two main characters (literally meaning "Locust" and "Son of Locust") make one feel that the factual basis, even if it exists, of this legend is of little consequence. The purpose is to explore the meaning of the destruction of the Second Temple.

At one level we can see this tale as a kind of theatrical farce that ends in tragedy. We begin with a simple situation of personal enmity. The unnamed "certain man" has a friend (Kamza) and an enemy with a similar name (Bar Kamza). Is it possible that these two are father and son? Our text does not tell us, though that raises interesting questions: Why might the anonymous man have such a complicated relationship with this father and son? And even if we are not speaking about a father and son here, what is the nature of the relationship between Kamza and Bar Kamza? Once again we are not told.

Of course, the key character is Bar Kamza and his relationship with the man who throws the party. All of this begins with a servant's simple error. Instead of tendering the invitation to Kamza, the servant has invited Bar Kamza in error. Why—given the situation of personal conflict—does Bar Kamza even bother to come to the party? My own reading is that he does *not* come with the intention of making a scene (after all he tries to soothe the host's feelings by paying for his own food, by paying for the whole party, in fact!), but rather when he receives the invitation, he sees it as a gesture of reconciliation offered by the host. He goes to the party with hopes for an end to the hostilities, but instead he is greeted with animosity. And perhaps this reversal of expectation increases Bar Kamza's disappointment and outrage. The host has no intention of letting his enemy remain, error or no error. Even when Bar Kamza tries to pay, the host will not accept his offer.

It's interesting to note that the host's claim about Bar Kamza is that the latter "tells tales about me." We are not told if Bar Kamza for his part has any complaints about the host. And the story raises the possibility that the host *is* justified in his original anger. Bar Kamza's reputation as a talebearer is borne out by the subsequent events in the story: After all, it is he who will go to the emperor with false tales about the Jews!

Still, it is clear that Bar Kamza is embarrassed by the way he has been treated, and, as we have discussed in chapter 6, public embarrassment (*malbin panim*) was considered a serious offense in rabbinic culture. The outcome of all of this is that Bar Kamza blames the rabbis at the party for not coming to his defense, and of course one wonders why they did not. Perhaps this is simply a matter of their not wanting to get involved. They preferred to look the other way, and in not living up to their principles, in not denouncing the host for his public shaming of Bar Kamza, they were indeed remiss. In fact, the version of this story that appears in Lamentations Rabbah emphasizes this point by referring not to the rabbis as a whole, but to one particular rabbi (R. Zechariah ben Avkilus, the same rabbi mentioned in the Talmud's version) and states that he "could have prevented" the host from his assault on Bar Kamza, "but did not intervene."

And yet, despite the possible grounds for Bar Kamza's anger, what happens next has no justification. To begin with, he takes the personal insult that happened to him and turns it into a generalized complaint against the rabbis as a whole. We can understand such a phenomenon; people do tend to think in such a way, irrational though it may be. But Bar Kamza went beyond that— he made his personal problem a matter of grievous national consequence by turning to the Roman authorities. By changing the terms of the discussion, by moving out of the domain of petty personal pride into the world of national affairs, Bar Kamza sets into play a chain of events that ultimately lead to a major tragedy.

His crime, of course, is more than talebearing; for he actually commits a deception and a vindictive act. He knows that Jewish law forbade using animals that had certain kinds of blemishes for sacrifice. He also knew that the Roman authorities would not understand the subtleties of such laws, that they would instead see the refusal of the rabbis to sacrifice the animal as an act of rebellion, and because of that Bar Kamza presented the matter as a kind of test of Jewish loyalty, a test the rabbis could not help but fail.

Yet there was a way out. The rabbis still could have sacrificed the blemished animal, despite the law, in the interest of self-preservation. But R. Zechariah intervenes. Indeed, he intervenes twice here—once to dissuade them from using the blemished animal and once to prevent them from killing Bar Kamza. The Lamentations Rabbah version of the story does not give us this detail. Indeed, it emphasizes the "farcical" side of the tragedy by concluding with the thought that the destruction of the Temple occurred because of the similarity of the names Kamza and Bar Kamza. Lamentations Rabbah, in other words, sees the servant's error at the beginning of the tale as the key to the tragedy.

The version above paints a different picture, placing the blame squarely on R. Zechariah. It is his strictness about the law that has caused the disaster: He neither allowed the rabbis to bend the rules about sacrifices, nor did he let them kill the traitor Bar Kamza. But Rabbi Yohanan's concluding line sums up this complex story a little too simply. Certainly R. Zechariah deserves a measure of blame, but equally responsible was the hatred between the unnamed host of the party and Bar Kamza. Without that vindictiveness—on both sides—none of this would have happened.

Thus, we are presented with two complementary explanations here: First, there is the danger that personal (and in this case petty), interpersonal conflict could lead to national disaster. It is a sentiment summed up elsewhere in the Talmud when it is asked: "Why was the Second Temple destroyed since in that time people occupied themselves with Torah, mitzvot and charity?" Because, answers the text, "groundless hatred prevailed" (*Yoma* 9b). Second, there is the role that the rabbis played in their own destruction. By refusing to bend the law, and by sticking to a kind of purity of religious fervor, the Temple was destroyed.

Both of these interpretations suggest the dangers of internecine struggle and the dangers of a refusal to compromise, and both are explored further in another story that addresses the same question —how did the Temple come to be destroyed?

> Now, when Vespasian came to destroy Jerusalem he said to the inhabitants: "Fools, why do you seek to destroy this city and why do you seek to burn the Temple? For what do I ask of you but that you send me one bow or one arrow, and I shall go off from you."
>
> They said to him: "Even as we went forth against the first two who were here before thee and slew them, so shall we go forth against you and slay you."
>
> When Rabban Yohanan ben Zakkai heard this, he sent for the men of Jerusalem and said to them: "My children, why do you destroy this city and why do you seek to burn the Temple? For what is it that he asks of you? All he asks of you is one bow or one arrow, and he will go off from you."
>
> They said to him: "Even as we went forth against the two before him and slew them, so shall we go forth against him and slay him."
>
> Vespasian had men stationed inside the walls of Jerusalem. Every word which they overheard they would write down, attach the message to an arrow, and shoot it over the wall, saying that Rabban Yohanan ben Zakkai was one of the Emperor's friends.
>
> Now, after Rabban Yohanan ben Zakkai had spoken to them one day, two and three days, and they still would not attend to him, he sent for his disciples, for Rabbi Eliezer and Rabbi Joshua.
>
> "My sons," he said to them, "arise and take me out of here. Make a coffin for me that I might lie in it."
>
> Rabbi Eliezer took hold of the head end of it, Rabbi Joshua took hold of the foot; and they began carrying him as the sun set, until they reached the gates of Jerusalem.
>
> "Who is this?" the gatekeepers demanded.
>
> "It's a dead man," they replied. "Do you not know that the dead may not be held overnight in Jerusalem?"
>
> "If it's a dead man," the gatekeepers said to them, "take him out."
>
> So they took him out and continued carrying him until they reached Vespasian. They opened the coffin and Rabban Yohanan stood up before him.

"Are you Rabban Yohanan ben Zakkai?" Vespasian inquired; "tell me, what may I give you?"

"I ask nothing of you," Rabban Yohanan replied, "except the town of Yavneh where I might go and teach my disciples and there establish a prayer house and perform all the commandments."

"Go," Vespasian said to him, "and whatever you wish to do, do."

Said Rabban Yohanan to him: "Lo, you are about to be appointed king."

"How do you know this?" Vespasian asked.

Rabban Yohanan replied: "This has been handed down to us, that the Temple will not be surrendered to a commoner, but to a king; as it is said, "And he shall cut down the thickets of the forest with iron, and Lebanon shall fall by a mighty one" (Isa. 10:34).

It was said: No more than a day, or two or three days, passed before messengers reached him from Rome, announcing that the emperor was dead and that Vespasian had been elected to succeed him as king. . . .

When Rabban Yohanan ben Zakkai heard that Jerusalem was destroyed and the Temple was up in flames, he tore his clothing, and his disciples tore their clothing, and they wept, crying aloud and mourning.

(Avot d'Rabbi Natan, Chapter 4) [18]

This famous story has even more of a "factual" ring than that of Kamza and Bar Kamza. After all, Vespasian *was* an historical figure; he was the Roman general—later emperor—who conquered Jerusalem in the year 70 C.E. And to the best of our knowledge Rabban Yohanan ben Zakkai was also a historical person. Yet this tale also is better read as a literary work than as a piece of historical reportage. [19]

The legend seeks to answer a number of questions: What caused the destruction of the Temple? Could that destruction have been avoided? How and why did the great study center in Yavneh come to be established?

At the heart of the legend is the role of Rabban Yohanan and, as he is portrayed here, we react to him with a certain degree of ambivalence. After all, here was a man who "went over" to the Romans at the time that they were the greatest enemy of the Jews. Yet the core of the legend itself presents a different view: Yohanan's journey outside the walls of the city in a coffin is an unforgettable symbolic image. He rises, quite literally, from the dead and establishes the community in Yavneh that will give birth to the leadership of rabbinic life, the community that will, in effect, create Judaism itself.

This tale, told years after the destruction itself, by implication asks the following question: What would have happened, where would we be today, had Yohanan joined those within the city who would not submit to Vespasian? Clearly, the answer is that there would have been no Judaism. It was, according to this tale, Yohanan who preserved the life of the Jewish people. It was Yohanan who saw that the rebels within the city, no matter how noble their cause, would only lead to Israel's destruction. And it was Yohanan's act of concession to Rome that created the future. Thus, despite the status of the rebellion and martyrdom at Masada in the consciousness of our own age, throughout Jewish history it was the different spirit symbolized by Yohanan's actions that was seen as heroic.

This story, I believe, speaks in two ways to our time and in particular to the situation of modern-day Israel. First, it tells something about the value of compromise; Yohanan was willing to accept the reality of Rome's power and to build something more lasting than the conquests of Vespasian. We today live in an age filled with almost messianic fervor; accommodation and compromise tend to be deprecated on all sides. Yet the model of Yohanan suggests that there may be other ways to act. Surely, as we read at the end of the story, he too wept at the destruction of the city; surely he too would have wanted, in an ideal world, for an end to Roman domination. But Yohanan understood that historical realities demanded another way. Thus, the calls for "no compromise" that one hears on all sides of the Arab–Israeli conflict seem to echo the rigid arrogance in the rabbinic legend of those within the city who eventually brought about its destruction.

Second, like the tale of Kamza and Bar Kamza, this story also deals with the internal battles of the Jews. Those within the walls would not listen to Yohanan; the conflict among the Jews was ultimately as dangerous as the threat from the outside. This too rings uncomfortably true for us today. And in that spirit another text comes to mind:

> Although the School of Hillel and the School of Shammai are in disagreement on the questions of marriage and betrothal in cases involving rivals, sisters, an old bill of divorce, a doubtfully married woman, a woman whom her husband had divorced and who stayed with him overnight in an inn, money, valuables, etc. The School of Shammai did not refrain from marrying women of the families of the School of Hillel, nor did the School of Hillel refrain from marrying those of the School of Shammai. This is to teach you that they showed love and friendship towards one another, thus putting into practice the biblical text "Love truth and peace" (Zech. 8:19).
>
> (Talmud, *Yevamot* 14b)

Hillel and Shammai, of course, were the two great rivals of early rabbinic times, and the text above outlines many areas of disagreement between the two schools they led. Nor are these disputes about trivial matters: Questions about divorce and marriage were crucial to rabbinic thinking. But the point the Talmud wishes to emphasize here is something else: *Despite* these enormous conflicts, and indeed despite the fact that the issues they argued over often concerned marriage, it is particularly striking that the children of one school would *marry* the children of the other. In other words, as the biblical quotation above would have it, both "truth" and "peace" are values, but of the two, peace seems the greater. For despite their disagreements over what is correct, the schools of Hillel and Shammai felt that the bonds of love that peace implies outweighed the battles between them.

For our own time the point here seems clear: At a time of great conflict among Jews within the community of Israel and between the Jews of Israel and those of other parts of the world, the behavior of Hillel and Shammai speaks to us quite directly. The dangers exposed in the story of Kamza and Bar Kamza and in the story of Yohanan and the fall of Jerusalem are all connected to a refusal to compromise, to an inability to put differences aside in the light of a greater good. What we learn from the story of Hillel and Shammai is precisely that openness to change that we do not see in the two other stories. Even about matters of great religious import these two warring factions were willing to put aside differences in the spirit of harmony. The fact that the question of marriage was what brought them together is a symbol that needs no further explication. Perhaps our own times will learn from their example.

NINE

GROWING

This book has been an attempt to look at the way that a body of sacred literature—the classical texts of the Jewish tradition—might speak to the religious concerns in a person's life today. Thus, while I have tried to touch upon what the meaning of those texts might have been in their own time, at heart my goal was something different: to move beyond historical reflection in order to explore the ways that those ancient writings might continue to live for us too. Because of that I have tried to choose those texts which, when read in the fashion I have proposed, seem to speak with special clarity to a contemporary reader. This enterprise—the attempt to reflect upon the contemporary meaning of traditional literature—can be seen as a new version of a very old Jewish concern, indeed something the Jewish tradition has considered one of the key preoccupations of a person's life—the study of Torah, perhaps the crown of all commandments. In the famous phrase of *Pirkei Avot,* "Turn it and turn it again, for everything is contained within it" (5:24).

Saying that Jewish texts should be seen as resources that can address the issues in one's own life leads us inevitably into one of the thorniest questions the study of Torah has always occasioned: How "pure" is Torah study? Is such study, in other words, some-

211

thing we "use," a means to an end—is it "instrumental"—or is its value somehow more ethereal or abstract?

Countless statements in rabbinic literature attempt to address this question. *Pirkei Avot* in particular supplies a number of examples:

> Antignos of Sokho . . . used to say: Be not like the slaves who serve the master in order to receive a reward, but be like the slaves who serve the master not in order to receive a reward. . . . (1:3)

> . . . Rabbi Yishmael said: One who learns in order to teach, is enabled to learn and to teach; one who learns in order to practice is enabled to learn, to teach, to observe and to practice. Rabbi Zaddok said: Do not make words of Torah a crown with which to magnify yourself, nor a spade with which to dig. And thus Hillel used to say: He who makes worldly use of the "crown" shall perish. From this you learn: One who uses words of Torah for his own benefit, removes his life from the world. (4:5)

> Rabbi Meir said He who occupies himself with Torah for its own sake (*Torah lishmah*) merits many things. Indeed, he is deserving of the whole world. He is called friend, beloved, a lover of God, one who gladdens God, one who gladdens humanity. . . . (6:1)

At first glance, the texts above seem to give a clear answer to our question: The emphasis is on the *noninstrumental* dimension of Torah study. The remarks of Antignos of Sokho, of course, have a broader application than to the issue of study alone. Any aspect of Jewish religious life could fit the rubric of serving "the master *not* in order to receive a reward," but certainly Torah study would stand high on the list.

The two other quotations above directly address the issue of study. In the first we see three rabbinic masters—Yishmael, Zaddok, and Hillel—deal with the question of study and its reward: Do not, we are warned, use Torah, either as a "crown" or as "spade." "Crown" seems to refer to those who use Torah for their own status, reputation, or self-importance; "spade" is even more utilitarian: those who would use Torah for material gain. In the statement attributed to Rabbi Meir we can see the words of praise heaped upon one who studies Torah "for its own sake" (*Torah lishmah* is the Hebrew term). We study, according to this view, for the sake of study itself. Indeed, historically, this idea was sometimes taken to an extreme: The more "irrelevant" the passage (such as the talmudic passages about performing the sacrifices in the Temple, something we can no longer do), the more valued was the act of study. There is in this an almost mystical belief in the power and importance of Torah study. We don't study Torah to learn any particular thing, the rabbis suggest, we study because Torah is God's gift to us.[1]

In fact, according to the Talmud, even God sets Himself a routine for learning—for the first quarter of every day, God devotes Himself to studying Torah (Talmud, *Avodah Zarah* 3b). But why should God do this? Certainly, the rabbis believed that God knows all there is to know and thus there can be no utilitarian end in God's study of Torah. But perhaps this activity is meant to serve as an example for human beings. God studies and so should we; even more than that, God—who surely does not study for practical reasons—is the model for all Jews who study Torah "for its own sake."

But is the matter so simple? In fact, *Torah lishmah* is a more complicated idea than it might appear on the surface. For example, in the second passage above, the remarks of Rabbi Yishmael suggest that Torah study *does* have a utilitarian purpose though that one goal is delineated quite specifically: A person learns in order to teach, or even more importantly, it appears, one learns in order to observe the commandments, as a famous debate reported in the Talmud indicates:

> Rabbi Tarfon and the Elders were once reclining in the upper story of Nitza's house in Lydda, when this question was raised before them: Which is greater, study or practice?
> Rabbi Tarfon answered: Practice is greater. Rabbi Akiva answered: Study is greater for it leads to practice. Then they all answered, saying: Study is greater, for it leads to practice.
>
> (Talmud, *Kiddushin* 40b)

Rabbi Tarfon appears to take the position that "practice"—religious deeds, in other words—is greater. Akiva, it is interesting to note, does not really reject Tarfon's view. Akiva claims that study is greater, but only *because* it leads to action! Ultimately, it seems, the most important quality for the rabbis was "practice" —performing the mitzvot. Study, as Rabbi Akiva views it, could lead a person to more informed observance of the command-ments. Study that does not lead to practice, we might infer from Akiva, is not necessarily praiseworthy. Thus, *Torah lishmah* is not really analogous to the concept in our culture of "art for art's sake": True, the goal of Torah study should not be for glory or material gain, but study *is* meant to lead one someplace—as indi-cated by this passage, toward fulfillment of the mitzvot.

Still, a midpoint may exist between the theoretical investigation of arcane passages and the practical knowledge that leads to ac-tion. Such a perspective may be found in the following talmudic text:

> A favorite saying of Rava was: The goal of wisdom is repentance and good deeds. A person should not study much Torah and much Mish-nah and then despise and kick at his father and mother and teacher or at one who is superior to him in wisdom and authority, as it is said "The fear of the Lord is the beginning of wisdom, a good understanding have all they that practice it" (Ps. 111:10). The Bible does not say "all they that *study* it," but rather "all they that *practice* it." That is, practice it for its own sake, and not from other motives. All who practice it for other reasons, it were better that they had not been created.
>
> (Talmud, *Berakhot* 17a)

This teaching attempts to make two different points. First, Rava argues that the goal of study is realized in the ethical behav-ior of human beings in the world. The person learned in Torah who mistreats his parents and elders, who lacks even common decency, is not to be admired. That person's knowledge is merely accumulated information, not true understanding. The real goal of study *is* instrumental; it is to lead us toward wisdom or right-eousness. When we try to find the ways in which the texts of the tradition speak to the concerns of our lives today, we are doing precisely what Rava had in mind. We are looking for the ways that, to play with the words of the Psalm that Rava uses, we can "begin" with wisdom and move toward deeds.

But Rava's statement has another goal as well. That "practice" which is the goal of studying Torah should be practice "for its own sake" (*lishmah*). In other words, Rava recognizes the dangers mentioned in our earlier text—those who study or practice for the sake of power or wealth or self-aggrandizement—and he tries to find a middle ground between the "pure," noninstrumental study and the deeds that people do. One should study for the sake of practice, but one should not forget the dangers of practice for inappropriate ends.

But there is a step beyond this as well. Ultimately, the study of Torah must be prompted by something even deeper than a desire for "repentance and good deeds," namely, the pure love of the endeavor itself. In that sense all Jews are commanded to be lovers of Torah, "amateurs" in the original sense of the word, those who do something simply because they love to do it. Thus this beautiful midrash from the Talmud:

> "That you may love the Lord your God and you may obey His voice and you may hold fast to Him." (Deuteronomy 30:20)
>
> That is, one should not say: "I will read Scripture that I may be called a Sage; I will study that I may be called Rabbi; I will teach to be an Elder and sit in the assembly of Elders." Rather, learn out of love, and honor will come in the end, as it is written, "Bind them upon your fingers, write them upon the tablet of your heart" (Prov. 7:3) and "Her ways are ways of pleasantness" (Prov. 3:17) and "She is a tree of life to those who grasp her and whoever holds on to her is happy" (Prov. 3:18).
>
> (Talmud, *Nedarim* 62a)

The three proof texts from Proverbs in the midrash above try to capture the joy of "occupying oneself with Torah," as the rabbis like to put it. One does not study for public acclaim or for social status, says this text; one studies because the words of Torah are written on the "tablet of your heart." That is, they become as much a part of you as your own inner life. And more than that, Torah is "pleasantness"—in the eyes of the ancient rabbis Torah was a joy that in the long run will lead to the personal happiness promised in Proverbs 3:18. If there is a reward to the study of Torah, it is that happiness that "those who grasp her" come to experience.

Of course, the joy of Torah is a step removed from Akiva's "study is greater for it leads to practice." And it explains, perhaps, why those obscure, "impractical" passages became so highly valued in Jewish culture. When you study those passages, it is clear that your motivation comes only out of pure love. Like most of us, the rabbis of the past also believed that it was somehow better to do a deed without ulterior motive, from sheer joy, even when the goal of the task was something as noble as performing a mitzvah.

But what about study and us today? The joy of studying Torah is a fine-sounding phrase, but does it have any meaning for a person who is not already part of the world out of which those words emanate? Study, without certain skills and experience, is no simple matter. In fact, the idea of individual study, one person without a community, is itself problematic. In midrashic literature we have the following sad tale which addresses that very issue:

> Rabban Yohanan ben Zakkai had five students. As long as he was alive, they stayed near him. When he died, they all went to Yavneh, except Rabbi Eleazar ben Arakh who joined his wife in Emmaus, a wonderful setting with beautiful waters.
>
> He waited for the others to come to him, but they did not come. When he saw that they did not come to him, he asked if he could go to them, but his wife would not let him.
>
> She said, "Who needs whom?"
>
> He said, "They need me."
>
> She said to him, "In the case of a container of food and mice, who goes to whom? Do the mice come to the container of food or does the container go to the mice?"
>
> He listened to her and stayed where he was, until he forgot his knowledge of Torah. A while later the rabbis came to him and asked him a complex legal question, but he did not know how to answer.
>
> (Ecclesiastes Rabbah 7:7, number 2)

216

As we have seen before, this story, like most rabbinic legends, deals with a number of different issues at the same time. As much as it is a story about the need for community, it is also a tale about the dangers of pride and even about the seductions of the "material" world. Yavneh, as we recall from the story told in chapter 8, was the community Rabban Yohanan ben Zakkai established for the perpetuation of Torah study after the destruction of the Temple in 70 C.E. It is there, we are told in the tale above, that four of his students gathered together after the death of the master. Our legend seems to suggest that while Yohanan was alive, his own charisma guaranteed the ongoing intellectual activities of the students, but after his death it was necessary for them to rely on each other for spiritual or intellectual support. Indeed, the example of Eleazar ben Arakh may be intended to show the dangers of leaving that kind of supportive community. Without the others he forgets all his Torah.

It is Rabbi Eleazar's wife who remains the shadowy figure in this tale. We are told that Rabbi Eleazar decides to join his wife in Emmaus, but other questions then come to mind: Why and for how long were they living apart? Was there some connection between the death of Yohanan ben Zakkai and Rabbi Eleazar's decision to go to his wife? None of this is explained directly by the tale. But one thing is clear: It is his wife who dissuades Rabbi Eleazar from joining his colleagues. "Who needs whom?" she asks, and by thus appealing to his pride, she convinces Rabbi Eleazar to stay. Did she indeed believe that Rabbi Eleazar was the "food" and the other rabbis the "mice"? Did she, in other words, honestly expect the other rabbis to join her husband because of his great learning? Or was she motivated simply by the "beautiful waters" of Emmaus, which she did not wish to leave.

One thinks of this legend as a kind of Jewish version of Homer's tale of the lotus-eaters in Book IX of the *Odyssey* in which Odysseus's sailors "wanted to stay there with the lotus-eating people feeding on lotus and forgetting the way home."[2] For Rabbi Eleazar, forgetting the way home was forgetting his learning. When he meets with his colleagues some time later—and we are not told, interestingly enough, how long it takes for this loss of knowledge to occur—he cannot answer their question of hala-khah. Indeed, the irony of the story is that while his wife's predic-tion has come true—the "mice" have come to the "food" after all —staying in Emmaus has cost him his ability to answer their question.

No matter what one's level of learning, this story seems to warn, the danger of being alone, of being without community, undermines a person's ability to learn Torah. The point is not only that study is enhanced or protected by community, as is indicated in the story of Rabbi Eleazar ben Arakh above; study also *defines* community. We become a community by studying together and the place where we live may define what our lives become. Thus, we have the example of Rabbi Yose ben Kisma as recounted in the sixth-chapter addendum to *Pirkei Avot*:

> Said Rabbi Yose ben Kisma: One time when I was walking along a road, I met a man who greeted me. I returned his greeting.
>
> He said to me: My teacher, where do you come from? I answered him: I am from a great city of sages and scribes.
>
> He said to me: My teacher, if you agree to live with us in our place, I will give you thousands of golden *dinars*, precious stones, and pearls.
>
> I answered him: Even if you give me all the gold, silver, precious stones and pearls in the world, I would only live in a place of Torah. So it is written in the book of Psalms by David, King of Israel, "I prefer the Torah You proclaimed to thousands of gold and silver pieces" (Ps. 119:72).
>
> Moreover, when a person dies nothing accompanies him, not sil-ver, gold, precious stones, nor pearls—rather his knowledge of Torah and his good deeds alone. . . . (6:9)

There is something haunting about this story. I picture Yose ben Kisma on the road, tempted by wealth and fame. All he has to do is leave his home. What characterizes that home for him is that it is a place where he can study Torah. I suspect that, as in the case of Rabbi Eleazar ben Arakh, that means he has colleagues there and that it is a place in which the study of Torah is encour-aged and nurtured. Of course, I put myself in Yose's position and wonder about my own answer to the question, and I wonder about what it means to value Torah so highly that the temptations of the world would have no meaning. We all face situations in which the temptations of money or fame or comfort push us toward decisions that conflict with our deeper values. What was it about Yose ben Kisma that allowed him to reject so unflinchingly the blandishments of the world?

Of course, Yose ben Kisma had that prior commitment to the importance of Torah learning which I've mentioned before. No one had to convince him of the importance of learning; it was part of the culture into which he was born. The world of the rabbis was built upon the principle of the deep importance of learning, and the literature of classical Judaism is filled with heroic tales about self-sacrifice and dedication to the ideals of learning. One early midrashic source tells the following story about one of Yohanan ben Zakkai's students:

What were the beginnings of Rabbi Eliezer ben Hyrcanus?

He was twenty-two years old and had not yet studied Torah. One time he resolved: "I will go and study Torah with Rabban Yohanan ben Zakkai." Said his father Hyrcanus to him: "Not a taste of food shalt thou get before thou hast plowed the entire furrow."

As he was walking along the road he saw a stone; he picked it up and put it in his mouth. And some say: It was cattle dung. He went to spend the night at a hostel.

Then he went and appeared before Rabban Yohanan ben Zakkai in Jerusalem and a bad breath rose from his mouth. Said Rabban Yohanan ben Zakkai to him: "Eliezer, my son, hast thou eaten at all today?"

Silence.

Rabban Yohanan ben Zakkai asked him again.

Again silence.

Rabban Yohanan ben Zakkai sent for the owners of his hostel and asked them: "Did Eliezer have anything to eat in your place?"

"We thought," they replied, "he was very likely eating with thee, master."

He said to them: "And I thought he was very likely eating with you. You and I, between us, left Rabbi Eliezer to perish."

Thereupon Rabban Yohanan said to him: "Even as a bad breath rose from thy mouth, so shall fame of thee travel for thy mastery of the Torah."

(Avot d'Rabbi Natan, Chapter 6)[3]

This is a peculiar story, no doubt, and what makes it strange is not only the obvious questions, such as why Rabbi Eliezer eats cattle dung. Or perhaps even more to the point: Why did the rabbinic sources pass down a tale about such odd behavior (and bad breath!) in one of their distinguished forebears?[4]

But even before we get to those details, we wonder about the opening lines of the legend: Why promise to talk about a person's "beginnings" and then not bother to tell them to you? Here is the future rabbi, Eliezer ben Hyrcanus, already twenty-two years old, and yet we learn nothing in this text about his upbringing, his formative years, what *we* would call his "beginnings." In our post-Freudian world it would be impossible to recount a great man's biography without telling about his upbringing, his relationship with his parents and siblings. But here we get none of that. What, then, is this story about?

This is a story about fathers false and true. Eliezer ben Hyrcanus is in search of a father who will understand his deepest desire—that unexplained, almost sudden desire to learn Torah. His natural father rejects him; indeed, he even denies him food. And that is the second symbolic pole of the story—food and its significance. Eliezer denies himself food in his haste to find a teacher (and in a sense it almost seems that he is trying to avoid disobeying Hyrcanus's statement "Not a taste of food shall you get," so he chooses not to eat) because for him the true nourishment he is seeking is not in food, but in something else: the study of Torah. Putting the stone or dung in his mouth is merely a way to stave off thirst or hunger.

It is fitting also that his search for a true father ends with meeting a sage, indeed the greatest sage of Eliezer's time, Yohanan ben Zakkai. For it is Yohanan who can provide him with Torah, with food for the inner life. For rabbinic Judaism one's father is one's teacher; and one's teacher is one's father (or even more important than one's father), a point elucidated in a number of talmudic texts.

What were the beginnings of Eliezer ben Hyrcanus? It was not his early life, his years on his father's farm. His life began the day he started to study Torah.

Another famous sage also "begins" his career late in life:

> What were the beginnings of Rabbi Akiva?
>
> It is said: When he was forty years of age he had not yet studied a thing. One time he stood by the mouth of a well. "Who hollowed out this stone?" he wondered.
>
> He was told: "It is the water which falls upon it every day, continually." It was said to him: "Akiva, hast thou heard, *The waters wear away the stones?*" (Job 14:19)
>
> Thereupon Rabbi Akiva drew the inference with regard to himself: If what is soft wears down the hard, all the more shall the words of the Torah, which are as hard as iron, hollow out my heart, which is flesh and blood. Forthwith he turned to the study of Torah.
>
> He went with his son and they appeared before an elementary teacher. Said Rabbi Akiva to him: "Master, teach me Torah."
>
> Rabbi Akiva took hold of one end of the tablet and his son the other end of the tablet. The teacher wrote down *aleph bet* for him and he learned it; *aleph taw,* and he learned it; the book of Leviticus, and he learned it. He went on studying until he learned the whole Torah.
>
> Then he went and appeared before Rabbi Eliezer and Rabbi Joshua. "My masters," he said to them, "reveal the sense of Mishnah to me."
>
> When they told him one *halakhah* (law) he went off to be by himself. "This *aleph,*" he wondered, "why was it written? That *bet,* why was it written? This thing, why was it said?" He came back and asked them—and reduced them to silence.
>
> (Avot d'Rabbi Natan, Chapter 6)[5]

The hard work exhibited by Akiva and the hunger of Rabbi Eliezer represent a kind of tradition of sacrifice in the cause of studying Torah that is not uncommon in rabbinic literature. Thus, as we shall see, there is a tale about Hillel, who endured freezing cold just to hear words of Torah. And of course there is the legend of the ten rabbis, one of whom was Akiva himself, who end their lives as martyrs because of their determination to study and teach Torah in the face of a Roman ban.[6]

But what interests me here is not so much the matter of sacrifice in order to study (although I'll say more about that a little later), but rather two other points. One is the utter centrality of study for the rabbis' very definition of Judaism: To be a Jew means to study Torah. The study of Torah is, after all, a mitzvah, a commandment, but more than that it is a way into the heart of God's message. Jewish sources abound with statements about study, and all Jews no matter what their piety or intelligence were enjoined to study Torah. For Eliezer ben Hyrcanus and for Akiva, it marked the very beginning of life.

But another point is also striking here: Both Eliezer and Akiva began their study of Judaism as adults. These two exemplary figures, it seems to me, gain a great deal of prestige in the tradition thanks to that fact. To enter the world of Jewish study as an adult is to take on a daunting and often frustrating task. It means wading through some difficult waters—some strange vocabulary and different cultural assumptions, for example.

Earlier I mentioned the issue of sacrifice and study. For most of us, studying Torah does not endanger our lives. For us sacrifice may take a different and far less dramatic form—simply the decision to put aside the time in our lives to study. What I mean to suggest is that we take quite seriously the principle that to be a Jew means to study Torah, and that we take upon ourselves that enterprise of study as a personal commitment. In *Pirkei Avot* we read two famous statements about finding time for study:

> Shammai said: Make your study of Torah a fixed habit. (1:15)

> Hillel said: . . . Do not say: When I have leisure I will study. Perhaps you will never have the leisure. (2:5)

I love the fact that both statements, so much in consonance, come from two famous *opponents* in early rabbinic times. It is almost as if the text in preserving both comments wants to say, "Look, I know Hillel and Shammai differ on just about everything, but on this matter they are in agreement."

Of course, Hillel spells the matter out a little more. Shammai, in his typical way, gives us the prescription with an unflinching eye—*do this*. But Hillel, perhaps a better psychologist, understands the real difficulty. All of us, he says, would like to put time aside for study. It will be part of our "leisure-time" activities, we think. But it's not so simple, Hillel tells us. Perhaps we will never find the leisure.

And I wonder: Does that mean all of us are just plain too busy —if you leave study out of the routine while you are waiting for the leisure time, you know very well that kind of leisure just never happens? Or is he saying something else: Study is not a leisure-time activity at all. It's serious business. It is a search for wisdom, and that is not the kind of thing one does in between tennis games. We lead hard and busy lives. Study will never be part of them unless we consciously make that decision.

According to the rabbinic tradition, one did not study in order to master a body of material and be done with it. The act of studying Torah was seen to be an integral part of one's life:

> Rabbi Meir says: If you have studied Torah with one teacher, do not say, "It is enough." Rather go study with another sage, also. However, do not go to study with just anyone; first, go to someone who from the outset is close to you, as it is said "Drink water from your own cistern, running waters from your own well" (Prov. 5:15).
>
> (Avot d'Rabbi Natan, Chapter 3)

One can never have "enough Torah," this teaching argues, but note that the text above does more than emphasize the lifelong nature of Torah study. Up to now we have spoken about the importance of community for learning to take place, but here Rabbi Meir raises another issue—the role of the teacher in the process of studying Torah. And Rabbi Meir chooses to emphasize not the teacher's authority or mastery of knowledge, but rather the quality of one's relationship to the teacher with whom one works. You should, according to this source, try to find someone who "from the outset is close to you."

To me that suggests the importance of the basic sympathy and connection one makes with the teacher's character. The relationship one forges with the teacher comes out of that original, almost instinctual, closeness that student and teacher feel. In other words, each person has to find the teachers who are right for him or her.

One need only recall the story discussed earlier of Rabbi Eliezer ben Hyrcanus and his search for a true "father" to see how significant a role the teacher played in the traditional Jewish consciousness. Indeed, the quotation that Rabbi Meir uses from Proverbs strikes that same note—"from your own cistern" and "from your own well" indicate the nature of the identification that happens between teacher and learner.

But it seems to me the end result of that relationship is something more than interpersonal closeness. It is through the connection with the close teacher that the learner moves into connection with Torah itself. Every sage is known as a *talmid hakham,* a "student of the wise," but the ultimate goal for each student is to become a teacher in his own right, that is, to go beyond the teacher into a kind of personal independence.

The best discussion of this topic that I know of is an essay by the educational philosopher Joseph Schwab entitled "Eros and Education."[7] There Schwab talks about the "eros"—deep personal connection—involved in the learning process. The goal for the teacher is to convert the students' liking (eros) for *him* or *her* into a liking for those *subjects* the teacher values. As Schwab puts it:

> He is to convert liking and respect for his person into pleasure in practicing what he is and does as a liberally educated person. . . .
> The student learns to like them (through being brought, originally, to like their possessor) because they are good, to enjoy their exercise and to desire them for himself.[8]

In a similar fashion, it seems to me, the closeness one feels for one's rabbi, according to the Jewish tradition, should lead one to an independent connection and regard for Torah. Thus, when we too think about learning with a teacher, it makes sense to remember that dependence on that one role model is only one step toward autonomy, toward what we might call religious adulthood. This is one of the underlying goals of Jewish religious consciousness: *growing within tradition.*

Of course, that growing does not come easily. Even with community and even with the right teacher, another element is significant as well—the hard work the task demands:

Rabbi Isaac said: If a person says to you, I have labored and not found, do not believe him. If he says, I have not labored, but still have found, do not believe him. If he says, I have labored and found —believe him. This is true for words of Torah, but in business a person must rely on the assistance of heaven. And even for words of Torah this is true only for sharpening one's learning; but in remembering what one has learned, one must rely on the assistance of heaven.

(Talmud, *Megillah* 6b)

Rabbi Isaac is quite specific about the nature of study and personal discovery. To "find" means to have "labored" in Torah. If a person claims to have "found" without hard work, don't believe him. Rabbi Isaac is equally confident that hard work will lead to a successful resolution. Indeed, he is skeptical of those who claim to have "not found" after laboring. Of course, the catch-22 here is that Rabbi Isaac can always claim to such a person, "You really haven't worked hard enough; otherwise you would have succeeded." And who is to judge what "laboring" really is? Perhaps he is right—the only proper way to evaluate the work is by the results you get. Still, in Rabbi Isaac's system there is an uncertainty factor: about some matters, such as business, one has no control. About those things, we must rely on the assistance of heaven. And even in the world of Torah some things are beyond our control. Remembering what one has learned is also outside of human control. It is a matter, in contemporary terms, of luck or genes or talent.

Recognizing, however, that there are things beyond our control does not undercut Rabbi Isaac's earlier point: Hard work is a requirement for learning, and no amount of talent on the one hand or personal excuses on the other will make up for a lack of effort. Thus, the Talmud outlines a whole set of personal excuses that people might make for *not* studying and rejects them all:

Our rabbis taught: The poor, the rich, the sensual come before the heavenly court. The court says to the poor: Why have you not occupied yourself with Torah? If he says: I was poor and worried about my sustenance, the court would say to him: Were you poorer than Hillel? It was reported about Hillel the Elder that every day he used

225

to work and earn one tropaik, half of which he would give to the guard at the House of Study, the other half he would spend for his food and for that of his family.

One day he found nothing to earn and the guard at the House of Study would not permit him to enter. He climbed up and sat upon the window to hear the words of the living God from the mouth of Shemayah and Avtalion. They say that day was the Sabbath eve in the winter solstice and snow fell down upon him from heaven. At dawn Shemayah said to Avtalion: On every day this house is light and today it is dark. Is it perhaps a cloudy day? They looked up and saw the figure of a man in the window. They went up and found him covered by three cubits of snow. They removed him, bathed and anointed him, and placed him opposite the fire and said: This man deserves that the Sabbath be profaned on his behalf.

(Talmud, *Yoma* 35b)

Following this example, the Talmud goes on to discuss the possible excuses of "the rich" and "the sensual" as each comes before the heavenly court. The rich are given the example of Rabbi Eleazar ben Harsom, a man so wealthy that it was said his father had left him a thousand cities and a thousand boats. Yet everyday he went from city to city and province to province, studying Torah day and night. The sensual are told of the biblical character Joseph, who resisted the temptations of Potiphar's wife as she tried to seduce him (Genesis 39).

Finally, the Talmud's elaborate attack on those who avoid the mitzvah of studying Torah concludes: "Thus the example of Hillel condemns the poor, Rabbi Eleazar ben Harsom condemns the rich, and Joseph, the virtuous, condemns the sensual."[9] There are no excuses good enough, in other words, and like the remark of Hillel mentioned earlier—"Do not say: When I have leisure I will study. Perhaps you will never have the leisure"—we cannot avoid the direct challenge to our own situation that these texts assert. As we've seen earlier in the chapter, a certain element of self-sacrifice is sure to be part of finding the time to study—though none of us is likely to end up like Hillel, crouched on the roof in a snowstorm—but learning Torah is what growing in Judaism is all about.

But how, when the task is so daunting?

226

> What does the unwise person say? "Who can learn the Torah? The
> section *Nezikin* ["Damages"] by itself is thirty chapters long! The
> section *Kelim* ["Vessels"] by itself is thirty chapters long!"
>
> What does the wise person say? "I will study two laws today and
> another two tomorrow until I have learned the entire Torah."
>
> (Leviticus Rabbah 19:2)

The passage above deals with the almost overwhelming wealth
of material that confronts the prospective learner. *Nezikin* and
Kelim are two "orders"—large sections—of the Mishnah, the
basic text of rabbinic study, and the words spoken by the "un-
wise person" must have been familiar ones to the rabbis' ears.
Merely contemplating all that one does not know is so daunting! And similar feelings of frustration are true for us today as
well. As we have pointed out earlier, the entry to the world of
Jewish study, particularly for an adult, is fraught with difficulty
and frustration.

Not long ago I spoke to a group and was asked by one man in
the audience, "How do you get over the feeling of never being
able to catch up?" I gave him the only honest answer I could:
"You don't." That's the bad news. The good news, if that's what
we should call it, is that *everyone*—even the greatest scholar—is
feeling the same thing. Too many texts; too little time.

Perhaps somewhere out there a scholar exists who feels that he
or she has the kind of mastery my questioner is talking about. But
I suspect that such individuals are rare indeed. Most of us realize
that the more you know, the more you understand how much
there is to know. In fact, learning in Judaism may be just that:
You learn that you'll *never* learn it all. And perhaps that is what
the rabbis meant when they talked about the "sea" of the Talmud
—it is endless, perhaps one could even drown from a sense of
discouragement.

What is interesting about our text above is the specific counsel
it offers for just such a sense of frustration. The task is enormous,
but take it slowly, the Talmud advises: "I will study two laws
today and another two tomorrow until I have learned the entire
Torah."

So what have we seen up to this point? To begin with, Torah

requires community, or at least it flourishes best in such a setting; otherwise one is in danger of ending up like Rabbi Eleazar ben Arakh—one's knowledge forgotten for lack of intellectual stimulation. Second, like Yose ben Kisma in his way and Eliezer ben Hyrcanus in his—and many others too—learning Torah requires sacrifice and hard work. This is not an easy task, nor does it come quickly. Indeed, its very difficulty suggests that if you wait for leisure time, you might never get to it. But we have seen two things that can help mitigate that sense of being overwhelmed— the assistance of a teacher and the good advice to take things slowly, step-by-step. If one accepts the rabbis' understanding that learning is a lifelong occupation, then one loses nothing by taking a measured pace.

Let us say I take all the comments above as good counsel, as practical recommendation. I try to find myself a community; I seek out teachers; I put aside the time and fight the urge to be overwhelmed. There still remains another element that it is important to recognize: Our relationship to the world of Jewish study and Jewish experience is tied to who we are as human beings and therefore it is bound to change and vary over the course of a lifetime. In recent years psychologists such as Erik Erikson and Daniel Levinson have tried to explore the developmental path of a person's life.[10] None of us, these researchers point out, becomes "adult" at a single moment and remains fixed in a specific mode of "adultness" forever. Yet we often tend to think of our relationship to Judaism precisely as something unchanging. Whether it be the Judaism we learned as children or that which we encountered in early adulthood, we often fail to recognize that our relationship to tradition must by necessity be a dynamic one, that ritual or prayer or study or communal life will have a different meaning (or lack of meaning) at different times in our lives. One passage in *Pirkei Avot* attempts to express this notion:

> At five years of age—the study of Bible
> At ten—the study of Mishnah
> At thirteen—responsibility for the mitzvot
> At fifteen—the study of Talmud

At eighteen—marriage
At twenty—pursuit of a livelihood
At thirty—the peak of one's powers
At forty—the age of understanding
At fifty—the age of counsel
At sixty—old age
At seventy—ripe old age
At eighty—the age of strength
At ninety—the bent back
At one hundred—as one dead and out of this world

(Pirkei Avot 5:23)

At first glance, this passage appears to be a presentation of a lifelong "curriculum" for Jewish learning—what should one study at which age. But soon it becomes clear that the text is trying to explore a larger context: the whole span of a person's life experience.[11] As people age, they view the world in different ways through the lenses of different strengths and weaknesses. It is not surprising, therefore, that our relationship to Judaism will take different paths and turns. Indeed, seeing one's experience of the tradition as something evolving and changing suggests that even a movement at one point in a person's life *away* from a living or meaningful relationship to Judaism does not mark the end of any possibility for a resumption of connection at some later point. Thus, in one midrashic text we read:

"An inheritance of the Congregation of Jacob."

(Deuteronomy 33:4)

This shows that the Torah is the inheritance of Israel. To what may this be compared? To a king's son who when small was taken away into captivity to a country across the sea. If he wants to return, even after a hundred years, he will not be embarrassed to do so, because he can say I am returning to my inheritance.

So also a sage who has turned away from the words of Torah in order to deal with other matters will not be embarrassed to return to them, if he wishes to even after a hundred years, because he can say I am returning to my inheritance. Therefore the Torah says, "An inheritance of the Congregation of Jacob."

(Sifre Deuteronomy, 345)

This passage talks about "a sage" who has turned away from the tradition "to deal with other matters," but it is not inappropriate to read the passage as speaking about *anyone* who wishes to reconnect to his or her "inheritance." I would read this text, in fact, even more broadly. This notion of change and evolution in one's relationship to the Jewish tradition is not limited by any means to those who have turned away from Judaism. To see it as such would be to focus only on the so-called *baalei teshuvah,* those who wish to "return" to Judaism.[12]

My point is something different: All of us—no matter how profound our connection to Judaism, no matter how deeply rooted it may be in our lives, the most Orthodox, the most committed—all of us are by necessity engaged in a dynamic relationship with the tradition. We cannot help it, because as human beings we are always changing. We hope that change is something positive; when it is, we call it growth. Growing implies reevaluation, new learning, and reflection. As one writer about psychological change has put it, "Far from going straight up, the stages of religious development proceed with a circling back that creates a spiraling effect."[13] Similarly, Hasidic writers talk about the flow between times of ordinary human experience and moments of profound connection in a person's relationship with God.[14] One never knows when the change from one state to the next will occur—"In an instant," as one source puts it, "the light of your soul will be kindled."[15]

When we speak of the "wisdom" of the Jewish tradition or of its "profundity," we avoid self-congratulatory cliché only to the extent that we honestly mean that we are willing to grow with that tradition and in the light of tradition. "Grow old and gray in Torah," one rabbi teaches. Why? Because, we would suggest, it is rich enough to sustain that growth. Seen in that light, the act of reading these texts becomes something more: an opportunity for reimagining who we are as human beings, a chance for rethinking our lives and our world.

Glossary

Aggadah: From the Hebrew for "telling." Nonlegal (cf. *Halakhah*) rabbinic literature: stories, theology, lore. Collected both in Talmud and midrashic works. *Aggadic* (adjective).

Aliyah: Literally, "going up." The term for moving to live in Israel.

Amidah: Literally, "standing." Central prayer in daily, Sabbath, and festival liturgies.

Avot: "Fathers," "Ancestors," or, as one scholar puts it, "Founders," a tractate of the Mishnah devoted entirely to statements of an ethical or spiritual nature. In the Mishnah, *Avot* consists of five chapters; a sixth chapter of similar antiquity and dealing with similar themes was added to the tractate to facilitate the custom of studying the work during the six Sabbaths between Passover and Shavuot. *Avot* is often known as *Pirkei Avot* ("Sayings" or "Chapters" of the Fathers), no doubt because of the aphoristic nature of the book.

B.C.E.: Before the Common Era. Used in place of *B.C.*, before Christ, in Jewish writing. *C.E.*, Common Era, is used in place of *A.D.*

Ben: "Son of" (same as Aramaic "bar" or Arabic "ibn"). Used in names: e.g., Eliezer ben Hyrcanus.

Berakhah: "Blessing."

Darshan: "Preacher." From the same Hebrew root as "midrash."

Ein Sof: Literally, "without end." In Kabbalah the mysterious, unknowable aspect of the divine.

Eretz Yisrael: The Land of Israel.

Etrog: Citron, lemonlike fruit used with lulav in ritual for festival of Sukkot. See chapter 2.

Gemara: Largely in Aramaic, the discussions and comments about the Mishnah that make up the bulk of the Talmud.

Halakhah: From the Hebrew verb meaning "to go, to walk"; hence "the way." Jewish law. *Halakhic* (adjective).

Hasidism: Jewish revivalist movement that began in the late eighteenth century.

Hokheah tokhiah: The commandment to rebuke your neighbor for doing wrong. See chapter 6.

Hukkim: "Statutes." According to Maimonides, these are the laws that seem to be unconnected to ordinary reason, "whose causes are hidden from us because

231

of our incapacities." In contrast to *mishpatim,* "laws," which, according to Maimonides are the "rational" commandments, "whose utility is clear to the multitude," such as the prohibition of killing and stealing. See chapter 6.

Kabbalah: Usually means Jewish mysticism, particularly medieval Jewish mysticism.

Kavvanah: From the Hebrew verb "to direct." Usually used to mean intentionality and concentration in prayer or in performing a mitzvah. See chapter 5.

Keva: The fixed liturgy or a fixed practice. Sometimes with negative connotation (when used in opposition to *kavvanah*), sometimes not. See chapter 5.

Kofer ba-ikkar: "One who denies the key principle." A nonbeliever.

Lashon ha-rah: "Evil speech." Gossip.

Lifnim mishurat ha-din: Going beyond the strict requirements of the law.

Lulav: Palm branch used with etrog in the ritual for the festival of Sukkot. See chapter 2.

Mahshava zara: In Hasidic literature, thoughts that distract one from *kavvanah* in prayer.

Malbin panim: Literally, "whitening the face." Public embarrassment of someone. See chapter 6.

Midrash: Classic Jewish literature that interprets Scripture. See Introduction for more on midrash. *Midrashim* (plural); *midrashic* (adjective).

Minyan: A quorum of ten needed in order to say certain prayers publicly.

Mishnah: The first major rabbinic book (c. 200 C.E.). Largely in Hebrew, a compilation of primarily legal traditions. Along with the Gemara, it forms the Talmud.

Mitzvah: Commandment. But sometimes simply used to mean "a good deed." *Mitzvot* (plural).

Mitzvot bein adam l'havero: Commandments that deal with issues between human beings. In contrast to *mitzvot bein adam l'makom*: Commandments between God and human beings. See chapter 6.

Peshat: The "plain meaning" of a text, particularly Scripture. The historical, contextual meaning, as opposed to *derash,* the fanciful or homiletical meaning.

Rabbinic age: Sometimes called the talmudic age, though this period precedes the compilation of the Talmud itself. Indeed, the rabbinic age culminates with the Talmud. Hence, roughly the period between the first and sixth centuries of the Common Era.

Rashi: Acronym for Rabbi Shlomo ben Isaac (1040–1105), famous French biblical exegete and key commentator on the Talmud.

Rebbe: Within Hasidism the religious leader or spiritual master for a particular group.

Sefirot: In kabbalistic writing the ten emanations of the divine world.

Shabbat: The sabbath.

Shema: Key prayer proclaiming God's oneness, from morning and evening services. The Shema is a compilation of sections from the Bible: Deuteronomy 6:4–9, 11:13–21; Numbers 15:37–41.

Siddur: The prayer book, from the Hebrew *seder,* "order."

Sifra: Midrashic commentary on Leviticus.

Sifre: "Books." One of two midrashic works: Sifre on Numbers, Sifre on Deuteronomy.

Sukkah: "Booth." Temporary dwelling in which Jews are commanded to dwell. Traditional Jews usually eat their meals in the Sukkah during the autumn festival of Sukkot ("Booths"). Also a tractate in the Talmud.

Taamei hamitzvot: Explanatory reasons for performing commandments. See chapter 2.

Talmid hakham: Literally, "student of the wise." Sage or rabbi. *Talmidei hakhamim* (plural).

Talmud: The key work of rabbinic Judaism (c. 500 *C.E.*), comprising the Mishnah and the Gemara.

Tanakh: Acronym for the three sections of the Hebrew Bible: Torah, Nevi'im ("Prophets"), Ketuvim ("Writings").

Tefillin: Phylacteries; small boxes containing biblical verses that are attached to one's arm and around one's head during morning service, so that, in the words of the Shema, God's words will be "as a sign upon your arm" and as "a reminder above your eyes."

Teshuvah: Literally, "turning." Usually means "repentance." *Baalei teshuvah* refers to Jews who have "returned" to their religion; generally used to refer to non-Orthodox who have become Orthodox. *Baal teshuvah* (singular).

Torah: Probably the central word in Judaism. It refers to many different things: the first five books of the Bible, the scroll in the synagogue that contains the first five books of the Bible, the Bible as a whole (the "written Torah"), the later sacred writings of Judaism (the "oral Torah"), the act of studying, etc.

Torah lishmah: Study for its own sake, not for an ulterior purpose. See chapter 9.

Tosefta: Aramaic for "supplement." A collection of early rabbinic writings, similar to the Mishnah.

Tzedakah: From the Hebrew *tzedek,* "justice." Usually means "giving charity." See chapter 7.

Yavneh: Town in which Rabban Yohanan ben Zakkai established his great study center after the destruction of Jerusalem in 70 *C.E.* See chapters 8 and 9.

Zohar: The central work of medieval Jewish mysticism (Kabbalah); traditionally attributed to the second-century rabbi Shimon bar Yohai.

Notes

INTRODUCTION

1. Gershom Scholem, *"The Meaning of the Torah in Jewish Mysticism,"* in his *On the Kabbalah and Its Symbolism* (Schocken Books, 1965), p. 65. The mystics talk about the 600,000 aspects of Torah, a number parallel to the traditional concept that 600,000 stood at Sinai to receive the Torah.

2. Franz Rosenzweig, *On Jewish Learning,* ed. Nahum N. Glatzer (Schocken Books, 1955), p. 98.

3. Ibid., p. 96.

4. Ibid., p. 99.

5. Israel Scheffler, "In Praise of the Cognitive Emotions," *Teachers College Record* 79, no. 2 (December 1977), pp. 171–86.

6. "Affective and cognitive processes cannot be readily separated," says Daniel N. Stern, one of the leading researchers in this area. See his discussion in *The Interpersonal World of the Infant* (Basic Books, 1985), pp. 38–42.

7. For more on this issue, see Janet Aviad, *Return to Judaism* (University of Chicago Press, 1983).

8. In the paragraphs that follow I try to make a few concise statements about a massive historical and literary phenomenon, rabbinic Judaism. For a more extensive introductory presentation on this subject, see chapters 2 and 3 in my (ed.) *Back to the Sources: Reading the Classic Jewish Texts* (Summit, 1984). See the bibliographies in those chapters for suggestions for further reading on these topics. See also the overview by Jacob Neusner, *The Oral Torah* (Harper & Row, 1986).

9. Joel Rosenberg, "Meanings, Morals, and Mysteries: Literary Approaches to Torah," *Response* 9, no. 2 (Summer 1975), p. 71.

10. To be sure, there were rabbinic sages who had their own skepticism about this hyperintensive mode of reading. In a famous statement Rabbi Ishmael declared, "The Torah speaks in human language" (Talmud, *Keritot* 11a), by which he meant that sometimes peculiarities or repetitions in the Bible are simply a matter of its literary style.

11. Martin Buber, "On National Education," in his *Israel and the World* (Schocken Books, 1963), p. 160.

12. Ibid., pp. 160–61.

13. Ibid., p. 161.

14. Ibid., p. 160.

CHAPTER ONE

1. *Avot*: a tractate of the Mishnah devoted entirely to statements of an ethical or spiritual nature. Also known as *Pirkei Avot* (see Glossary).

2. Robert Goldenberg, "Law and Spirit in Talmudic Religion," in *Jewish Spirituality*, vol. I, ed. Arthur Green (Paulist Press, 1986), p. 232.

3. See the recent study by Samuel C. Heilman and Steven M. Cohen, *Cosmopolitans and Parochials: Modern Orthodox Jews in America* (University of Chicago Press, 1989), particularly pp. 18–21 and their discussion of issues such as attitudes toward premarital sex among the Orthodox, pp. 174–79. Some research, (such as Heilman's in a forthcoming work and the studies done by Menahem Friedman of Bar Ilan University in Israel) has suggested that the questions raised by modernity affect even the most "insulated" of Jews, the ultra-Orthodox, though they are framed in different language. Thus, the incongruity one can witness any day in New York of a black-frocked, bearded Hasid wearing a Sony Walkman over his sidelocks!

4. I have always thought of this story as exemplifying the peculiar relationship between the world of "fact" and the world of law. We see the same concept, to use a more mundane metaphor, in the way rules of play work in games. Let's say we are watching a baseball game. The runner is racing to the base, the ball is thrown, the decision must be made—is he safe or out? It is the umpire, the "rabbi" at the ballpark, we might say, who will decide. Now we all know that sometimes in the realm of fact or "truth" that decision will be wrong. We see the replay on television. The runner is safe, yet he is called out. But "truth" in the divine sense is irrelevant. We do not wait for the divine voice of judgment, the instant replay's eye. Truth is in the human world—even if it is wrong. In similar fashion, the rabbis asserted their own responsibility for determining the law: It is not in heaven, they proclaim.

5. "The Proem in the Aggadic Midrashim," in *Studies in Aggadah and Folk-Literature,* ed. Joseph Heinemann and Dov Noy (Jerusalem: Magnes Press, 1971), pp. 100–123. My translation here uses the emendation of the talmudic text presented in Heinemann's article.

6. Ibid., p. 103.

7. Note that this same impulse operates among "centrist Orthodox" Jews. Writing about this group in their recent study of American Orthodox Jewry, sociologists Samuel C. Heilman and Steven M. Cohen state: "They remain rather individualist and even eclectic in their willingness to accept religious authority, often preferring not to 'ask the rabbi' but to interpret for themselves what Judaism demands of them." *Cosmopolitans and Parochials,* pp. 18–19.

8. Unfortunately, as far as I know this story has not been translated into English. It can be found in Hebrew in vol. 6 (*Samukh V'Nireh*) of the *Complete Stories of Agnon* (Tel Aviv: Schocken Publishing House, 1974), pp. 5–54.

9. For example, Rabbi Ishmael's rules of interpretation from the midrashic text Sifra, which are listed toward the beginning of the daily morning service in a traditional prayer book such as the one edited by Philip Birnbaum (Hebrew

Publishing Company, 1949), pp. 41–45. Even more dramatic are the wordplays permitted by rabbinic interpretation because of the rabbis' profound belief in the sacred quality of the biblical text. That flexibility of interpretation will often break the boundaries of contextural meaning in startling ways. It would be, as I have written elsewhere, tantamount to a reader's interpreting the word "be" in Shakespeare's "To be or not to be" as an allusion to honeybees! See my discussion of this whole issue in *Back to the Sources,* in particular pp. 187–97.

10. Jerome Bruner, *Actual Minds, Possible Worlds* (Harvard University Press, 1986), p. 123.

CHAPTER TWO

1. Translation is from *Your Word is Fire: The Hasidic Masters on Contemplative Prayer,* ed. Arthur Green and Barry W. Holtz (Schocken Books, 1987), p. 101.

2. Maimonides, *Guide of the Perplexed,* trans. Shlomo Pines (University of Chicago Press, 1963), pp. 508–9.

3. For more on this, see Gershom Scholem, "Tradition and New Creation in the Ritual of the Kabbalists," in his *On the Kabbalah and Its Symbolism* (Schocken Books, 1965), pp. 118–57.

4. Robert Darnton, *The Great Cat Massacre* (Basic Books, 1984), p. 4.

5. In Leviticus 23:10–11: "When you enter the land which I am giving to you and you reap its harvest, you shall bring the first sheaf of your harvest to the priest. He shall wave the sheaf before the Lord for acceptance in your behalf; the priest shall wave it on the day after the sabbath."

6. The translation is from William Braude, *Pesikta Rabbati* (Yale University Press, 1968), p. 857.

7. See, for examples of this kind of experience, Eugen Herrigel, *Zen and the Art of Archery* (Random House, 1971), and Mark Salzman, *Iron and Silk* (Random House, 1987).

8. Peter Berger, *The Heretical Imperative* (Anchor/Doubleday, 1972), pp. 13–20 *passim.*

9. "On the Training of Rabbis: Scholarship, Belief, and the Problem of Education," in *The Seminary at 100,* ed. Nina Beth Cardin and David Wolf Silverman (Jewish Theological Seminary, 1987), pp. 195–205.

10. See Heilman and Cohen, *Cosmopolitans and Parochials,* for more on this matter.

11. In one example, discussed in *Sanhedrin* 21b, the rabbis tell what happened to the great King Solomon when he reflected on the reasons behind certain commandments. The Talmud imagines Solomon in his pride thinking that since he knows the reasons behind these mitzvot he can certainly afford to ignore them. But the text shows how precisely what Solomon thought he could avoid actually came to pass, with terrible consequences. Thus, Rav Isaac says: "Why were the reasons of the commandments not revealed? Because the reasons of two commandments were revealed to the greatest man in the world [Solomon] and he stumbled on account of knowing them."

CHAPTER THREE

1. The classic scholarly account of the history of Jewish mysticism is Gershom Scholem's *Major Trends in Jewish Mysticism* (Jerusalem: Schocken Publishing House, 1941; 3rd ed., Schocken Books, 1961). For a reliable introduction with a more popular feel, see the chapter on Kabbalah by Lawrence Fine in *Back to the Sources*. Interestingly, the latest research on Jewish mysticism stresses the orientation toward religious *experience* that I have been speaking about in this chapter. See, for example, the approach of the recent major study by Moshe Idel, *Kabbalah: New Perspectives* (Yale University Press, 1988).

2. See *The Kuzari* I, pp. 86–88.

3. A readable account of the question of Biblical authorship can be found in Richard Friedman's *Who Wrote the Bible?* (Summit Books, 1987).

4. This theme of the conflict between modern and "primitive" culture has been played out in numerous contexts. See, for example, the amusing film *The Gods Must Be Crazy*; for an illuminating example of the issue of *texts* moving across cultures, see the anthropologist Laura Bohannan's "Shakespeare in the Bush," in which the author describes her attempt to tell the story of Hamlet to an African tribe who hear it with their own cultural "ears." The essay originally appeared in *Natural History* (August/September 1966) and has been anthologized in James P. Spradly and David W. McCurdy, eds., *Conformity and Conflict* (Little, Brown, 1971), pp. 22–32.

5. See R. J. Z. Werblowsky's *Joseph Karo: Lawyer and Mystic* (Oxford University Press, 1962) for a study of this seminal thinker in Jewish history and his angelic visitations.

6. For a concise presentation of the contrast between Judaism and Christianity in this matter, see W. D. Davies, "Torah and Dogma: A Comment," *Harvard Theological Review* 61, no. 2 (1968), pp. 87–105.

7. Theodore Roszak, "On the Contemporary Hunger for Wonders," originally published in the *Michigan Quarterly Review* and anthologized in Bill Henderson, ed. *The Pushcart Prize, VI: Best of the Small Presses, 1980–81* (Avon, 1981); see pp. 108–12.

8. See, for example, Mary Douglas and Steven M. Tipton, eds., *Religion and America* (Beacon Press, 1983); Charles Y. Glock and Robert N. Bellah, *The New Religious Consciousness* (University of California, 1976); and Robert N. Bellah et al., *Habits of the Heart* (University of California, 1985).

9. For example, they assert that God's "might" lies precisely in His suppression of His anger against the nations; hence, it is still correct to call Him "mighty."

10. Berger, *The Heretical Imperative,* pp. 112–13.

11. Erik Erikson, *Toys and Reasons* (Norton, 1977), p. 39.

CHAPTER FOUR

1. For example, there is the famous midrash about Moses' intelligence as an infant in Pharaoh's court. When tested by the king, the young boy reached out to choose the jewel instead of the burning coal and was only saved from revealing his extraordinary capacities when an angel moved his hand onto the coal. In

touching the hand with coal to this mouth, Moses injured his tongue and thus we have the origins of his slowness of speech! (Exodus Rabbah 1:10)

2. For more on this idea, see the chapter on midrash in *Back to the Sources*.

3. According to this famous midrash, found in many versions throughout rabbinic literature, Abraham's father Terah was an idol-maker. Abraham, who has discovered the idea of monotheism through the powers of his own reason, smashes all the idols of his father's shop except one, which he leaves holding an ax. When Terah enters the shop and asks what has happened and how have all the idols been destroyed, Abraham tells him to blame the idol holding the ax, since that is the one who had smashed all the other idols in the course of a fight!

4. See Jastrow's *God and the Astronomers* (Norton, 1978) or Steven Weinberg's *The First Three Minutes* (Basic Books, 1988).

5. Einstein–Solovine letter, March 30, 1952, quoted in Yehuda Elkana, "The Myth of Simplicity," pp. 68–69, a paper presented at the Jerusalem Einstein Centennial Symposium, March 14–23, 1979.

6. For a good introduction to this literature, see the anthology *On Nature,* ed. Daniel Halpern (North Point Press, 1987).

7. In the Finkelstein edition, (1983) vol. 2, pp. 17–18.

8. From "My Credo," quoted in Elkana, "The Myth of Simplicity," pp. 63–64.

9. There is the famous rabbinic story in the Talmud (*Hagigah* 14b) about the four rabbis who "entered the garden" of mystical speculation. Only Rabbi Akiva returned unscathed.

10. Oliver Sacks, *The Man Who Mistook His Wife for a Hat* (Summit Books, 1986); A. R. Luria, *The Mind of a Mnemonist* (Basic Books, 1968), and *The Man with a Shattered World* (London: Jonathan Cape, 1972).

11. Sacks, *The Man Who Mistook His Wife for a Hat,* p. 147.

12. When we read rabbinic literature today, we must be aware of the complicated—and in many ways *unclear*—history of the transmission of these texts. If a text says it was spoken by Rabbi X, are we really sure that that rabbi actually said those words? And in similar fashion we cannot be sure if the tales about particular figures have consistency from one tale to the next or any historicity whatsoever.

13. Sir John Eccles, the neurophysiologist who received the Nobel Prize in medicine in 1963, has made an even stronger argument than I am prepared to make—that the individual psyche is "divinely infused between conception and birth." (See his article in *Teachers College Record* 82, no. 3 [Spring 1981].) My point is that consciousness is illustrative of, or perhaps indicative of, the mystery we call God. Eccles believes that an individual's consciousness is God's actual creation. Other works that deal with this question include Eccles' book *The Human Mystery* (Springer-International, 1979); his book with Karl Popper, *The Self and Its Brain* (Springer-International, 1977); and Wilder Penfield, *The Mystery of the Mind* (Princeton University Press, 1975).

14. The various perceptions of the manna's taste are explored in the Talmud, *Yoma* 75a.

15. William Braude, *Pesikta de Rav Kahana* (Jewish Publication Society, 1975), pp. 249–50. My translation here differs from Braude's in a number of other places.

16. See Erik Erikson, *Childhood and Society* (Norton, 1963), *Adulthood* (Norton, 1978), and *The Life Cycle Completed* (Norton, 1982). Daniel J. Levinson, *The Seasons of a Man's Life* (Ballantine, 1978), and James Fowler, *Stages of Faith* (Harper & Row, 1981).

17. For more on this notion of metaphor and the classic Jewish sources, see Arthur Green, "The Children in Egypt and the Theophany at the Sea," *Judaism* 24, no. 3 (Fall 1975), pp. 446–56.

18. Peter Abbs, "Education and the Living Image: Reflections on Imagery, Fantasy, and the Art of Recognition," *Teachers College Record* 82, no. 3 (Spring 1981), p. 491.

19. In recent years attempts to create a consistent theology out of diverse rabbinic statements about God have been criticized on scholarly grounds for a number of reasons. On the one hand, such thinking is problematic because, as we have seen before, it is difficult to know for certain if any particular statement in rabbinic literature can be consistently attributed to the rabbi who appears to have said it. And on the other hand, such attempts are seen as misrepresentative of the nature of rabbinic Judaism because, unlike a Maimonides or a Thomas Aquinas, theological statements in rabbinic literature are always *contextual,* that is, they appear almost reactively in a particular moment of biblical interpretation, and we cannot really know the weight to give each individual statement if we try to build a consistent "rabbinic theology." How can we know, for example, if one particular view about God implied by a midrash on a verse in Leviticus is intended to have great seriousness for an overall rabbinic theology or was merely the interpretive flourish given in a moment of midrashic enthusiasm?

CHAPTER FIVE

1. Siddur, from the Hebrew *seder,* "order," is the traditional name for the prayer book.

2. Abraham Joshua Heschel, *God in Search of Man* (Meridian Books, 1959); see pp. 306–36.

3. The term can also be used with a positive connotation, as in the dictum that there should be "fixed" times for study (*Avot* 1:15).

4. See, for example, the classic study by H. G. Enelow, "Kavvanah: The Struggle for Inwardness in Judaism," in *Studies in Jewish Literature in Honor of Kaufmann Kohler* (Berlin, 1913); and Martin Buber, *Hasidism and Modern Man,* ed. and trans. Maurice Friedman (Harper Torchbooks, 1966), pp. 98–110. In reading the rabbinic selections in this chapter, one must also keep in mind that they come from a time before the liturgy was completely fixed and established. The basic themes of the blessings had been determined, but the particular language of each blessing was more or less left up to the individual worshiper, or at least to the particular leader of the service. In addition, one should also remember that these comments date from a time before printed books. Thus, R. Zera's concern about

his mind becoming confused may be connected to the need to recite the blessings from memory, without the aid of a written text.

5. Joseph Heinemann, *Prayer in the Talmud,* trans. Richard S. Sarason (Walter de Gruyter, 1977), p. 241.

6. See the discussion in Heinemann, chapters 2, 3, and 9.

7. Of course, there are differences among the various "Orthodox" liturgies as well, some of which seem also to emanate from ideological points of view, but these variations are subtle and the polemical point being made (if any) may not be readily apparent.

8. The issue is discussed in the Talmud, *Berakhot* 11b.

9. This is not the only example of "hidden midrash" in the liturgy. During the ritual for festivals the following phrase is chanted: "The Lord! The Lord—a God compassionate and gracious, slow to anger, abounding in kindness and faithfulness, extending kindness to the thousandth generation, forgiving iniquity, transgression and sin, and giving pardon to the penitent." This verse, often known as the thirteen attributes of God, is taken directly from the Bible, Exodus 34:6, when God passes before Moses on Sinai after Moses has carved the second tablets of stone following the incident of the Golden Calf. However, in the version in Exodus the verse continues, "Yet he does not remit all punishment, but visits the iniquity of fathers upon children and children's children, upon the third and fourth generation." Thus, the full meaning of the text in the Bible has been reversed, or at least ignored, in the liturgical context.

10. The translation is from Arthur Green and Barry W. Holtz, eds. and trans., *Your Word Is Fire: The Hasidic Masters on Contemplative Prayer* (Schocken Books, 1987), p. 28. "Cast us not into old age" is from Psalm 71:9.

11. Abraham Joshua Heschel, *Man's Quest for God* (Scribners, 1954), p. 28.

12. Green and Holtz, *Your Word Is Fire,* p. 93.

13. Ibid., p. 95.

14. Ibid., p. 46.

15. Ibid., p. 51.

16. Ibid., p. 65.

17. The approach to saying the Amidah is somewhat different. In this case the congregation says the entire prayer silently and then the leader essentially repeats it in its entirety.

CHAPTER SIX

1. That is, there are large sections of the Talmud that deal with the sacrifices in the Temple, which have had little practical relevance since the destruction of the Temple in the first century.

2. For example, R. Joshua of Siknin's comment in the Talmud, *Shabbat* 88a. But not all talmudic sources use the term in that fashion. For some, *hukkim* is merely another way of saying "decree." See the discussion in Ephraim E. Urbach, *The Sages: Their Concepts and Beliefs,* trans. Israel Abrahams, vol. I (Jerusalem: Magnes Press, 1976), pp. 376–81.

3. Maimonides, *Guide of the Perplexed* III, 26. Of course, one can argue that

some of the "God-oriented commandments" are also *mishpatim*, laws "whose utility is clear to the multitude," but in general the commandments necessary for the functioning of a community are those that make up the majority of the *mishpatim*, the "rational" commandments.

4. For an interesting discussion of the political theory of classic Jewish thought, see the essays in Daniel J. Elazar, ed., *Kinship and Consent: The Jewish Political Tradition and its Contemporary Uses* (Ramat Gan and London: Turtledove Publishing, 1981).

5. Within Judaism there is a whole tradition of *musar* literature, ethical writing, which emanated from the classical rabbinic sources and flourished in the Middle Ages. For a brief introduction to those works, see Joseph Dan, *Jewish Mysticism and Jewish Ethics* (University of Washington Press, 1986).

6. The page number refers to the edition of the text edited by Mordecai M. Kaplan (Jewish Publication Society, 1936). The translations of this excerpt and the following one are my own and differ from Kaplan's.

7. Thus, to choose a simple example, although we all grow up chanting the phrase "Finders keepers, losers weepers," in point of fact within Judaism the concept of *hashavat avedah*, the requirement to *return* lost property to the rightful owner, is an important ethical principle. The loser is not to "weep," since the finder is not supposed to keep what has been lost! The matter is discussed in great detail in the Talmud, particularly in the Tractate *Bava Metzia*, chapter 2.

8. Lawrence Kohlberg, *The Psychology of Moral Development*, vol. 2 (Harper & Row, 1984), pp. 174–76. For an interesting religious critique of Kohlberg, see Gabriel Moran, *Religious Education Development* (Winston Press, 1983). Of course, classical Judaism too saw the possibility of going beyond the law, *lifnim mishurat ha-din* as it is called in the rabbinic texts. (See, for example, in the Talmud, *Bava Metzia* 24b.) Thus, the question can be raised: Does the law *encompass* going "beyond the law" or is it an extralegal category? This problem can be explored further by looking at two interesting scholarly articles: J. David Bleich, "Is There an Ethic Beyond Halakha," in *Proceedings of the Ninth World Congress of Jewish Studies* (Jerusalem: World Union of Jewish Studies, 1986), pp. 55–63; and Aharon Lichtenstein, "Does Jewish Tradition Recognize an Ethic Independent of Halakha," in Marvin Fox, ed., *Modern Jewish Ethics* (Ohio State University Press, 1975), pp. 62–89.

9. For more on this idea, see the chapter on midrash in *Back to the Sources: Reading the Classic Jewish Texts*.

10. Rabbi Shlomo ben Isaac (1040–1105). The acronym of his name is Rashi and as such he is usually known. Rashi's commentary on the Bible often mixes classic talmudic and midrashic materials with his own comments. (Sometimes, in fact, it is not immediately clear which is which.) As the most widely used Jewish Bible commentary, those rabbinic comments often loosely became identified as "Rashi's view," and, more importantly, they became the basic standard understanding of the Bible known by most Jews.

11. A very similar explanation is given in the Talmud, *Yoma* 23a.

12. The infinitive absolute form of the verb is placed directly before the verb itself, producing a kind of doubling effect.

13. In a sense a hard case to prove since so much of prophetic fury was dedicated to an attack on the oppression of the poor and the helpless, surely *mitzvot bein adam l'havero!*

CHAPTER SEVEN

1. And of course in advocating such a view, the rabbis provide an important justification for their own continued financial support as scholars!

2. The term "religion" itself is a problematic one in connection with Judaism. The Bible has no term for "religion" in our sense of the word, and even later rabbinic sources had to find a foreign word—*dat,* from the Persian—to express the concept. When we talk about Judaism as a "religion," we have redefined it in a term familiar to Western languages, but which in and of itself may have changed classical Judaism's own self-understanding.

3. For example, there is a tale told about one sage, Abba Tahnah, who found a man suffering from boils at the gate of the city. When asked by the man for help, Abba Tahnah chose to help him into the city and thus was forced to leave behind the package that he, the sage, was carrying. When he went back to pick up the package, it was already after sunset and therefore Abba Tahnah was in violation of the prohibition against carrying on the Sabbath. When the people of the city pointed out this surprising violation of the law by such a pious man, God miraculously caused the sun to shine, thus preserving Abba Tahnah's saintliness both in matters of *tzedakah* and in punctiliousness about ritual law (Ecclesiastes Rabbah 9:7). Of course, what is interesting here is not the miracle per se, but the fact that before the miracle had occurred, the sage chose to violate the Sabbath in order to perform an act of *tzedakah*.

4. Maimonides, Mishneh Torah, *Hilkhot Matanot Aniyim* 7:10.

5. Ibid., 10:7–14.

6. For more on this topic, see note 7 of the previous chapter.

7. Maimonides' viewpoint is based on the discussion in the Talmud, *Ketubot* 67b.

8. The translation is by Judah Goldin in his English-language edition, *The Fathers According to Rabbi Nathan* (Yale University Press, 1955), pp. 158–59.

9. See, for example, the Mishnah, *Peah* 4:10.

10. We should also point out that another translation of the line "Is he so delicate?" that is also reasonable in this context would be "Is he so accustomed to such treatment?" and in that case we could read the story as an example of the need to let the poor live at the level to which they had previously been living. Here Mar Ukva is simply following the rabbinic principle—later codified by Maimonides as we have seen earlier in this chapter—to respect the poor person's dignity and self-respect.

11. This story, which appears in the Talmud immediately following the tale of the poor man calling for wine, may add an additional dimension to the relation-

ship between Mar Ukva and his son. Perhaps the son feared that the father was intent on giving away too much of the family wealth and that's why he reported the incident of the poor man's fakery (or maybe the whole story was the son's fabrication?). On his deathbed Mar Ukva indeed lived up to the son's "worst" expectations, or perhaps seeing his son's stinginess the father wished to make sure that the needy would get something after he was gone. As usual with these tales, readings and interpretations multiply!

12. Talmud, *Bava Batra*, 9a.

13. Marc Saperstein, *Jewish Preaching 1200–1800: An Anthology* (Yale University Press, 1989).

14. Ibid., p. 59.

15. Ibid., p. 61.

16. Ibid., pp. 276, 277.

17. Ibid., p. 272.

18. Ibid., pp. 399–400.

19. Ibid., p. 400.

20. Ibid.

21. Ibid., p. 401.

22. Ibid.

23. That is, the experience of being victimized by pogroms and massacres in our past—and having governments disclaim responsibility for such events by saying they were not "directly" responsible—should make us sensitive to such events when they happen to others.

24. The report looked at the case of the murdered person found in a field and the biblical ritual described in Deuteronomy 21 to deal with the question of guilt. In particular, the commission was interested in the talmudic explication of the ritual (found in the Babylonian Talmud, *Sotah* 38b), which deals with the issue in terms of the question of indirect responsibility for the death.

CHAPTER EIGHT

1. For a contemporary presentation of the history of the connection of Judaism to Eretz Yisrael, see the excellent collection of essays by Judaica scholars edited by Lawrence Hoffman, *The Land of Israel: Jewish Perspectives* (University of Notre Dame Press, 1986).

2. Thus, in his essay on Kabbalah and the land of Israel, Moshe Idel writes: "Some Hasidic masters considered the place where they established their court as the 'Land of Israel,' an assertion closely related to their emphasis on the possibility of individual salvation, which (for them) is independent of both the Messiah and the actual geographical Land of Israel." In "The Land of Israel in Medieval Kabbalah" in Hoffman, cited above.

3. Will Herberg, *Protestant-Catholic-Jew: An Essay in American Religious Sociology* (Doubleday, 1955).

4. Abraham J. Heschel, *Israel: An Echo of Eternity* (Farrar, Straus & Giroux, 1967), p. 59. Heschel's book is an excellent example of contemporary writing about Israel from a religious perspective. For a collection of texts that relate to

the issue of Israel throughout Jewish history, see Benjamin J. Segal, *Returning: The Land of Israel as Focus in Jewish History* (Jerusalem: Department of Education and Culture, World Zionist Organization, 1987); or (in Hebrew only, unfortunately) Joseph Zahavi, *Eretz Yisrael in Rabbinic Lore* (Jerusalem: Tefilla Institute, 1962).

5. See, for example, Baruch M. Bokser, *The Origins of the Seder* (University of California Press, 1984).

6. For a study of the history of the complex relationship between homelessness and return throughout Jewish literature and philosophy, see Arnold M. Eisen, *Galut: Modern Jewish Reflection on Homelessness and Homecoming* (Indiana University Press, 1986).

7. For more on this theme, see the early chapters of Alan Mintz, *Hurban: Responses to Catastrophe in Hebrew Literature* (Columbia University Press, 1984).

8. The translation is from Reuven Hammer, *Sifre on Deuteronomy* (Yale University Press, 1986), pp. 134–35.

9. See the study by Marc Saperstein in his essay "The Land of Israel in Pre-Modern Jewish Thought: A History of Two Rabbinic Statements," in Hoffman, *The Land of Israel*, pp. 195–204.

10. Saperstein reads it as such, p. 195.

11. See Saperstein's discussion, pp. 190–95.

12. Ibid., p. 192. *Tosafot* ("Additions") is actually a plural noun and refers to the commentaries, beginning with Rashi's sons-in-law and grandsons and continuing throughout France and Germany into the fourteenth century. They appear stitched together as a kind of running commentary, opposite Rashi's comments, on the outer margin of the typical Talmud page.

13. Ibid., pp. 192–94.

14. Talmud, *Ketubot* 110b–111a.

15. Eating bread symbolizes a full meal; thus, the full Grace is recited after a meal in which bread has been eaten. After a meal in which one has eaten one of the special foods associated with Eretz Yisrael (such as grapes, figs, wheat, etc.), the shorter Grace, called in Hebrew the Berakhah Aharonah, the "Final Blessing," is said.

16. As is common in rabbinic writing, the story also appears in another version, in this case in a midrashic text, Lamentations Rabbah (4:2, number 3). There the story is told with slightly different details, but for our purposes we will focus on the version that appears in the talmudic tractate *Gittin,* using details from the other version where appropriate.

17. See the discussion of this notion in Jacob Neusner's *Judaism: the Evidence of the Mishnah* (Scholars Press, 1988), pp. 307–28.

18. Judah Goldin, trans., *The Fathers According to Rabbi Nathan* (Yale University Press, 1955), pp. 35–36.

19. See the discussion in Neusner, *Judaism,* pp. 319–22.

CHAPTER NINE

1. In other words, the specific content of the words on the page is less important than the very act of study itself. See the discussion by Robert Goldenberg in *Back to the Sources: Reading the Classic Jewish Texts,* (1984) pp. 163–67. The cultural meaning of Talmudic study is explored by Samuel C. Heilman in *The People of the Book* (University of Chicago Press, 1983); see in particular pp. 74–110 and 248–59.

2. *The Odyssey of Homer,* trans. Richard Lattimore, Book IX, lines 96–97 (Harper & Row, 1967), p. 139.

3. Goldin, *The Fathers According to Rabbi Nathan,* p. 43.

4. See the discussion in Neusner, *Judaism,* pp. 307–28.

5. Goldin, *The Fathers According to Rabbi Nathan,* pp. 41–42.

6. Based on a number of midrashim, this tale is retold in poetic form as the "Eleh Ezkerah" ("These I Remember") in the Yom Kippur liturgy each year.

7. In his *Science, Curriculum, and Liberal Education: Selected Essays,* ed. Ian Westbury and Neil J. Wilkof (University of Chicago Press, 1978), pp. 105–32.

8. Ibid., pp. 116–17.

9. To our eyes the example of Joseph is less effective than the other two. After all, the issue in the text is a person's excuses not to study Torah, and Joseph's personal integrity was in the realm of sexual ethics. Still, the idea that Joseph retained the virtues valued by the Torah in the face of Potiphar's wife's attempts to seduce him is close enough to fit the Talmud's main argument.

10. See Erikson's classic account in *Childhood and Society* (Norton, 1950) as well as in his other books, such as *Adulthood* (Norton, 1978); Levinson, *The Seasons of a Man's Life* (Ballantine, 1978).

11. See the discussion by Levinson of this passage in *The Seasons of a Man's Life,* pp. 318–40.

12. For more on this, see the study by Janet Aviad, *Return to Judaism* (University of Chicago Press, 1983). Recent fiction has also looked at this phenomenon: Philip Roth's *The Counterlife* (Farrar, Straus & Giroux, 1987) and Anne Roiphe's *Lovingkindness* (Summit Books, 1987).

13. Gariel Moran, *Religious Education Development: Images for the Future* (Winston Press, 1983), p. 133.

14. Called *katnut* and *gadlut* respectively, literally "smallness" and "largeness."

15. See Arthur Green and Barry W. Holtz, eds. and trans., *Your Word Is Fire: The Hasidic Masters on Contemplative Prayer* (Schocken Books, 1987), p. 65.

Index

Aaron, 101
Abaye, 71, 201
Abbahu, 201
Abbs, Peter, 106
Abraham, 11, 12, 17, 84–85, 87
  Job contrasted with, 165–68
aggadah, 12, 64–66, 182–83
  definitions of, 11, 231
  mystical texts as, 66
Agnon, S. Y., 33
Aha, Rabbi, 160, 162
Akiva ben Joseph, 41, 42, 78, 80, 81,
  82, 88–89, 185, 213–14, 216
  martyr's death of, 29, 30–31, 221
  Moses and, 26–32, 35, 47
  Torah study by, 221, 222
aliyah, 196–97, 231
Amidah, 117, 123, 197–98, 231
Amos, 143
Amram, 201
angels, 70, 77, 89, 98
animal sacrifices, 205
Anim Zemirot ("Sweet Melodies"),
  107–8
Antignos of Sokho, 212
Arab-Israeli conflict, 188, 201
Aristotle, 34
Ashkenazim, 133
associative reverie, 126–30, 134
Avihu, 101
Avodah begashmiut, 40
Avot, 17, 61, 137, 231
Avot d'Rabbi Natan, 166, 168–69,
  206–7, 219, 221, 223

baalei teshuvah, 9, 73, 230
Babylonia, 12, 183, 189, 194, 196
Babylonian Talmud, 12, 196
Bahya ibn Pakuda, 112–13, 118
Barbuhin, 164
Bar Kamza, 202–5, 207, 208, 209
Bar Kokhba revolt, 96, 201
Ben Porat Yosef, 129
Berger, Peter, 54, 56, 57, 78
Beston, Henry, 87
Bible, 4, 11, 23–24, 98, 121, 140,
  143–44
  human origins of, 67–68
  laconic style of, 84, 150
  translations of, 150
  as word of God, 67, 68
  see also Torah
"big bang theory," 85
biology, 68, 69
blackmail, 196
blessings, 59, 119, 121, 124, 125, 127–
  28
Braude, William, 101
"Breath of Every Living Thing, The"
  (Nishmat Kol Hai), 115–17
Bruner, Jerome, 35
Buber, Martin, 13–14
business ethics, 40, 42, 139, 145,
  149

cantors, 132
charity, see tzedakah
Christianity, 72, 73, 106, 147, 188–
  89, 191

civil rights movement, 5, 190
class structure, 70
Commentary on Leviticus (Ibn Ezra), 151–52
Conservative Judaism, 120
criminal behavior, 42, 140, 141, 158
Cronkite, Walter, 68, 69
culture:
conditioning by, 69–70, 71, 77–78, 79, 81
definition of, 35
primitive, 69, 71, 76–77
Western, 140, 141, 144–46, 183, 184, 185–86

damage, liability for, 136–37
Daniel, 74–76, 103–4, 122, 125
Darnton, Robert, 47
darshan, 23–24, 231
David, King, 84, 93, 94, 218
Deborah, 84
Degel Mahane Ephraim, 127
democracy, 185
Deuteronomy, 36, 60, 65, 74, 91, 160, 162, 193, 215, 229
devotional practices, 33, 45, 46, 47–53, 55, 59
Diaspora, 189–90, 194–96
dietary laws, 33, 43, 72, 139
Dillard, Annie, 87
divorce, 40, 42, 196, 209
Duties of the Heart (Bahya ibn Pakuda), 112–13

Ecclesiastes, 23–24, 36
Ecclesiastes Rabbah, 216
ecological system, 86–87
education, *see* learning
Egypt, 116
Eilat, 88
Ein Sof, 89, 105, 231
Einstein, Albert, 85–86, 89, 90
Eleazar ben Arakh, 216–18, 228

Eleazar ben Azariah, 22–26, 32, 33, 75, 155–56, 170–72
Eleazar ben Harsom, 226
Eliezer ben Hyrcanus, 20–22, 26, 32, 111, 219–20, 221, 222, 224, 228
Elijah, 21, 96
Emancipation, 5, 62
Emmaus, 216, 217, 218
Enlightenment, 70, 190
envy, 149
Eretz Yisrael, 188–200, 231
duty of living in, 192–200
prayers referring to, 197–200
Erikson, Erik, 81, 102, 228
"Eros and Education" (Schwab), 224
Esther Rabbah, 164
ethics, 136–59, 183, 214
etrog, 46, 47–53, 63, 231
evil, 30, 121–22
Exodus, 11, 23–24, 25, 79, 88, 96, 99, 103, 153
Exodus Rabbah, 102
experience, 67–70
biological limitations and, 68, 69, 81
cognitive vs. affective, 7–8
cultural conditioning and, 69–70, 71, 77–78, 79, 81
free will vs. divine determinism of, 80–82
past experiences and, 68, 69
perceptions of, 68–71, 76–77, 82
psychological interpretations of, 70, 77, 80, 81–82
rational vs. nonrational, 70–71, 77–78
"story" concept of, 81–82
Ezekiel, 201
Ezra, 74–75, 123

Falangists, Christian, 185–86
famine, 116

fanaticism, 22
Festival Morning Service, 115, 117
Feuerbach, Ludwig, 70
Finch, Robert, 87
forgiveness, 138–39
fraud, 170–76, 185
free will, 80–82
Freud, Sigmund, 70, 77
fundamentalism, 22, 73

Gamaliel, Rabban, 146, 147
Gemara, 111, 231
Genesis, 4, 11, 83–84, 162, 226
Genesis Rabbah, 4–5, 11, 43, 83, 86
God:
    attributes of, 74–76, 82, 85, 91, 93,
        104–5, 115–17, 122, 213
    belief and faith in, 67–68, 71–72,
        78–79, 97, 105–6, 109, 115, 135
    central questions about, 66–67, 72,
        74–76, 79, 96–97
    creation of humanity by, 90–91
    creation of the universe by, 85–88,
        115–16, 122, 128
    discussion and thought on, 64–82,
        89, 92–93
    doubt and denial of, 69, 70, 71–72,
        73, 97, 106
    forgiveness from, 138–39
    human interaction with, 21–22, 92,
        97, 99–104, 108–9
    individual and personal perceptions
        of, 68–69, 70, 71, 77–78, 100–
        106, 108–9
    message of, 98–101
    metaphors for, 65, 98–99, 105–6,
        109, 137
    mitzvot in service of, 42, 43, 44,
        48, 58, 59, 63, 72, 137, 138–40,
        142, 147–48, 151, 159, 164
    mystery of, 91, 92, 97, 105, 108,
        130
    nature of, 97–109, 115–17

ontological vs. phenomenological
    perception of, 107
rational approaches to, 83–109, 135
gossip, 141, 145, 149
Grace After Meals, 198
Greek language, 98
Greek Orthodoxy, 188
Guide of the Perplexed (Maimonides),
    44
guilt, 151, 153

halakhah, 12, 19–20, 182–83, 185,
    218, 221
    definitions of, 11, 231
Halevi, Judah, 67
Hama, 162
Hamakom, 105
Hamnuna, 201
Hanina, 59, 162, 170–73, 185, 201
Hasidim, 8, 12, 19, 40–42, 45, 58–59
    definition of, 231
    teaching and texts of, 40–41, 105,
        129, 130, 134, 230
hasidut, 142
Hebrew language, 37, 60, 98, 101,
    121, 133, 147, 161, 200
Heinemann, Joseph, 23–24, 115
Hellenism, 93, 183
Herberg, Will, 188
Heretical Imperative, The (Berger), 54
Heschel, Abraham Joshua, 111, 129,
    190
Hillel, 146, 209–10, 212, 221, 222–23,
    225–26
Hiyya, 160, 161
Hiyya bar Abba, 104
hokheah tokhiah, 151–52, 153–55, 156,
    159, 231
holiness, 39–63
    daily life and, 40–42, 44
    religious texts as source of, 66, 137,
        140, 144
    role models and, 41–42, 65, 136–37

Holocaust, 191
Homer, 217
hukkim, 140–41, 231
human rights, 185
Hymn of Glory, 107–8

Ibn Ezra, 150–53, 155
idolatry, 84, 98–99
ikkar, 76
ikonin, 98
Iran, 22
Isaac, 201, 225
Isaiah, 78, 95, 96, 121–22, 143
Islam, 188
Israel (ancient), 189–90, 201–9
Israel (modern state), 87, 139, 159,
    185–86, 187–89
  creation of, 191
  "going up" to, 196–97
  Jewish identification with, 187–
    91
  media focus on, 187–88
  size and population of, 187–88
Israelites, ancient, 37, 68, 99, 104,
    179–80, 183

Jacob, 4–5, 6, 12
Jacob ben Idi, 111
Jastrow, Robert, 85, 87
Jeremiah, 74–76, 79, 122, 125, 143–
    44, 197, 201
Jeremiah, Rabbi, 162
Jerusalem, 9, 19, 197–98, 207
  destruction of, 201–3, 206
Jerusalem (Palestinian) Talmud, 11–
    12
Jewish law, 10–11, 20
  discussion and disagreement on,
    20–22, 33
  revelation vs. human deliberation
    on, 21–22
Jewish Publication Society (JPS),
    150

Jews:
  aspirations vs. reality of, 6–7, 58–
    59
  assimilation of, 5–6, 54, 141, 191
  Babylonian exile of, 183, 189
  as chosen people, 120
  differing practices among, 72, 133
  dispersal of, 189–90, 194–96
  ethnic self-identification of, 189–91
  as holy people, 6, 39
  nonreligious, 9, 55, 62, 189
  ordinary vs. expert, 36–37
Job, 165–68
Job, Book of, 30
Jonestown tragedy, 101
Joseph, 4, 226
Joseph, Rabbi, 111–12
Joshua, 17
Joshua, Rabbi, 21, 41, 221
Joshua ben Levi, 165
jubilee years, 193
Judah, 136–37, 196–97, 201
Judah HeHasid, 107–8
Judaism, 104, 105
  Ashkenazic rites in, 133
  belief vs. behavior in, 18–19, 39–
    40, 47, 71–72
  central questions in, 66–67
  characteristics of, 39–40, 47, 71–72,
    99
  classic values of, 124, 147
  community life and, 56–57, 136–59
  as community of blood lines, 189–
    91
  Conservative, 120
  conversion to, 189
  criticism of, 139
  debate and deliberation in, 35, 64–
    65, 66, 145–46, 148–49
  deed vs. belief in, 71–72
  definitions of, 188, 222
  ethical values of, 136–59, 183, 214
  ethnicity and, 190–91

evolution of, 47, 93
history of, 84, 127, 183
intellectualism of, 64
Israel and, 187–210
lifelong relationship with, 228–30
messianic speculation in, 188
poetic theology of, 106
Rabbinic, 10
returning to, 9, 73, 230
sacred vs. secular distinctions in,
    40–41, 42, 45, 136–59
secularity vs., 63
Sephardic rites in, 133
sermonic tradition in, 178
teaching vs. historicity in, 10
tradition and, 13–14, 32, 63, 137,
    139, 224
varying commitments to, 9, 55, 62,
    71–72, 73
Western culture vs., 140, 141, 144–
    46, 183, 184, 185–86
see also Orthodox Judaism
justice, 147, 159, 160–86

Kabbalah, 105, 106, 232
Kahana, 41, 42
Kahan Commission, 185–86, 187
Kamza, 202–5, 207, 208, 209
Karo, Joseph, 70, 77–78
katan, 37
kavvanah, 59, 112–13, 114, 134, 232
Kelim, 227
Kennedy, John F., 5
Keter Shem Tov, 130
keva, 111, 112, 113, 114, 127, 134,
    232
koah, 101–2
kofer ba-ikkar, 72, 232
Kohlberg, Lawrence, 146–47
kosher foods, 43, 139

Lamentations, 201
Lamentations Rabbah, 205

lashon ha-rah, 141, 232
learning, 57, 202
    cognitive vs. affective experiences
        and, 7–8
    community and, 218, 227
    emotional response to, 7–8
    joyfulness of, 61
    new insights vs. traditional ideas
        and, 8–9, 13, 32–33
    purposes of, 13
    thinking vs., 64–65
    traditional commitment to, 36
Leib, Rabbi, 42
Levi, 91, 97–98, 99–100
Levinson, Daniel, 102, 228
Leviticus, 50, 101, 149–50, 153, 155,
    169, 193, 221
Leviticus Rabbah, 50, 93, 160, 227
Lewis, Flora, 42
lifnim mishurat ha-din, 167, 232
Likkutim Yekarim, 129, 132
Lopez, Barry, 87
Low, Judah, 180–85, 187
lulav, 46, 47, 53, 63, 232
Luria, A. R., 94
Luzzatto, Moshe Hayim, 142–44
l'zakot etkhem, 60

maggid, 70, 77
Maggid of Mezeritch, 42
Maharal of Prague, 180–85, 187
mahshava zara, 129, 232
Maimonides, 30, 66–67, 79, 105, 183
    on charity, 163–64, 167, 168, 174–
        75
    on ethical practices, 155–59
    jewish law codified by, 12, 155–59,
        174–75
    on mitzvot, 43–45, 141
malbin panim, 153, 204, 232
manna, 99, 100
Man Who Mistook His Wife for a Hat,
    The (Sacks), 94

Man with a Shattered World, The
    (Luria), 94
marriage, 40, 42, 163, 209–10
martyrs, 29, 30–31, 221
Mar Ukva, 172–76, 185
Marx, Karl, 70
Masada rebellion, 208
masorah, 17
Meir, Rabbi, 212–13, 223, 224
melave malke, 45
"melting pot" concept, 190
memory, 15–17, 53, 90, 190
Men of the Great Assembly, 17, 74–
    76, 123
Mesilat Yesharim (Luzzatto), 142
metaphors, 24–25, 28, 65, 98–99,
    105–6, 109, 137
Middle Ages, 8, 43, 67, 112, 141, 163,
    164, 177
Middle East, 128, 188
midrash aggadah, 11
midrash halakhah, 11
midrashim, 4–5, 10–12, 33, 36–37,
    64–65, 178, 229, 232
    characteristics of, 12
    definition of, 10–11, 232
    disharmony and confrontation
        addressed in, 149–59
    interpretive methods of, 34
    introductory commentary of, 23–
        24
    metaphor in, 87
    oral aspects of, 23–24, 121–22
    study of biblical figures in, 84–85
Midrash Psalms, 90–91
Midrash Tanhuma, *Parshat Emor,* 46
Mind of a Mnemonist, The (Luria), 94
miracles, 21–22, 26, 71, 86, 99
Mishnah, 111, 114, 137, 227, 228
    Berakhot, 114
    definition of, 232
    Yoma, 138
Mishneh Torah (Maimonides), 12

Hilkhot Deot, 155–56, 157, 158
Hilkhot Matanot Aniyim, 163, 167,
    174
mishpatim, 141
mitzvot, 42–63
    actualities vs. generalities of, 44–
        48
    business and social relationships
        and, 40, 42, 136–59
    choice vs. command of, 54, 57, 58,
        59, 73, 146–48, 159
    classic concepts of, 42, 55, 59, 61,
        164
    clear vs. hidden meanings in, 139–
        41, 145–46
    communal aspects of, 56–57, 62–
        63
    concentration and intentionality in,
        51–52, 59
    definitions of, 18, 232
    Eretz Yisrael and, 193–94, 196–
        97
    experiential vs. intellectual
        dimension of, 43, 51–52, 53, 57,
        61–62
    forgiveness and restitution required
        by, 138–39
    generations connected by, 46–48,
        52, 54, 61, 73
    human experience integrated with,
        46–47, 54, 61–62, 63, 72–73
    individual temperament and, 56,
        57, 61
    interpersonal vs. spiritual, 136–76
    joyfulness of, 61, 63
    meaning and purpose of, 42–44,
        46, 47–58, 60
    mitzvot inspired by, 61, 62
    motivation for, 47, 54–59, 61–62,
        72, 146–48, 164
    negative, 42
    obligatory aspects of, 42, 48, 58,
        59–60, 138, 146–48, 164–76

order and discipline of, 58
purification through, 43, 44, 46
rationality of, 43–45, 48, 51–58,
    140–41
rewards and punishments of, 60–
    61, 63
service of God's will in, 42, 43, 44,
    48, 58, 59, 63, 72, 137, 138–40,
    142, 147–48, 151, 159, 164
support of others as, 160–76
symbolism of, 49–52, 55, 56, 63
Torah study and, 214, 216, 222,
    226
vertical vs. horizontal dimensions
    of, 63
violation of, 60, 72
mitzvot bein adam l'havero, 137–42,
    144, 148, 159
definitions of, 137, 232
mitzvot bein adam l'makom, 137, 138–
    40, 142, 159
definitions of, 137, 232
modern world:
    primitive cultures vs., 69, 71, 76–
        77
    rationalism of, 70–71
    religious hunger of, 73–74, 88
    religious skepticism of, 68–71
    tradition vs., 19–20, 26, 36, 45, 52,
        54–56, 57, 59, 77–78, 104, 123,
        184, 186, 187
moon landing, 68, 69
Morning Service, 115, 117, 121, 122,
    124, 125, 128
mortality, 90–91
Morteira, Saul ha-Levi, 179–80
Moses, 34, 37, 47, 185
    prayer of, 74–76, 122
    teaching and mission of, 26–32, 35,
        84, 193
    Torah received by, 10, 17, 29, 96
Moses Hayim Ephraim of Sudylkov,
    127

Mount Sinai, 10, 17, 21, 23–25, 27–
    29, 31, 34, 37, 67, 96, 99–100
Muir, John, 87
music, 131–33
mystery, 88–92, 97, 105, 108, 130
mysticism, 4, 44, 66, 89, 96, 130
mythology, 98

Nadav, 101
nature, 87–88, 116
Nazis, 191
Nehemiah, 74
New Deal, 194
Nezikin, 227
1984 (Orwell), 151
Nishmat Kol Hai ("The Breath of
    Every Living Thing"), 115–17,
    118
Noah, 84

Odyssey (Homer), 217
ontology, 107
Or Ha-Meir, 131
Orthodox Judaism, 20, 57, 123, 159,
    230
    revitalization of, 6, 33
Orwell, George, 151
Oshaiah, 111
Outward Bound, 88

Papa, Rav, 71
Passover, 72
Paul, 147
peace, 128, 184, 201, 209
peshat, 96, 232
Pesikta de Rav Kahana, 95–96, 97–
    98, 104, 165, 176–77
Pesikta Rabbati, 50
Pharaoh, 179
philanthropy, 163–65
Pirkei Avot, 145–46, 211–12, 218,
    222, 228–29
populism, 33–35

Potiphar's wife, 226
poverty, 164–76, 187
Prayer for the State of Israel, 123
prayers, 10, 12, 40–41, 64, 70–73,
    74–76, 107–8, 109, 110–35, 162,
    228
  answering of, 135
  chanting of, 133
  communal, 63, 72, 126, 132–34
  discussion of, 64, 109
  distractions in, 129–30, 134
  editing and deleting of, 120, 121–
    23, 125, 132, 134
  emotional response to, 131–32,
    134
  Eretz Yisrael and, 197–200
  focusing in, 112–13, 118, 124–25,
    128
  God as source of, 117, 118
  innovation vs. routinization in,
    111–13, 119–21, 126–27
  meditation and reflection in, 126–
    30, 134
  modern problems with, 114–15,
    123
  music and, 131–33
  nature of, 110
  nonrational aspects of, 118, 129–32,
    134–35
  nontraditional models of, 133
  personal experience of, 118–121,
    124–32, 133, 134, 135
  petitionary, 110, 113–14, 118, 134,
    198
  renewal in, 125, 127
  requirements of, 118
  "second-order" nature of, 118, 119,
    123–24
  sense of inadequacy and, 116–17
  study vs., 118, 122
  tension in, 121–22, 124
  thanksgiving and worship in, 110,
    113–17, 125

  values asserted in, 124–25, 128, 134
  see also specific prayers
proem form, 23
proof texts, 34, 215
prophets, 17, 74–76, 84, 143–44, 159
Protestant-Catholic-Jew (Herberg), 188
Protestantism, 188
Proverbs, 169, 215–16, 224
Psalm 29, 101, 102
Psalm 92, 88
Psalm 103, 94
Psalm 111, 214, 215
Psalm 118, 107
Psalms, Book of, 121, 123, 127, 218
psychology, 19, 77, 78, 81–82, 138,
    146–47
psychotherapy, 80

Rabbinic Judaism, 10
rabbis, 8
  changing role of, 19
  definition of, 35
  literature of, 10–13, 27, 31, 48–50,
    64, 107, 111–12
  oral tradition of, 10, 23–24, 33, 67
  ordinary Jews vs., 36–38
  as role models, 41–42, 65
  sermons of, 177–83
  theology of, 106–7
  traditional authority of, 19, 27, 33
  traditional beliefs of, 92
Rashi, 152–53, 195, 197, 232
rationalism, 70–71, 78
  approaches to God through, 83–
    109, 135
Rav, 43, 62, 136
Rava, 111–12, 136, 137, 154–55, 214–
    15
rebuke, 154–59, 169, 182, 202
Red Sea, 103–4
responsive reading, 132
revelation, 10, 11, 17, 21, 96, 99–104,
    177

righteousness, 4–5, 6, 18–19
ritual, 47–53
  adult vs. childhood experience of, 53–54, 228
  allegorical vs. primitive aspects of, 49–52, 54, 60
  casting off of, 53–54, 60
  motivation and, 54–59, 61–62, 72, 146–48, 164
  self-consciousness and, 50–52
ritual purity, 20–21, 43, 44, 46
role models, 41–42, 65, 136–37
Roman Catholicism, 188, 189
Roman Empire, 30, 201–8, 221
Rosenzweig, Franz, 5–7
Roszak, Theodore, 73–74

Sabbath, 11, 45, 53, 55, 107, 115, 117, 139, 158, 159, 163, 202
sabbatical years, 193
Sabra and Shatila massacres, 185–86
Sacks, Oliver, 93–95
sacrificial wave offering, 48–49
Sages, 65, 111, 230
Samson, 84
Sanhedrin, 36–37
Saperstein, Marc, 178–79, 180
Scheffler, Israel, 7–8
Schwab, Joseph, 224
science, 70, 71, 78, 79, 85–86, 87–88, 90
se'ahs, 195
secularism, 20, 45–46, 54, 63, 73, 90
Seder Eliahu Rabbah, 86
Seder Nezikin, 136, 137, 227
Seders, 55
Sefirot, 105
selas, 195
Sephardim, 133
sermons, 23–24, 177–83
sexual behavior, 33
Shakespeare, William, 34
Shammai, 209–10, 222

Shem, 84
Shema, 108, 117, 123, 201, 232
Sheshet, 136
Shimon, 195
Shimon ben Azzai, 89
Shimon ben Gamaliel, 146
Shimon ben Yohai, 95–97
Shimon the Just, 146
Shlomo ben Issac *see* Rashi
siddur, 110, 113, 121, 124, 126, 133, 134, 198–200, 232
Sifra *Dibura Dinedava,* 89
Sifra on Leviticus, 147, 152, 153, 192, 232
Sifre, 64–65, 193–94, 233
Sifre Deuteronomy, 36–37, 192, 229, 233
  Ekev, 64, 65
  Parshat Zot Haberakhah, 91–92
Simeon bar Abba, 201
Simhat Torah, 131
Simlai, 194
Song of Songs, 105
Spinoza, Baruch de, 67
"stage theory," 146–47
Sukkot, 46, 47, 52, 53, 233
synagogues, 9, 15, 123, 126, 131, 132–34

taamei hamitzvot, 51–58, 233
taamim, 52, 57
talmidei hakhamim, 33, 224, 233
Talmud, 11–12, 20–23, 82, 178, 227
  Arakhin, 153–54, 155
  Avodah Zarah, 213
  Bava Batra, 195
  Bava Kamma, 59, 136
  Bava Metzia, 21, 153, 154
  Berakhot, 41, 71, 111, 136, 137, 214
  definition of, 233
  Gittin, 202–3
  Hagigah, 22–23
  Jerusalem vs. Babylonian, 11–12

Talmud (*cont.*)
  Ketubot, 170, 172, 174, 194, 196
  Kiddushin, 213
  Megillah, 225
  Menahot, 26, 29
  Nedarim, 215
  organization of, 12, 137
  Pesahim, 62
  Shabbat, 79–80, 96, 201
  Sota, 162–63, 193
  Sukkah, 39, 48–49, 80, 233
  topical orders of, 12, 137
  Tosafot, 196
  Yevamot, 156–57, 209
  Yoma, 60, 74, 75, 122, 206, 225–26
Tanhum, 160, 161
Tarfon, 155–56, 213–14
teachers, 19, 223–24, 228
technology, 68, 69, 70
Temple, 75, 195
Temple, First, 189
Temple, Second, 192, 201, 203, 205–
  6, 217
Ten Commandments, 11, 23, 99
tithes, 193
Torah, 3–7
  community and national relevance
    of, 6–7
  contemporary relevance of, 176–
    86
  contradictory aspects of, 24–25
  definitions of, 4, 233
  excuses for avoidance of, 225–26
  fulfillment of mitzvot and, 214,
    216, 222, 226
  hard work requirements of, 224–
    25, 228
  joyfulness of, 215–16
  literal meaning of, 17
  as literature, 7–8
  metaphor and, 24–25, 28
  mitzvot connected with, 214, 216,
    222, 226

modern neglect of, 7
as monumental code, 34, 85
multiple interpretations of, 4, 10–
  11, 21–22, 25–26, 28–32, 34
oral vs. written, 10, 233
personal and ancestral connection
  to, 8–9, 99–100
proscribed uses of, 212–214
relationship of life to, 4–7, 8–9,
  20–22
as revelation, 10, 11, 17, 21, 99–104
"reverse order" learning from, 5–6
self-reflection and, 176–77
study of, 11, 66, 160–62, 211–30
teaching of, 19, 223–24, 228
traditional authority of, 7, 9
two-sided nature of, 60
wilderness setting and, 176–77,
  183
Torah lishmah, 61, 212, 213, 214, 215,
  233
Tosefta, *Shevuot,* 72
tradition, 13–38
  ambivalence and, 18, 49, 50, 52
  authority and demands of, 17–20,
    31–32, 33, 39
  continuity and evolution of, 14,
    26–33, 35–36, 39, 47
  custom, sentiment and stability of,
    17–18, 20, 46
  definition of, 17
  denial and rejection of, 13, 53–54,
    55, 62
  "errors" of, 78
  handing down of, 13–14, 17–18,
    27–32, 46–48
  having vs. living of, 13–14, 36, 46–
    48
  human vs. divine interpretation of,
    20–22, 25–26, 32–33, 37–38,
    59
  Judaism and, 13–14, 32, 63, 137,
    139, 224

limitations of, 33–35, 67
memory and, 15–17, 53, 90,
    190
modern world vs., 19–20, 26, 36,
    45, 52, 54–56, 57, 59, 77–78,
    104, 123, 184, 186, 187
past preserved in, 16–17, 26–27,
    46–49, 52, 54, 78–79, 103
power of, 34, 35, 46, 54
reliability of, 67
as self-enclosed system, 67
three approaches to, 13–14
"Two Sages Who Lived in Our
    Town" (Agnon), 33
Tzava'at Rivash, 40
tzedakah, 48, 61, 163–76, 193
    activism and, 165–68
    approach of Abraham vs. Job to,
        165–68
    Christian charity vs., 147–48
    complexities of, 170–74
    definition of, 233
    eight levels of, 164
    fraud and, 170–76, 185

Ulla, 201

Vespasian, Emperor of Rome, 206–8
visions, 70

West Beirut, 185–86
wilderness, 176–77, 183
Will, George, 42
wisdom, 8–9, 36–38, 230
wordplay, 34, 60, 161–62
World War II, 189

yakim, 160, 161
Yavneh, 207–8, 216–17, 233
yeshivot, 9
Yishmael, 212, 213
Yohanan ben Zakkai, Rabban, 39,
    80–81, 203, 205–9, 216–17, 219,
    220
Yom Kippur, 132, 135, 138
Yose bar Hanina, 99–100
Yose ben Kisma, 218–19, 228

Zaddok, 212
Zechariah ben Avkilus, 202–3, 204–5
Zera, 112
Zionism, 200
Zohar, 96, 233